2025年度版

京都市の
英語科

過 去 問

協同教育研究会 編

協同出版

本書には，京都市の教員採用試験の過去問題を
収録しています。各問題ごとに，以下のように5段
階表記で，難易度，頻出度を示しています。

難 易 度

非常に難しい　☆☆☆☆☆
やや難しい　☆☆☆☆
普通の難易度　☆☆☆
やや易しい　☆☆
非常に易しい　☆

頻 出 度

◎　　　ほとんど出題されない
◎◎　　あまり出題されない
◎◎◎　普通の頻出度
◎◎◎◎　よく出題される
◎◎◎◎◎　非常によく出題される

※**本書の過去問題における資料，法令文等の取り扱いについて**
　本書の過去問題で使用されている資料や法令文の表記や基準は，出題さ
れた当時の内容に準拠しているため，解答・解説も当時のものを使用して
います。ご了承ください。

はじめに〜「過去問」シリーズ利用に際して〜

　教育を取り巻く環境は変化しつつあり，日本の公教育そのものも，教員免許更新制の廃止やGIGAスクール構想の実現などの改革が進められています。また，現行の学習指導要領では「主体的・対話的で深い学び」を実現するため，指導方法や指導体制の工夫改善により，「個に応じた指導」の充実を図るとともに，コンピュータや情報通信ネットワーク等の情報手段を活用するために必要な環境を整えることが示されています。

　一方で，いじめや体罰，不登校，暴力行為など，教育現場の問題もあいかわらず取り沙汰されており，教員に求められるスキルは，今後さらに高いものになっていくことが予想されます。

　本書の基本構成としては，出題傾向と対策，過去5年間の出題傾向分析表，過去問題，解答および解説を掲載しています。各自治体や教科によって掲載年数をはじめ，「チェックテスト」や「問題演習」を掲載するなど，内容が異なります。

　また原則的には一般受験を対象としております。特別選考等については対応していない場合があります。なお，実際に配布された問題の順番や構成を，編集の都合上，変更している場合があります。あらかじめご了承ください。

　最後に，この「過去問」シリーズは，「参考書」シリーズとの併用を前提に編集されております。参考書で要点整理を行い，過去問で実力試しを行う，セットでの活用をおすすめいたします。

　みなさまが，この書籍を徹底的に活用し，教員採用試験の合格を勝ち取って，教壇に立っていただければ，それはわたくしたちにとって最上の喜びです。

協同教育研究会

CONTENTS

第1部

京都市の
英語科
出題傾向分析

京都市の英語科　傾向と対策

中高共通

　2024年度は，リスニング問題，文法・語法問題，読解問題，英作文問題，英語指導に関する問題が出題された。とにかく問題量が多いので，試験時間内にすべてを解答するためには，英文を読むスピードと理解力を充分養っておくことが不可欠である。英作文および英語指導に関する問題を除くと，大半は選択式の解答となっている。

　リスニング問題は，全部で4つのセクションに分かれている。このうち，AからCまでは1回のみの放送である。Aは短い会話文であるが，選択肢も音声で聞き取ることが求められる。一方で，BとCは選択肢が文字で与えられているものの，音声がやや長いものとなっている。さらに，Dは放送が2回あるが，音声が非常に長く，かつ日本語で要約をする問題である。そのため，全体的に難易度が高いと言えるだろう。Dについては，全体の要旨をつかみながらも，要約に必要な語彙を適切にメモしなければならない。リスニング問題としては特殊であるため，形式に慣れるためにも，新聞記事のようなまとまった内容の音声を聞いて，指定語数でまとめる学習をしておくことが必要である。「BBC 6 minutes English」のようなサイトを活用することをおすすめする。

　文法・語法問題は，空所補充・正誤判断・同意語選択・整序などの形式で出題された。語彙やイディオム，文法事項のレベルを確認するつもりで過去問題を解くほか，大学入試対策問題集を1冊仕上げておくことで十分に対応可能である。

　読解問題は，長文問題が3題出題された。長いもので500語程度からなる。設問は内容把握，空所補充，一部英文記述などである。内容把握問題と空所補充型問題の難易度は大学入試レベルで，特に難しい単語や構文も見当たらず，問題文自体も比較的短い。確実に得点できるよう，集中力をもって臨みたい。ただし，ダブルパッセージの問題も出題されており，TOEICのPart7のような形式にも慣れておく必要がある。過去問題を解くほか，同レベルの長文問題集で読解力をつけておくと同時に，英

語をたくさん読むことに対する抵抗感を極力なくしておくことが必要である。「English e-Reader」ではレベル別に物語文を無料で読むことができ，おすすめである。

　英作文問題は，年度により，整序英作文，自由英作文，和文英訳のいずれか，あるいはすべてが出題されている。自由英作文は教育関連のトピックで「生徒が日常的な話題についてスピーチするような授業を行うとき，英語教師が留意すべき点について，3つ以上の項目を80語で述べる」という出題であった。下書きの段階で，文型や時制，前置詞，接続詞などの関係を丁寧に見て，誤文がないように仕上げることが重要である。どんなテーマでも意見を述べることができるようになるためには，日頃から新聞や学術書などに広く目を通して情報を多く取り入れ，いろいろなテーマについての賛成意見，反対意見の両方を考える習慣をつけることが必要である。英作文問題は，語数制限内で手早くまとめる必要があるので，読解問題中の英作文も含め，過去問題の中の英作文問題の制限語数をチェックし，その語数で英文をまとめられるよう学習しておくことが必要である。

　また英語指導に関する問題では，教師としての文法知識と説明力が問われており，教室での実践的な対応が重要視されている。文法に関する深い知識を身につける際には文法書だけでなく，辞書の記述も有用である。電子・アプリ・紙のいずれでもよいが，参考書代わりに繰り返し引いて適宜メモを取っておくとよいだろう。

　近年，学習指導要領に関する出題はないが，今回の学習指導要領の改訂に伴い出題も予想される。過去には実際の授業を想定して自分の考えを記述する問題などが出題されているが，当然のことながら，新学習指導要領のねらいに沿った解答が求められているので，改訂の経緯，趣旨や要点など熟読しておくことが望ましい。

高等学校

　共通問題以外に，高等学校では読解問題が2題課せられている。どちらも教育に関する話題である。設問は適語・適文補充が主である。読解問題内に課されている自由作文はいずれも英語による解答である。解答時

間は40分であり，中高共通の読解に比べるとかなり長い英文(700語と800語程度)を読まなければならない。読解力，文章力，授業構成力など総合的な能力が試されることになる。自由英作文では書く内容に関する専門知識はもちろんであるが，段階を踏んで慣れていくとよい。まずは，和訳を用いた逆翻訳から始めることをおすすめする。英作文では「言いたくても言えない」ということが多い。ここで重要なのがパラフレーズ思考である。「やさしい英語ニュース」のように和訳が提示されているサイトを用いて，先に和訳をみて自分で英語を作る練習をすると自身で英語を書くハードルが下がる。英語を書く機会を増やすことが肝要である。

過去5年間の出題傾向分析

中学＝● 高校＝▲ 中高共通＝◎

分類	設問形式	2020年度	2021年度	2022年度	2023年度	2024年度
リスニング	内容把握	◎	◎	◎	◎	◎
発音・アクセント	発音					
	アクセント					
	文強勢					
文法・語法	空所補充	◎	◎	◎	◎	◎
	正誤判断	◎	◎	◎	◎	◎
	一致語句	◎		◎	◎	◎
	連立完成					
	その他	◎	◎			
会話文	短文会話					
	長文会話					
文章読解	空所補充	◎ ▲	◎ ▲	◎ ▲	◎ ▲	◎ ▲
	内容一致文	◎	◎ ▲	◎ ▲	◎ ▲	◎ ▲
	内容一致語句	◎ ▲	◎ ▲	◎	◎	▲
	内容記述					◎
	英文和訳					
	英問英答	◎	◎	◎ ▲	◎ ▲	◎
	その他	◎ ▲	▲	◎	◎ ▲	◎ ▲
英作文	整序	◎	◎	◎	◎	◎
	和文英訳					
	自由英作	◎ ▲	◎ ▲	◎	◎ ▲	▲
	その他					
学習指導要領						

第2部

京都市の
教員採用試験
実施問題

2024年度　実施問題

【中高共通】

Script

[There are three speaking roles for the test: Directions , Man(M), and Women(W).]

Directions : Please turn the test paper over. The Listening Comprehension Test will now begin. You may take notes while listening.

【1】Section A

Please listen to the following conversations. After each conversation, a question will be asked, and four possible answers will be read. Choose the best answer and circle the corresponding letter on your answer sheet. Each conversation, the question, and the answers will be read only once.

Conversation 1

M : What do you think of our new boss?

W : Well, I have negative impressions of him. He asked me to work, or I should say, he told me to work last Saturday without asking if I'd already made plans.

M : That's too bad. Had you made plans yet?

W : Yeah, but it didn't make any difference. I was going to visit my friend. I told him that she was one of my best friends from childhood and she had a wedding party last Saturday. I was expected to speak. But he didn't even care.

M : Really? I can't believe it. You should let him know how you feel.

QUESTION : What does the woman imply?

A)   She is going to quit her job.

B)   The new boss is inconsiderate.

C)   She will talk with her boss.

D)   The new boss will be replaced.

Conversation 2

W : Takeshi, I've got three official job offers.

M : Wow, good for you!

W : Yes, but I can't decide which to take. Dalton Company offers the highest paying job to me. On the other hand, it seems I have few holidays.

M : I see. Tell me the other offers.

W : Second choice is Smith IT Corporation, but the office is at Tokyo. Living in Tokyo sounds fun and I want to enjoy urban life. But it offers the smallest salary and I don't think I can make ends meet on a meager salary. The third one is Summers Industry, but the job description doesn't attract me very much. Well, I'll think it over for a while.

M : If you need some advice, let me know. You have to make a tough life decision.

QUESTION :   What will the woman do?

A)   Spend more time before making a decision.

B)   Ask her friends for advice.

C)   Take the best paying job.

D)   Enjoy urban life.

Conversation 3

W : So, what did you think of the apartment we viewed privately this morning?

M : Well, I liked it the first time I saw it and the facilities are good. But it's a bit far away from the nearest station, and the rent seems a bit high.

W : Yeah, maybe a little. But the kids liked it very much, because there is a huge playground.

M : Doesn't your friend Saki live near there? Maybe she can give us some advice.

W : Good idea.

QUESTION :　What does the couple decide to do?

A)　Decide to rent the apartment.

B)　Visit the playground to see if their children enjoy playing there.

C)　Choose a more conveniently located apartment.

D)　Consult the woman's friend about the apartment.

Conversation 4

M : Hey, Nami. How do you plan to spend the summer holidays?

W : Actually, I'm going to Australia with my family.

M : Australia! I have many pleasant memories of it because I spent my childhood there. Have you ever been before?

W : No, never. This is my first time. You know, I love shooting scenery photos, so I'm really looking forward to visiting there. Where do you recommend?

M : Melbourne, Tasmania, and Ayers Rock. But I left when I was 18, which is 20 years ago. I'm not sure they are what they used to be.

W : I can imagine. You should go back sometime.

QUESTION :　What do we learn about the man?

A)　He loves to take photographs.

B)　He grew up in Australia.

C)　He wants to go abroad with the woman.

D)　He has never been abroad.

(☆☆◎◎◎)

12

【 2 】 Section B

Please listen to the following two passages. After each passage, two questions will be asked. Four possible responses to each question are listed on the answer sheet. Choose the best one and circle it. Each passage and question will be read only once.

Passage 1

Thanks to the development of mobile phones, we can talk with people around the world, anywhere, anytime. Not only at home but also while driving, many people use mobile phones. This practice often causes serious and tragic traffic accidents. As a result, using mobile phones while driving is prohibited in many countries. But can you imagine how dangerous it is? An experiment conducted at the University of Utah has shown some insightful stories.

In the experiment, 200 students were asked to carry out tasks on a mobile phone while taking part in a computer based driving simulator. Not surprisingly, most students experienced great difficulty in doing both tasks at the same time. However, 2.5 percent of the subjects managed to do two tasks just as well as one. Remarkably, some of the subjects performed even better when doing so. The experiment shows that for most people talking and driving at the same time is dangerous. Yet, it suggests that in the near future, people may eventually be able to learn how to do two or more tasks at the same time, including using a mobile phone and driving.

QUESTION ： 1. What was the aim of the experiment at the University of Utah?

A) To prove how dangerous it is to use a mobile phone while driving.

B) To see the difference of the ability of young drivers and old drivers.

C) To estimate the ability of university students to use new technology.

D) To check how to react when young drivers are in a car accident.

13

QUESTION : 2. How did a small fraction of students differ from the majority?

A) As they concentrated on driving, their driving improved.

B) They were good at learning new skills using a mobile phone.

C) They refused to use a mobile phone while driving.

D) They proficiently carried out two tasks simultaneously.

Passage 2

Research indicates that people tend to adjust calorie intake at fast-food restaurants when they know the amount of the calories a particular menu item has. Economists from Stanford University observed customers ordering food in New York City, where to post calorie information on their menu boards is mandated. What they found was that customers decreased their calorie consumption by an average of 6 percent after viewing calorie information. Heavier customers cut back even more. However, the research found that beverage choices are unaffected by calorie posting. That is, calorie posting leads consumers to buy fewer food items, and to switch to lower calorie food items. On the other hand, the results were different at a leading coffee chain that offered high-calorie drink options. Customers who normally consumed drinks over 250 calories cut their calorie intake by 26 percent when calorie notices were listed on the menu.

This latest study contradicted discoveries of a preceding study, which found that customers of 14 fast-food outlets located in low-income neighborhoods of New York City did not cut back their calorie intake when calories were posted. Researchers explain the discrepancy in research results by indicating that the more recent study is more inclusive, surveying neighborhoods that range from low to high incomes. Consumers in wealthier neighborhoods, who generally have a high level of education, make the biggest reductions.

QUESTION : 1. How did consumption at fast-food restaurants compare with consumption at a coffee chain when calorie contents were posted?

A)   Drink orders were less affected at fast-food restaurants.

B)   Drink consumption significantly dropped at both places.

C)   Food orders remained relatively unchanged at the coffee chain.

D)   Food consumption sharply decreased at both places.

QUESTION : 2. Why do researchers believe previous research findings conflict with new findings?

A)   The later study included drinks as well as food.

B)   The earlier study focused on higher income groups.

C)   The earlier study was seriously flawed.

D)   The later study was more comprehensive.

(☆☆☆○○○○)

【3】 Section C

Please listen to the following two conversations. After each conversation, two questions will be asked. Four possible responses to each question are listed on the answer sheet. Choose the best one and circle it. Each conversation and question will be read only once.

Conversation 1

M : Alice, I need your help. An important trading partner is flying in from Tokyo next Friday, and I'm hosting her as a guest. I'm planning to take her to a fancy Japanese-style restaurant, but she doesn't eat meat. Do you know of a place that serves good vegetarian food in Kyoto?

W : I know some. What about the one on Kiyamachi Street — Kaiseki Miyako? They offer vegetarian food, which is appetizing. Have you ever been there?

M : No, but I think I read a review about it on Instagram recently. But I'm not sure if I read anything about vegetarian options.

15

W : If you want, I can drop by the restaurant and get a menu on my way to work tomorrow morning. So you can get a clear idea of the dishes they serve before your trading partner comes on Friday.

QUESTION : 1. How does the man know about Kaiseki Miyako?

A)   He took an instagrammable photo there.

B)   He read a review about it.

C)   His friend lives nearby.

D)   He has eaten there once before.

QUESTION : 2. What does the woman offer to do?

A)   Make a reservation

B)   Talk with the owner

C)   Buy a magazine

D)   Pick up a menu

Conversation 2

M : Hello, Ms. Suzuki? I'm calling from the Kyoto Business School. I understand that you recently took one of our management seminars. We're surveying attendees so that we can improve future events. I would really appreciate if you could kindly answer some of our questions. Did you find the course helpful?

W : Oh, yes. I've been working in a management post for a number of years, but I wanted to make sure I'm up-to-date on the latest developments. I found the discussion about management and leadership skills particularly helpful.

M : I'm pleased to hear that. Now, is there anything you'd recommend for future courses?

W : Well, it'd be helpful if the classes started later in the evening. I don't get out of work until five-thirty, so it was hard for me to make it to a six o'clock class on time.

16

QUESTION : 1. Why is the man calling?

A) To introduce a new course

B) To register for an event

C) To confirm a class schedule

D) To ask survey questions

QUESTION : 2. What does the woman suggest?

A) Offering a different payment method

B) Starting at a later time

C) Making the seminar longer

D) Having more instructors

(☆☆☆○○○○)

【4】 Section D

The following article will be read twice. Write a summary of the contents in Japanese. The summary should be between 150 and 200 characters. You may take notes and begin summarizing while listening. Now, please listen to the article.

In the northeastern village in Thailand, Siriporn Sapmak starts her day by doing a livestream of her two elephants on social media to raise money to survive.

The 23-year old, who has been taking care of elephants since she was in school, points her phone to the animals as she feeds them bananas and they walk around the back of her family's home.

Siriporn says she can raise about $27.46 of donations from several hours of livestreaming on TikTok and YouTube but that is only enough to feed her two elephants for one day.

It is a new - and insecure - source of income for the family, which before the pandemic earned money by doing elephant shows in the Thai city of Pattaya.

17

They top up their earnings by selling fruit.

Like thousands of other elephant owners around the country, the Sapmak family had to return to their home village as the pandemic decimated elephant camps and foreign tourism ground to a virtual halt. Only 400,000 foreign tourists arrived in Thailand last year compared with nearly 40 million in 2019. Some days, Siriporn doesn't receive any donations and her elephants are underfed.

Edwin Wiek, founder of Wildlife Friends Foundation Thailand, estimates that at least a thousand elephants in Thailand would have no "proper income" until more tourists return.

Thailand has about 3,200 to 4,000 captive elephants, according to official agencies, and about 3,500 in the wild.

Wiek said the Livestock Development Department needs to find "some kind" of budget to support these elephants.

"Otherwise, it's going to be difficult to keep them alive, I think, for most families," he said.

The government has sent 500,000 kilograms of grass across multiple provinces since 2020 to help feed the elephants, according to the Livestock Development Department, which oversees captive elephants.

Elephants, Thailand's national animal, eat 150 to 200 kg each day, according to the Wildlife Conservation Society.

Siriporn and her mother, however, said they have not yet received any government support.

While the government is expecting 10 million foreign tourists this year, some say this may not be enough to lure elephant owners back to top tourist destinations, given the costs involved. Chinese tourists, the mainstay of elephant shows, have also yet to return amid COVID-19 lockdowns at home.

Wiek expected more elephants to be born in captivity over the next year, exacerbating the pressures on their owners.

"Some days we make some money, some days none, meaning there's going to be less food on the table", said Siriporn's father.

"I don't see a light at the end of the tunnel."

(出典　Voice Of America Sep 11 2022:

https://www.voanews.com/a/streaming-to-survive-thailand-s-out-of-work-elphants-in-crisis/6738210.html)

(☆☆☆☆◎○○○)

【5】次の(1)〜(10)の英文の＿＿に入る最も適切な語(句)を，ア〜エの中からそれぞれ1つ選び記号で答えなさい。

(1)　Bauer liked Audrey, so he often smiled at her, and spoke warm words to her, but his efforts were not ＿＿. For Audrey, Bauer was just one of her colleagues.

　ア　extinguished　　イ　reciprocated　　ウ　deliberated

　エ　reconciled

(2)　People told me how difficult Mrs. Gibson was. Later I met her and found that she was a little eccentric but a gentle person. Finally I thought people had ＿＿.

　ア　confined　　イ　justified　　ウ　exaggerated　　エ　proclaimed

(3)　A : Ann often says she is a vegetarian, but yesterday she ate lamb with me.

　　　B : It is true that she does not eat beef, but she eats other meats. I think she just ＿＿ to be a vegetarian or that she does not know vegetarianism well.

　ア　pursues　　イ　exclaims　　ウ　urges　　エ　professes

(4)　Since an unexpected volcanic explosion happened, several airports in South America were ＿＿ every day with many people waiting for flights for depart.

　ア　complemented　　イ　congested　　ウ　swelled

　エ　accommodated

(5)　The lady wore the scent of many flowers like lily, orchid and lavender ＿＿＿ with something like amber, which I had never smelled.

ア　mimicked　　イ　mumbled　　ウ　triggered　　エ　mingled

(6)　A : I'm fed up with listening to Elliott these days.

B : Yeah, me too. Whenever he opens his mouth, he ＿＿＿.

ア　grumbles　　イ　censors　　ウ　endows　　エ　inflicts

(7)　The contract of the movie ＿＿＿ the actor from appearing in a commercial for two years in the U.K. but not in Canada.

ア　licenses　　イ　precludes　　ウ　mobilizes　　エ　dislocates

(8)　I needed to purchase a new car but could not afford to pay for it all at once, so I decided to pay in monthly ＿＿＿ over the next 36 months.

ア　installments　　イ　reputations　　ウ　declarations

エ　calamities

(9)　The transfer pupil outperformed everybody else in every ＿＿＿ way. He aced all the tests, had a great sense of humor and was a great athlete.

ア　concealable　　イ　courteous　　ウ　considerate

エ　conceivable

(10)　A : Could I have your number again? I couldn't get through to you no matter how many times I tried.

B : Oh, gosh. I changed my number last week. Actually I don't remember mine yet. Let me ＿＿＿ your number. I'll call you when I get home.

ア　step down　　イ　jot down　　ウ　get down　　エ　flag down

(☆☆☆☆○○○○)

【6】次の(1)～(5)の英文において，下線部に最も近い意味の語(句)をア～エの中からそれぞれ1つ選び記号で答えなさい。

(1)　The doctor is prominent in her field of liver surgery. Other surgeons come from afar to observe her techniques and learn from her.

ア　subsequent　　イ　evident　　ウ　eloquent　　エ　famous

20

(2)   The government <u>dispatched</u> four naval ships to the island as soon as the hurricane was over to help out with relief efforts.

ア   sent off   イ   resolved   ウ   diminished   エ   resigned

(3)   No matter how many times I told the salesperson at my porch that I wasn't interested in his goods, he wouldn't leave. He was <u>persistent</u> to the point of being rude.

ア   fraudulent   イ   stubborn   ウ   redundant   エ   expectant

(4)   Sofia often buys things from door to door salespeople. Her husband gets frustrated with her because she is <u>gullible</u>, believing almost everything they tell her.

ア   liable   イ   easily fooled   ウ   affable   エ   credible

(5)   The lifestyle of the rich and famous seems <u>enviable</u> at first, but they are commonly no happier than average people, and they often suffer from a lack of privacy.

ア   impassive   イ   insightful   ウ   enlightening
エ   desirable

(☆☆☆◎◎◎◎)

【7】次の(1)～(5)の英文において不適切な箇所を，下線部ア～エの中からそれぞれ1つ選び記号で答え，正しい形，または，適切な語(句)にしなさい。

(1)   Though ア<u>it</u> may vary slightly during the day, イ<u>human</u> body temperature remains ウ<u>relative</u> constant エ<u>at</u> 37.0 degrees Celsius.

(2)   The Spanish language ア<u>provided</u> the common basis イ<u>for</u> Hispanics to unite ウ<u>ourselves</u> politically エ<u>during</u> the 1980's.

(3)   The ア<u>thickest</u> Arctic ice is イ<u>close</u> the North Pole, ウ<u>where</u> the temperature remains low エ<u>whole</u> the year.

(4)   Alligators have the same ア<u>bodily</u> structure イ<u>than</u> crocodiles, but their heads are broader and ウ<u>their</u> snouts エ<u>blunter</u>.

(5) Passenger pigeons ア<u>had become</u> uncommon by the end of the 19th

21

century, イand ウsoon after エbecoming extinct.

(☆☆☆○○○○)

【8】次の(1)～(3)の英文において，〔　　　〕内の語(句)を正しく並べかえて文章を完成するとき，〔　　　〕内の語(句)の4番目と7番目にくる語を，ア～キの中からそれぞれ1つ選び記号で答えなさい。ただし，文頭に来る文字も小文字になっている。

(1)　A : Leo? Is that you? You have changed〔ア　hardly　イ　can　ウ　I　エ　that　オ　much　カ　so　キ　recognize〕you!

　　B : Yeah, I used to be very short and skinny, but then I joined the rugby team.

(2)　A : Where is Oliver? Is hope he didn't get into an accident or anything.

　　B : Let's〔ア　rule　イ　the possibility　ウ　not　エ　he　オ　is　カ　out　キ　that〕just lost. I'm sure he's fine.

(3)　A : I was so surprised at how high the deduction was.

　　B : So was I. Tax rates are〔ア　is　イ　really　ウ　high　エ　so　オ　left　カ　much　キ　not〕for our take-home pay.

(☆☆☆○○○○)

【9】次の英文において空欄(1)～(3)に入る最も適切な語(句)を，ア～エの中からそれぞれ1つ選び記号で答えなさい。

　　We find that many sorts of animals, especially the younger, engage in doings that seems like play. Actually, we don't know the reasons why animals play. For one thing, observation of animals playing is considerably difficult. Most animals play a lot, but it's almost impossible to make them play at the time desired by researchers. Therefore, to observe animals playing, all we can do is (1). Thanks to scientists' long time study, we can find some likely purposes of animals' play.

Animals, like human beings, sometimes need to assume control, and sometimes follow. Animals seem to learn this lesson through playing. For instance, scientists have realized that when two monkeys are play-fighting, (2). One will be on top, and he seems to win. Then all of sudden, he will give the other a chance to take charge of the action. This kind of play is thought to help monkeys learn to take different roles when they are older.

Another possible reason is to let animals learn how to get along with others of their own age. Scientists have noticed that while baby rats kept with their siblings engage in a lot of rough play, those raised alone with their mothers play just a little. However, when rats that have only been with their mothers are put with other young rats, they play (3) those brought up in a large family. It seems that they try to adapt to the new circumstance in less time.

More things may remain to be discovered about animal play, but studies by scientists seem to show that animals learn some very basic social skills by participating in play.

(1) ア buy the right zoos
　　 イ tame animals in the zoo
　　 ウ just sit patiently waiting for such moments
　　 エ make a quick observation of animals the wild
(2) ア they take turns winning
　　 イ one always dominates the other
　　 ウ they fight till one of them surrenders
　　 エ a lot of monkeys join them
(3) ア not so much as　　イ as much as
　　 ウ a lot more than　　エ with their mothers

(☆☆☆◎◎◎◎)

【10】次の英文を読み，以下の各問いに対する答えとして，あるいは問いの文に続くものとして最も適切なものを，ア～エの中からそれぞれ1つ選び記号で答えなさい。

23

Some people look like they've always been happy, which gives fodder to the belief that our level of happiness is determined in our genes. The happy adults we see were simply born that way, or so the argument goes. Other people are just lucky, with winning looks or winning circumstances, hitting the great jackpot called a successful life.

However, present-day psychologists believe that the majority of factors behind our smiles or frowns have little to do with either genes or luck. Feeling good is a skill, just like swimming or sewing. Harvard University is convinced of this concept to the point that they offer a course on how to be happy, with 800 students enrolled, it is the university's most packed classroom. Harvard's super achievers are focusing their attention on learning how to feel remarkable satisfaction with their lives. Course instructor and psychologist Tal Ben Shahar argues, "When you give yourself permission to be human, you are more likely to open yourself up to positive emotions."

Psychologists didn't always believe this. Until the last decade, most assumed that, over the long run, life satisfaction levels remained rather stable, returning to a "set point" after a particularly gratifying or troubling event. However, researchers at the University of Illinois found that our set point can shift over the years, and that there are things that we can do to push that set point up on the happiness scale. One of those things is to be more appreciative of what we have, and not always look for our next thrill in a new handbag, automobile, or plastic surgery. Like digging into the world's biggest chocolate sundae, material things are great at first, but lose their strong appeal the more we consume.

(1)　Psychologists now believe that happiness is primarily a result of the

　　ア　emotional dispositions we have inherited from our ancestors.

　　イ　unknowable factors at play in the world.

　　ウ　efforts we make to pursue a state of happiness.

　　エ　physical skills we develop to overcome many of life's challenges.

(2)　In what way have psychologists' views of one's happiness set point changed over the last decade or two?

ア　Research has led psychologists to believe that our set point is bound to change over the years, and there is little we can do to influence such fluctuations.

イ　Psychologists now assume that an individual's set point is not set in stone and there are things we can do to proactively change it.

ウ　The emotional shifts observed by earlier psychologists were short-lived: psychologists now know happiness returns to a stable level in the long term.

エ　The earlier concept of a set point has been invalidated, for our swings in happiness are simply too large to support the theory.

(3)　Which of the following is NOT mentioned as a commonly held belief about happiness?

ア　There is a genetic component to happiness.

イ　People have a base-line level of happiness, to which they naturally return after certain highs or lows.

ウ　Faith in a higher being increases the set point of one's happiness.

エ　Some people's happiness is the result of being born lucky.

(4)　In the second paragraph, the writer describes

ア　an innovative university class, which has gained considerable popularity.

イ　a potential pitfall to finding long-term happiness.

ウ　one of the most common misconceptions about the modern system of universities.

エ　a strategy for getting a spot in Harvard University's most popular class.

(5)　Which of the following statements would Tal Ben Shahar most likely agree with?

ア　The most effective strategy for happiness is to wait for a return to one's own set point.

イ　Modern genetic science has created a paradigm shift in our understanding of happiness.

ウ　One's happiness is not set in stone.

エ　Gaining material items is the most realistic means to achieving happiness.

(☆☆☆☆◎◎◎◎)

【11】次の2つの資料を読み，以下の各問いに対する答えとして最も適切なものをア～エの中から1つ選び記号で答えなさい。

TKI Planning Inc. Business Plan

Table of Contents

1.0 Executive Goals

    1.1 Goals

    1.2 Summary

    1.3 Market Predictions

2.0 Products

    2.1 Online Service Summary

    2.2 Projections

3.0 Market Analysis

    3.1 Target Market

    3.2 Strategies

4.0 Financial Plan

    4.1 3-year Projections

TKI Planning Inc. provides high-tech business solutions to online companies. The company now has a total of 600 corporate clients, and is expecting to increase that number to 1,500 by the year's end.

To: Olivia Astley

From: William Garland

Subject: TKI Planning's Business Plan

Dear Olivia,

Thank you for taking the time to go over TKI's business plan with us yesterday. The response to your presentation was overwhelmingly positive, and now we have a better idea of TKI's corporate goals.

As you know, our marketing director, Michael Hardy' could not attend the meeting. But he examined the meeting minutes and was particularly intrigued with the market predictions section of the business plan. It seems that he would like to make a few additions to that section and would like to meet with you. He has a long history of doing top-notch analysis of marketing research, so I think his additions will be of value to your company.

Please let us know at your earliest convenience when you would be able to meet with Michael. I look forward to hearing from you.

Regards,

William

(1) What is the main purpose of Mr. Garland's email to Ms. Astley?

　ア　To offer to sell the parts for her company's products for a reasonable price

　イ　To introduce her to Michael Hardy

　ウ　To inform her about additions made to her plan

　エ　To set up a meeting with Michael Hardy

(2) What is one of the things the plan's market analysis covered?

　ア　Data on the kinds of employees the company will have

　イ　Data on the types of customers the company is trying to attract

　ウ　Data about online services and products

　エ　Data on the ecological impact of their business model

(3) What was detailed in the financial plan section of the business plan?

　ア　How much money the company expects to take in over the next few years

　イ　How the company will serve its 600 corporate clients in three years

ウ　What kind of projector to use during presentations

エ　Details of the legal regulations regarding corporate taxes

(4)　What can Michael Hardy do for TKI?

　ア　He can take over the duties of the chief executive officer.

　イ　He can become the company's top man.

　ウ　He can improve its business plan.

　エ　He can set up meetings with its staff.

(5)　What would Mr. Garland like Ms. Astley to do?

　ア　Give another presentation based on the changes he proposed

　イ　Come to the meeting earlier

　ウ　Contact him as soon as possible

　エ　Make some additions to his plan

(☆☆☆◎◎◎)

【12】次の英文を読み，以下の各問いに答えなさい。

　The tiny but elegant fish, tree, and horseshoe designs engraved neatly on old stone seals comprise the few and scattered examples of an ancient Indian script. Almost 4,000 years old, the seals have been circulating in the academic world for over 130 years, but despite intense scrutiny, researchers have so far been unsuccessful in unlocking their meaning.

　The mystery began in the 1870s, when ancient Indus symbols were first discovered in Pakistan. Then in 1921, engraved seals were unearthed at Harappa in Pakistan's northeast. As excavations continued, archaeologists became impressed with the size and scope of what became known as the Indus Valley Civilization, for they uncovered over 1,000 settlements. The unearthing also revealed some 2,000 seals with what appears to be fascinating writing. Believed by many to be one of humanity's first writing systems, its symbols comprise the most famous undeciphered script in the world, a script that performed an as-yet undefined function.

　While much is known about the ancient Egyptian and Mesopotamian languages, researchers are comprises in the dark about what language the Indus valley people spoke, this lack of understanding comprises one of the many stumbling blocks to deciphering the symbols. The others are the brevity of the seal inscriptions, the average having just five symbols, and that there is no known bilingual inscription to help decipher the script like the famous Rosetta Stone. Yet another problem is the number of symbols discovered, some 200 to 400, a number too large for an alphabetic system, but too small for a logographic system like that of written Chinese.

However, most researchers theorize that the writing system is a logophonetic system, in which signs are used to express meanings but also have phonetic values. One hypothesis holds that the underlying language was part of the Dravidian family, still spoken in the region but unrelated to other tongues. Based on decades of computer analysis, University of Helsinki Indologist Asko Parpola concludes: "The Indus script was essentially similar to the other pictographic scripts created before the middle of the third millennium B.C., and the language of the Indus people was Dravidian."

A very different view is held by controversial American historian Steve Farmer, who takes umbrage at the notion that the symbols are a writing system. He argues that this notion is nothing more than a scholarly myth that has persisted for over a century, noting that, "No ancient literate civilizations are known — not even those that wrote extensively on perishable materials — that did not also leave long texts behind on durable materials," Farmer and his colleagues have even put forth a $10,000 prize for an Indus inscription containing at least 50 symbols, believing that the chance of such an inscription materializing is vanishingly small.

Despite Farmer's argument, it seems unlikely that a sophisticated urban society like the one found at the Indus cities would have flourished without writing, one of the distinguishing features of civilization. Ongoing fieldwork at Harappa and other sites may yet yield insights. Until then, the exquisitely carved symbols will continue to conceal their secrets, as they have through the centuries.

(1)　次の①，②の問いに対する答えとして最も適切なもの，③につい
ては，文に続くものとして最も適切なものをア～エの中から1つ選
び記号で答えなさい。

①　What is one of the reasons the Indus symbols have yet to be
deciphered?

ア　The number of symbols suggests that they have no phonetic value.

イ　Though most researchers are familiar with the language of the
Indus Valley, its writing system is fundamentally different.

ウ　Scholars are not aware of any translations of the symbols into other
languages.

エ　Computer analysis of the discoveries has produced contradictory
results.

②　What fact does Steve Farmer use to support his theory?

ア　No examples of a large number of Indus symbols being written
together on a long-lasting surface have been discovered.

イ　Excavations show that the Indus Valley Civilization was certainly
sophisticated enough to develop a vibrant literary culture.

ウ　The analysis by Asko Parpola was fundamentally flawed from a
technological standpoint.

エ　It is wrong to assume the symbols are part of a writing system
when researchers have completely failed to decipher them.

③　The writer of this passage implies that

ア　most researchers are oblivious to the fact that the symbols are
logophonetic and so express both sounds and meanings.

イ　the symbols are probably related to ancient languages in Egypt and
Mesopotamia.

ウ　it is quite unlikely that the meaning of the symbols will ever be
unraveled by researchers.

エ　the symbols are probably part of a writing system because they were developed by an advanced civilization.

(2) 次の各英文を，本文中で述べられている順番に並び替え，記号で答えなさい。

　ア　It is commonly assumed that the symbols are a logophonetic representation of a Dravidian language.

　イ　There are several impediments to deciphering the symbols used by the Indus Valley people.

　ウ　Around 2,000 seals have been unearthed in the the northeast region of Pakistan.

　エ　A controversial historian from America asserts that the symbols do not represent a writing system.

(3) 本文のタイトルとして最も適当なものをア〜エの中から1つ選び記号で答えなさい。

　ア　A 10,000 Dollar Prize

　イ　The Accomplishments of a Leading Indologist

　ウ　A 4,000-Year-Old Riddle in Writing

　エ　Writing on Perishable Materials

(4) 本文中の下線部a scholarly mythについて，本文内容と関連付けながら20語以上30語以下の英語で説明しなさい。

(☆☆☆☆◎◎◎)

【13】 The Course of Study states that English teachers have to develop the qualities and abilities necessary for communication through language activities. Write an English composition about three or more important points that English teachers need to be aware of if they want to have a class where students give speeches about daily topics based on their opinions and feelings. The composition should be 80 words or more.

(☆☆☆☆◎◎◎)

【14】授業中に生徒が次の(1)と(2)の質問をした。あなたは英語の教員と
　　してどのように説明するか。それぞれについて日本語で答えなさい。
　　(説明の一部に英語を交えても差し支えない)

　(1)　thinkは不定詞を目的語に取ることができないと思っていました
　　が，think to doがあり得ると聞きました。例をあげてその意味と用
　　法を教えてください。

　(2)　「the＋比較級…, the＋比較級…」の構文はすべてif節を使って書き
　　換えられるのでしょうか。例を示して教えてください。

（☆☆☆☆◎◎◎◎）

【高等学校】

【１】Read the passage and answer the questions below.

Collaborative Communities that Research, Reflect, and Revise

　　At Rochester High, science teacher Amy Blackburn has her students use a
suite of options, including e-mail, discussion forums, Google Docs, and
Google Sites to communicate with each other in real-time on projects. Google
Docs registers each team member's contributions to a project just as it does in
genuine office settings - eliminating the thorny he-said, she-said debates of
years past.

　　Similarly, at the *¹Science Leadership Academy, tenth graders in English
teacher Larissa Pahomov's linked English and history class use Wikispaces, a
free online educational tool, to create poetry portfolios. Pahomov knows it
will be motivating for students, given their enthusiasm for social networking.
Students use the program to write their own poems and a forum allows them
to edit and comment on each other's writing, and then comment on other
students' feedback. Meanwhile, Pahomov can monitor the exchanges and
offer extra help only when needed; for instance, if a student seems stalled in
his or her writing, or if a critic needs suggestions on how to be more
diplomatic. This learning tool helps writing become a more communal
process and mirrors something that is also happening more and more on

campuses and in professional settings.

Technology has the ability to shift traditional power dynamics in educational settings. At their discretion, teachers can free themselves from constantly being the primary (　ア　). Instead they remain at a distance, monitoring conversations to make sure the feedback is constructive and not hurtful, and stepping in only occasionally as the students learn to take responsibility for their own and each other's progress. More broadly, technology spurs collaboration by creating and strengthening virtual communities that give students and their teachers new ways and different modes of trading ideas and providing feedback.

"Technology creates opportunities to make the work real," says David Grant, the technology integrator at*²King Middle School. "If you are working in the world today, there's little chance you won't be working on a computer. For anything that is complex, requires an outcome product, needs collaboration, communication, research, etc., there will be software or hardware in the middle. Without ₐthis, school is ᵦpretend." While other teachers may still ask kids to keep private journals of their reflections in class in notebooks, Grant encourages them to post them online, to "make their thinking visible" and invite other students to respond.

Many Deeper Learning schools rely heavily on student presentations as a means for students to share their work with the school community and to demonstrate their understanding of the academic concepts involved in a project. Rather than just reading aloud a written speech, students are encouraged and often required to create more complex, engaging presentations using PowerPoint, Prezi, and webinars, or even by making a DVD. These schools also encourage students to use the technology many of them already have regular access to, in the form of now less expensive cell phones and digital cameras, for school-related projects. Supporting students to feel like, and behave like, professional documentarians, they can venture out into their communities to conduct all kinds of research and gather material.

(ウ) strategically, technology can give students (イ) <u>novel</u> opportunities to practice reflection and revision, both critical to the Deeper Learning process, by making those pursuits more authentic and engaging. Simply through an ability to save (digitally), track, and time stamp, technology can help students better reflect on and revise their work. (エ) how many homework papers get lost in backpack transit between school and home in traditional schools, eliminating that factor is a big deal in itself. (オ) to this is the advantage that as students build their digital portfolios, they can go back an unlimited number of times to revise what they've done. Naturally, when students can search through their work in one place (as opposed to behind bureaus, under car seats, and hidden by parents in attics), they can also play a more active role in reviewing their own progress over the course of their school career. Essentially, technology allows for work to be archived, which in turn enables more efficient and fruitful reflection and revisions. In this way, Hull says, digital portfolios encourage students to keep asking, "What will I do next time that will make my learning better?"

*¹ Science Leadership Academy: a high school in Philadelphia, Pennsylvania

*² King Middle School: a high school in Portland, Maine

1. Choose the best option which describes Larissa Pahomov from among the choices. Write the number of the answer.

① Her class reflects what happens in real life and helps students get the skills which they need in society.

② To help students develop their creativity, Pahomov observes students' activities and gives them feedback on a frequent basis.

③ Through her class, students have a lot of enthusiasm for social networking.

④ Through learning how to compose poetry, students get effective communication skill which they can use on campuses and in professional settings.

2.   Choose the best option for (ア   ) from among the choices. Write the
     number of the answer.

     ① coaches   ② interlocutors   ③ motivators   ④ observers

3.   What does "(A   )<u>this</u>" refer to? Write the number of the answer.

     ① an outcome product   ② collaboration   ③ communication

     ④ software

4.   Choose the meaning of "(B   )<u>pretend</u>" from among the choices. Write
     the number of the answer.

     ①   as good as possible, or the best of its kind

     ②   not real, imaginary

     ③   showing care and effort in your work or duties

     ④   very important because what happens in the future depends on it

5.   Choose the meaning of (イ   )<u>novel</u> from among the choices. Write the
     number of the answer.

     ①   believing in old or traditional ways

     ②   done secretly or kept secret

     ③   not like anything known before, and unusual or interesting

     ④   suitable, acceptable or correct for the particular circumstances

6.   Choose the best pair of the words from among the choices for (ウ   ),
     (エ   ) and (オ   ). Write the number of the answer.

     ①   ウ   Managed   エ   Considered   オ   Added

     ②   ウ   Managing   エ   Considering   オ   Adding

     ③   ウ   Managing   エ   Considered   オ   Adding

     ④   ウ   Managed   エ   Considering   オ   Added

7.   The author emphasizes the importance of student presentations in this
     passage. Do you agree with the author or not? Write your opinion and
     idea(s) in 50 to 100 words in English referring to your own experience.

                                        (☆☆☆☆☆◎◎◎)

【2】 Read the passage and answer the questions below.

MALCOLM X SHABAZZ AND THE FUTURE PROJECT

　　The minute you set foot in Malcolm X Shabazz High School in Newark, New Jersey, you notice something different. In a school that for years held spot on the list of our country's most troubled high schools, kids walk down halls with confident smiles and a sense of purpose. In the past couple of years, attendance rates have jumped dramatically. (ア)<u>Kids now come to school on snow days</u>. And during lunch, groups of kids take their lunch trays to sessions tutoring them on things like writing skills.

　　The Newark school system has long been viewed as Ground Zero for education reformers. Several, including Bill Gates, Mark Zuckerberg, the Waltons, and Eli Broad, set out to transform Newark schools and make them a national model. Zuckerberg announced a $100 million gift to Newark education on the Oprah Winfrey show, timed to coincide with the documentary *Waiting for Superman*. But, as the *New Yorker* reported, this heavily funded reform initiative accomplished nothing other than lining the pockets of consultants. In a telling line from Vivian Cox Fraser, the president of the Urban League of Essex County, "Everybody's getting paid, but Raheem still can't read."

　　Gemar Mills, the principal of Shabazz, explains, "When I took over as principal in 2011-2012, I was the fourth principal over the course of four years, the state had recommended the district close the school, and the media dubbed the school 'Baghdad.' I couldn't begin to count the problems at this school. Nothing was working." So what's different now about Malcolm X Shabazz, if reform policies had no impact? Principal Mills teamed up with The Future Project, which hired an extraordinary visionary named Divine Bradley. Bradley is the head Dream Director at Shabazz, and part of the audacious nonprofit called The Future Project. He walks the halls of Shabazz, gets to know the students, and engages them on the question of "What's something big and bold you'd like to do with your life to make your world

36

better? I'm here to help you." Most students have never been asked about life goals before. As a result of this kind of engagement, students at Shabazz rise to challenges, take on ambitious projects, and approach education and life with newfound purpose.

In the 2013-2014 school year, the Shabazz girls' basketball team hadn't lost a home game in thirty years and was ranked number two in the nation by *USA Today*. Though most players had never been on an airplane before, the team dreamed of playing in the national tournament in California, in which they had been invited to compete for two consecutive years. They approached their Dream Director for support, who responded, "I'm here to help, but you need to lead this effort, figure out your plan, and make it happen." Well, they did research and learned that former NBA star Shaquille O'Neal was born in Newark. They found a time he'd be in town. They worked with Bradley and Principal Mills to figure out a way to convince *¹ Shaq to come to their school and help them paint a mural. In advance, they prepared their pitch asking him to support their trip, complete with well-written backup. When he was at Shabazz, the team made their case, and O'Neal committed the funds to make the team's dream a reality. Principal Mills explains, "The impact on these girls, and on the rest of the school, was transformational. Under different circumstances, many would have dropped out of high school. However, this team served as an example of what could happen when you dream big and work hard. Of the five seniors on the team, all five graduated from Shabazz with diplomas three with high honors. Moreover, all five seniors received scholarships to top colleges throughout the country. We now call our school Possibility High."

This school year, The Future Project launched an initiative called FutureU, as it expanded to high schools all over the country. Students spend time during lunch hours, before school, after school, or on Saturdays learning the skills required to accomplish their dreams: effective communication skills, how to manage projects, how to collaborate, and how to critique and exchange feedback. FutureU makes other school classes more compelling for the students and more effective for the teachers, since the link between a class and life is more apparent. Principal Mills reports that The Future Project doesn't just transform his students. He notes, "Our teachers and our staff all have dreams of their own, and Divine and his team help them achieve what they strive for. I knew just how special this program is when one of our security guards put up a huge picture of himself, alongside other students, which said his dream is to be a Newark policeman."

Not yet three years old, The Future Project is one of the fastest-growing and most successful nonprofit start-ups since the founding of Teach For America in 1990. Possibility High? That's the point of The Future Project. If the top priority of our education system were engaging and inspiring kids — not testing and measuring them — all sorts of things would be possible.

*¹ Shaq: nickname of Shaquille O'Neal

1. What does the sentence (ア) imply?

　① Even on snow days, some kids at Malcolm X Shabazz High School take sessions to improve their writing skills.

　② It snows a lot in Newark, so kids at Malcolm X Shabazz High School must often come to school on snow days.

　③ Kids in Malcolm X Shabazz High School enjoy their school life.

　④ There is a lot of trouble in Malcolm X Shabazz High School because of the heavy snow in winter.

2. What is true about the Newark school system?

　① In spite of monetary support, education reformers failed to transform Newark schools.

　② Several donors including Mark Zuckerberg provided financial support, which succeeded in making Newark schools a national model.

　③ The documentary *Waiting for Superman*, filmed by Oprah Winfrey, made a feature of how Zuckerberg announced a $100 million gift to Newark education.

④　Vivian Cox Fraser, one of the principals of a Newark school complained that teachers should get paid more.

3.　What is true about Divine Bradley?

①　He is a student who started The Future Project with Principal Mills, and helps his friends to think about their future.

②　He is an entrepreneur who is employed by The Future Project and helps students in Malcolm X Shabazz High School to take on projects.

③　He is one of the best teachers in Malcolm X Shabazz High School and launched The Future Project.

④　He stimulates students to tackle aspirational projects and provides full support.

4.　What is true about the Shabazz girls' basketball team?

①　According to Principal Mills, all students of the girls' basketball team graduated and three students could obtain scholarships from colleges.

②　Thanks to the funds of Shaquille O'Neal, the team could travel to California without an airplane.

③　Their Dream Director made a systematic plan in advance and had students carry it out.

④　What the team achieved with their Dream Director had a beneficial influence on other students in their school.

5.　According to this passage, The Future Project emphasizes four skills: effective communication skills, how to manage projects, how to collaborate, and how to critique and exchange feedback. Among these four skills, which do you think is the most important for students to realize their dreams? As an English teacher, how will you cultivate that skill in class? Write your opinion and idea(s) in 50 to 100 words in English referring to your own experience.

6.　The author claims that the top priority of our education should be engaging and inspiring students, not just testing and measuring them. Do you agree with the author or not? Write your opinion and idea(s) in 50 to

100 words in English referring to your own experience.

(☆☆☆☆◎◎◎)

解答・解説

【中高共通】

【１】Conversation 1　B　　　Conversation 2　A　　　Conversation 3　D
Conversation 4　B

〈解説〉Conversation 1　設問は「女性は何を暗示しているか」。女性は，新しい上司が女性の予定を尋ねることなく，土曜日に仕事をするように言ったことに対して否定的印象を持っているので，B「新しい上司は思いやりがない」が適切。　Conversation 2　設問は「女性はどうするだろうか」。女性は3社から採用通知をもらったが，どこに行くべきか迷っていて，しばらく考えてみると言っているので，A「決断する前に時間をかける」が適切。　Conversation 3　設問は「夫妻は何をすることに決めたか」。男性が，近所に住んでいる女性の友達にアドバイスをもらおうと言っているので，D「そのアパートについて女性の友達に相談する」が適切。　Conversation 4　設問は「男性について何がわかるか」。男性は，幼少期をオーストラリアで過ごしたので，楽しい思い出がたくさんあると言っている。よって，B「彼はオーストラリアで育った」が適切。

【２】Passage 1　Question 1　A　　　Question 2　D　　　Passage 2　Question
1　A　　　Question 2　D

〈解説〉Passage 1　Question 1　設問は「ユタ大学での実験の目的は何だったか」。前半は，運転中の携帯電話使用が引き起こす事故の可能性について述べられているので，A「運転中に携帯電話を使用することがどれほど危険であるかを証明するため」が適切。　Question 2　設問

は「ごく一部の学生は大多数の学生とどのように違っていたか」。後半に，被験者の2.5％が運転と携帯電話の操作の2つのタスクを同時にこなすことができたとあるので，D「彼らは2つのタスクを同時に巧みに実行した」が適切。　Passage 2　Question 1　設問は「カロリー表示がなされたとき，ファストフード店での飲食とコーヒーチェーン店での飲食を比較してどうだったか」。前半に，ファストフード店では飲料の選択はカロリー表示の影響を受けないことがわかったとある。よって，A「ファストフード店では，飲み物の注文にはあまり影響がなかった」が適切。　Question 2　設問は「研究者が，以前の研究結果と新しい発見が矛盾すると考えるのはなぜか」。以前の研究では，低所得者層が住む地域では顧客はカロリー表示を気にせず，摂取カロリーを控えないという結果が得られたと述べられており，所得者層別に研究が行われたことがわかる。しかし，最近の研究では，低所得者層から高所得者層までの顧客が混在していたと説明しているので，D「後の研究はより包括的であった」が適切。

【3】Conversation 1　Question 1　B　　Question 2　D　　Conversation 2　Question 1　D　　Question 2　B
〈解説〉Conversation 1　Question 1　設問は「どうしてその男は懐石Miyakoのことを知っているのか」。男性は，最近Instagramでそれについてのレビューを読んだ気がすると言っているので，Bが適切。Question 2　設問は「女性は何をしようと申し出ているか」。女性は「レストランに寄ってメニューをもらってくると言っているので，Dが適切。　Conversation 2　Question 1　設問は「男性はなぜ電話をしているのか」。男性は，マネジメント・セミナーの参加者にアンケートを行っていると言っているので，Dが適切。　Question 2　設問は「女性は何を提案するか」。女性は「授業が夕方遅くに始まってくれると助かる」と言っているので，Bが適切。

【4】パンデミックにより外国人観光客が事実上ストップしたため，タイで象のショーをすることで収入を得ていた一家にとって，SNSが新たな収入源である。2019年には4,000万人近い外国人観光客がタイを訪れたのに対し，2020年は40万人だった。タイで飼育されている象をサポートするために予算が必要である。政府は2021年に1,000万人の外国人観光客を見込むが，それでは十分ではないかもしれない。(192字)

〈解説〉400語程度の英文を聞いて，要旨を150〜200字の日本語で記述する形式。放送は2度流れる。「タイで象のショーをして生計をたてていた家族」→「パンデミックによる外国人観光客受け入れ停止」→「政府による支援と観光客回復の兆し」という流れ。「トンネルの先に光が見えない」というような内容で締めくくる。

【5】(1) イ　　(2) ウ　　(3) エ　　(4) イ　　(5) エ　　(6) ア
(7) イ　　(8) ア　　(9) エ　　(10) イ

〈解説〉(1)「BauerはAudreyのことが好きだったので，よく彼女に微笑みかけ，温かい言葉をかけた。しかし彼の努力は報われなかった」。reciprocate〜「〜に報いる」。　(2)「人々はGibson夫人がどれほど気難しい人かを私に話した。後で会ってみると，彼女は少し風変わりだが優しい人だった。結局，みんな大げさに言っていたのだと思った」。exaggerate「誇張する」。　(3) B「確かに彼女は牛肉を食べないが，他の肉は食べる。彼女はベジタリアンを公言しているだけか，菜食主義をよく知らないのだと思う」。profess「〜を公言する，〜と自称する」。　(4)「予期せぬ火山爆発が起きて以来，南米のいくつかの空港は出発便を待つ多くの人で連日大混雑だ」。congested「混雑した」。(5)「その女性は，ユリ，ラン，ラベンダーなど多くの花の香りに，私が嗅いだことのないアンバーのようなものが混ざった香りをまとっていた」。mingle with〜「〜と混ざる」。　(6)「A：最近，Elliottの話にはうんざりしているよ。B：ああ，僕も。彼は口を開けばいつも文句ばかり言う」。grumble「ぶつぶつ不平を言う」。　(7)「映画の契約により，この俳優はイギリスでは2年間CMに出演できないが，カナダで

はそうではない」。preclude「排除する，妨げる」。 (8)「新車を購入する必要があったが，一度に支払う余裕がなかったので，36カ月にわたる分割払いにした」。installment「分割払い(の1回分)」。 (9)「その転校生は，考えられるあらゆる点で他の生徒より優れていた」。conceivable「考えられる，想定される」。 (10)「B：実はまだ自分の番号を覚えていないんだ。あなたの番号を控えさせて。家に帰ったら電話するから」。jot down「メモする」。

【6】(1) エ (2) ア (3) イ (4) イ (5) エ

〈解説〉(1)「その医師は肝臓手術の分野で著名である」。famous「有名な」。 (2)「政府はハリケーンが過ぎるとすぐに，救援活動を支援するために4隻の海軍の艦船を島に派遣した」。send off「送り出す」。 (3)「彼は無礼なまでにしつこかった」。stubborn「頑固な」。 (4)「彼女は騙されやすく，彼らの言うことをほとんどすべて信じてしまうので，夫は彼女にイライラしている」。easily fooled「騙されやすい」。 (5)「金持ちや有名人のライフスタイルは一見羨ましく思えるが…」。desirable「望ましい」。

【7】(1) 記号…ウ 語…relatively (2) 記号…ウ 語…themselves (3) 記号…イ 語…close to (4) 記号…イ 語…as (5) 記号…エ 語…became

〈解説〉(1)「人間の体温は，日中多少変化することはあっても37℃で比較的一定である」。relativelyはconstantを修飾する副詞。 (2)「スペイン語は，1980年代にヒスパニック系住民が政治的に団結するための共通の基盤となった」。uniteの目的語はHispanicsなのでthemselvesにする。 (3)「最も厚い北極地方の氷は北極により近く，年間を通して気温が低い場所にある」。be close to～「～の近くにある」。 (4)「アリゲーターはクロコダイルと同じ体の構造をしているが，頭はより広く，鼻先はより丸みを帯びている」。the same A as B「Bと同じA」。 (5)「伝書鳩は19世紀末には滅多に見られなくなり，やがて廃れてしまった」。

soon after「その後すぐに」。and soon after (passenger pigeons) became extinctとなる。

【8】(1)　4番目…ウ　　7番目…キ　　(2)　4番目…イ　　7番目…オ
(3)　4番目…キ　　7番目…オ
〈解説〉(1)　整序すると，You have changed so much that I can hardly recognize you.「あなたはあまりに変わってしまって，私はあなたを見分けられません」。　(2)　整序すると，Let's not rule out the possibility that he is just lost.「ただ道に迷っているだけという可能性を排除しないようにしよう」。　(3)　整序すると，Tax rates are really high, so not much is left for our take-home pay.「税率が本当に高いから，手取りはあまり残らない」。

【9】(1)　ウ　　(2)　ア　　(3)　ウ
〈解説〉(1)　「ほとんどの動物はよく遊ぶが，研究者が望むような時間に遊ばせることはほとんど不可能だ。したがって，動物が遊んでいるのを観察するには，『その瞬間をじっと待つしかない』」。just sit patiently waiting for such momentsが入る。　(2)　「動物たちは，遊びを通してそのこと(主導権を握ったり，従ったりすること)を学んでいるようだ。例えば，科学者たちは2匹のサルがケンカごっこをしているとき，『交互に勝ち負けを決めている』ことに気づいた」。they take turns winningが入る。　(3)　「しかし，母親としか一緒にいなかったネズミを他の若いネズミと一緒にすると，大家族で育ったネズミ『よりもたくさん』遊ぶ。より短い時間で新しい環境に適応しようとするようだ」。a lot more thanが入る。

【10】(1)　ウ　　(2)　イ　　(3)　ウ　　(4)　ア　　(5)　ウ
〈解説〉(1)　第2段落参照。「気分の良さは水泳や裁縫と同じように技術だ。ハーバード大学では「幸せになる方法」を学ぶコースを設けるほどこのコンセプトを確信していて…」から，「心理学者たちは現在，

幸福とは主に幸福な状態を追求するための努力の結果であると考えている」が正しい。　(2)　質問は「この10年，20年の間に，心理学者たちの幸福のセットポイントに対する見方はどのように変化したか」。第3段落のイリノイ大学の研究者たちの見解参照。「心理学者たちは現在，個人のセットポイントは決まっておらず，それを積極的に変えるためにできることがあると仮定している」が正しい。　(3)　質問は「幸福に関する一般的な考え方として挙げられていないものはどれか」。ア「幸福には遺伝的要素がある」，イ「人には幸せのベースラインがあり，ある種の絶頂期や低迷期を過ぎると自然にそのレベルに戻る」，エ「生まれながらにして幸運に恵まれている人もいる」は第1段落，第3段落で述べられている。ウ「高次の存在への信念は，自分の幸福のセットポイントを高める」が誤り。　(4)　第2段落で筆者が述べていることは，ア「非常に人気がある，ある革新的な大学の授業」。(5)　質問は「Tal Ben Shaharが最も同意しそうな記述はどれか」。Tal Ben Shaharは「幸せになる方法」を学ぶコースの講師。ア「幸福のための最も効果的な手段は，自分自身のセットポイントに戻るのを待つことである」，イ「現代の遺伝子科学は，幸福についての理解にパラダイムシフトをもたらした」，エ「物質的なものを得ることは，幸福を得るための最も現実的な手段である」はあてはまらない。ウ「人の幸福は定まったものではない」が正しい。

【11】(1)　エ　　(2)　イ　　(3)　ア　　(4)　ウ　　(5)　ウ
〈解説〉(1)　「Mr. GarlandがMs. Astleyに送ったメールの主な目的は何か」。メール後半の文面から，エ「Michael Hardyとの面談を設定するため」。(2)　「このプランの市場分析で扱われたことのひとつは何か」。株式会社TKIプランニングが法人顧客を増やそうとしていることから，イ「会社がどのような顧客を獲得しようとしているかについてのデータ」。(3)　事業計画書の財務計画セクションに書かれている内容としては，ア「今後数年間で，その会社がどれだけの収入を見込んでいるか」が適切。(4)　「Michael HardyはTKIのために何ができるか」。

メール中ほど参照。ウ「事業計画を改善することができる」が適切。
(5)　「Mr. GarlandはMs. Astleyに何をしてほしいか」。メールの最後の2
文から「できるだけ早く自分に連絡すること」。

【12】(1)　①　ウ　　②　ア　　③　エ　　(2)　ウ→イ→ア→エ
(3)　ウ　　(4)　Steve Farmer says that the idea that the Indus symbols are a
writing system is simply a delusion of academia.

〈解説〉(1)　①　「インダスの記号がいまだに解読されていない理由のひ
とつは何か」。第3段落中ほど参照。「…ロゼッタ・ストーンのように
文字を解読するのに役立つ対訳碑文が知られていない…」から，ウ
「学者たちは，記号が他の言語に翻訳されていることを把握していな
い」。　②　「Steve Farmerが自説の根拠にしている事実は何か」。第5段
落中ほど参照。Steve Farmerは，耐久性のある素材に長い文章を書き残
さなかった文明は知られていないという理由で，この記号が文字体系
であるという考え方に賛同していない。ア「長期保存可能な表面上に
インダスの記号の多くが一緒に書かれた例は発見されていない」が適
切。　③　最終段落参照。この文章の著者が示唆していることは，エ
「記号は高度な文明によって開発されたものなので，おそらく文字体
系の一部である」。　(2)　ウ「パキスタン北東部で約2,000点の印章が
発掘された」→イ「インダス渓谷の人々によって使用された記号を解
読するには，いくつかの障害がある」→ア「記号はドラヴィダ語の音
声表現であると一般的に考えられている」→エ「物議を醸しているア
メリカの歴史家は，記号は文字体系を表すものではないと主張してい
る」。　(3)　未だ解明されない印章に刻印された文字と思われるもの
についての文章であるので，タイトルは，ウ「4,000年続く文字の謎」
が適切。　(4)　a scholarly myth「学術的神話」の内容は「インダスの
記号が文字体系であるという考え」を指す。「そのような考えは『学
術的神話』であるとSteve Farmerが主張している」とまとめる。

【13】 English teachers should keep the following three attention points in mind when we have classes where students give speeches. The first one is to help students make the speeches' goal clear like giving listeners chances to think or to let them take actions by telling thoughts or feelings about facts in which students are interested. The second is to help students think about the order of the facts or thoughts you want to tell. The third is to help students give speeches that are considerate for listeners. (87 words)

〈解説〉設問の文意は「学習指導要領では，英語教師は言語活動を通してコミュニケーションに必要な資質・能力を育成しなければならないとされている。生徒が自分の意見や感じたことに基づいた日常的な話題についてスピーチするような授業を行うとき，英語教師が留意すべき点を3つ以上挙げて英作文を書きなさい。英作文は80語以上とする」。解答例では，スピーチの目的を明確にすること，伝えたい事実や考えの順番を考えさせること，聞き手に配慮したスピーチをさせることを挙げている。中学校学習指導要領解説外国語編および高等学校学習指導要領解説外国語編・英語編を参照のこと。使用する語句や文，発話例を示すこと，視覚的な補助を作成するなど準備のための時間を確保すること，情報や考え，気持などを整理し，理由や根拠とともに話すことなどに触れて書くこともできる。

【14】 (1) 一つ目は intend, hope, plan to doのように「～するつもりだ」という意味を表し，二つ目はit occurs someone to doのように「(～しようという考えが)頭をよぎる」という意味を表します(他に「～することを思いつく」think of doingや「忘れずに～する」remember to doの意味を表す)。一つ目の用法としては，He thinks to get a job.「彼は仕事を得ようとしている」。二つ目の用法は，I didn't think to learn sign language at first.「手話を習うなんて考えてもみなかった」などのようになります。 (2) 確かに The longer he has to wait, the angrier John gets.はif節を使って，If he has to wait a long time, John gets angry.とすることができます。しかしすべてif節を使っては書き換えられません。例えば，The

more I thought about the plan, the less I like it.などは，実際に起きたこと
を述べているので，if節への書き換えは不可能です。

〈解説〉(1)　think to doは「(否定文・疑問文で)予期する，予想する」や
「しようとする」という意味で使われることがある。　(2)　解答例の，
The more I thought about the plan, the less I like it.のような文は，as〜「〜
するにつれて」等で書き換える。

【高等学校】

【１】１　①　　　２　②　　　３　④　　　４　②　　　５　③　　　６　④

7　High school students' presentations are crucial as they enhance essential
skills like communication, public speaking, and critical thinking. These
abilities are essential for academic success, future careers, and personal
development. Presentations enable students to articulate ideas, engage with
diverse audiences, and boost self-confidence. Moreover, they foster teamwork
and research skills while promoting creativity and problem-solving. By
mastering presentation techniques in high school, students are better prepared
for higher education and professional environments, where effective
communication and presentation prowess are highly valued and can
significantly impact their overall success. (88 words)

〈解説〉1　Larissa Pahomovに関する記述のうち，最も適切なものを選ぶ
問題。第2段落参照。Larissa Pahomovは，生徒たちがソーシャル・ネッ
トワーキングに熱中していることから，それが生徒たちのやる気を引
き出すと考えた。生徒たちは，自分の詩を書き，お互いの詩を編集し，
他の生徒にコメントする。その間，Larissa Pahomovは必要なときだけ
手助けをすると述べられている。よって，①「彼女の授業は実生活に
即しており，生徒が社会で必要とされるスキルを身につけるのに役立
つ」が適切。　2　空所を含む文の文意は「テクノロジーは，教育現
場における伝統的なパワー・ダイナミクスを変化させることができ
る。教師は自分の裁量で，常に主要な『対話者』であることから解放
される。その代わり，教師は距離を置き…」となる。interlocutor「会

話者，発問者」。　3　David Grantは「今日の世界で働くなら，コンピュータを使わない可能性はほとんどない。複雑なもの，成果物が必要なもの，共同作業やコミュニケーションや研究が必要なものなどには，その途中でソフトウェアやハードウェアが存在する(＝ソフトウェアやハードウェアが必要だ)。これがなければ，学校は見せかけである」と言っている。「これ」はソフトウェアを指す。　4　「見せかけ」を言い換えると，②　not real, imaginary「本物ではない，架空の」。

5　novel「新しい，新奇な，奇抜な」なので，③「これまで知られていたものとは違う，珍しい，興味深い」が正しい。　6　ウ　Managed strategically「戦略的に活用されれば」。　エ　Considering how many homework papers get lost in backpack transit between school and home「学校と自宅を往復するリュックサックの中で宿題用紙が紛失することが多かったことを考えると」。　オ　Added to this is the advantage that…「これに加えて，…という利点もある」。　7　設問の文意は「著者はこの文章で生徒のプレゼンテーションの重要性を強調している。あなたは著者の意見に賛成ですか，反対ですか。あなたの意見と考えをあなた自身の経験を踏まえて，50～100語の英語で書きなさい」。解答例は賛成の立場で意見を述べている。プレゼンテーションは，生徒が考えを明確にし，多様な聴衆と関わり，自信を高めることを可能にすること，プレゼンテーションのテクニックを習得することで，高等教育や職業環境に，よりよく備えることができることなどを理由として挙げている。

【2】　1　③　　2　①　　3　④　　4　④　　5　Among the four skills, I believe effective communication skills are the most crucial for students to realize their dreams. I cultivate this skill in class by incorporating various interactive activities. These activities help students express their ideas confidently, actively listen to others, and constructively exchange feedback. I provide individualized feedback to help them improve their communication techniques. Additionally, I encourage them to participate in extracurricular activities like public speaking contests or joining the school newspaper. By mastering effective communication, students can effectively advocate for their dreams, engage with opportunities, and build connections that propel them towards their goals. (98 words)　　6　In foreign language education, prioritizing student engagement and inspiration is paramount for successful language acquisition. For instance, instead of solely focusing on grammar drills and assessments, teachers can incorporate interactive language games, cultural activities, and immersive experiences. By organizing language exchange programs or virtual interactions with native speakers, students become enthusiastic about communicating in the target language authentically. Such approaches not only enhance language proficiency but also foster a genuine appreciation for the culture and its nuances. Inspired learners are more likely to continue their language journey beyond the classroom and pursue careers that require multilingual skills. (97 words)

〈解説〉1　前後の「ここ数年で出席率は劇的に上昇した」や「昼食時には，子どもたちのグループがランチトレイを持ってライティングスキルなどを指導するセッションに参加する」などから，Malcolm X Shabazz High Schoolの子どもたちが学校生活を楽しんでいることを示している。　2　設問の文意は「ニューアークの学校制度についてどれが正しいか」。第2段落参照。多額の資金を投入されたニューアークの改革構想は失敗に終わったので，①「金銭的な支援にもかかわらず，教育改革者たちはニューアークの学校を変革することができなかった」が適切。　3　第3段落後半参照。Divine Bradleyは将来について考えさせ，生徒の手助けをしている。その結果，Shabazz High Schoolの生徒たちは課題に立ち向かい，野心的なプロジェクトに取り組み，新たに見つけた目的を持って教育や生活に取りかかるようになった。よって，④「学生が野心的なプロジェクトに取り組むように仕向け，全面的にサポートする」が正しい。　4　第4段落参照。Shabazz girls' basketball teamは，大きな夢を持って一生懸命取り組み，結果，本人たちと学校の他の生徒たちに与えた影響は変革をもたらすものになっ

た。よって，④「チームがドリームディレクターとともに成し遂げたことは，学校の他の生徒に有益な影響を与えた」が正しい。　5　設問の文意は「この文章によると，The Future Projectでは，効果的なコミュニケーション・スキル，プロジェクトの管理方法，協力方法，批評とフィードバックの交換の方法という4つのスキルを重視している。これら4つのスキルの中で，生徒が夢を実現するために最も重要なのはどれだと思うか。英語教師として，授業でそのスキルをどのように培うか。あなた自身の経験を踏まえて，あなたの意見や考えを50〜100語の英語で書きなさい」。解答例では，効果的なコミュニケーション・スキルを最も重要なものとして取り上げている。その理由は，効果的なコミュニケーションは，自分の夢を効果的に主張し，チャンスに恵まれ，目標に向かって進むための人脈を築くのに役立つからである。そして，このスキルの育成のために，授業にさまざまな対話型アクティビティを取り入れることや，個別のフィードバックを生徒に与えることなどを述べている。　6　設問の文意は「著者は，教育の最優先事項は単に生徒をテストして測定することではなく，生徒を魅了し刺激を与えることであるべきだと主張している。あなたは著者に同意するか。あなた自身の経験を踏まえて，あなたの意見や考えを50〜100語の英語で書きなさい」。解答例は，著者の意見に同意する立場であり，生徒の関与とインスピレーションを優先することが最も重要だとしている。授業にインタラクティブな言語ゲーム，文化活動，没入型の体験や，言語交換プログラム，ネイティブスピーカーとのバーチャル交流などを導入することで，生徒が本物のコミュニケーションをとることに熱心になり，言語の熟練度と文化の差異に対する認識が生れること，これに感化された学習者が，その後も多言語スキルを必要とするキャリアを追求する可能性が高くなることを述べている。

2023年度　実施問題

【中高共通】

Script

[There are three speaking roles for this test: Directions , Man(M), and Woman(W).]

Directions : Please turn the test paper over. The Listening Comprehension Test will now begin. You may take notes while listening.

【 1 】 Directions : Section A.

Please listen to the following conversations. After each conversation, a question will be asked, and four possible answers will be read. Choose the best answer and circle the corresponding letter on your answer sheet. Each conversation, the question, and the answers will be read only once.

Directions :　Conversation 1.

W : All right, Ms. Brown. I'm happy to tell you that you've passed all the medical examinations. Now you're almost ready for your transfer to the business office in Chicago. All you have to do is to take several vaccinations.

W : OK, can I take them here or do I have to go to the city hospital?

M : I'm afraid we don't stock the kind of vaccines you need. You'll have to go to the city hospital.

W : I see. Do I need some kind of letter from you to show the staff at the city hospital?

M : Yes, you do. I'll write a letter of reference for you now. You can pick it up at the reception desk when you leave.

Directions : What will the man most likely do next?

A. Perform an examination.

B. Make a phone call.

C. Prepare a document.

D. Renew the woman's policy.

Directions : Conversation 2.

M : Meg? It's David. I can't log in to my computer today. Has the IT section done anything to the network?

W : No, just the regular maintenance — nothing that should cause you any troubles. Have you tried restarting your computer?

M : Yes, but it hasn't improved yet. You know, I'm kind of in a hurry. I'm making a presentation of the announcement of our new product at the board meeting this afternoon, and I have to finish up my slides by then. Could you come here and take a look right now?

W : OK, I have to visit the advertising section anyway to update some software. I'll be there in 5 minutes.

Directions : Why does the man call the woman?

A. To ask for technical assistance.

B. To register a child's birth.

C. To request a vacation.

D. To announce a change of policy.

Directions : Conversation 3.

W : My father's not satisfied with me.

M : But Stephanie, I thought you are close to him.

W : Yes, but I don't have a job yet even though I'm going to graduate in two months.

M : A lot of students haven't been offered for employment yet. Don't let him stress you out.

W : I know, but it's because of my way of thinking, I guess. I told him I'm not motivated to hunt for a job and that I may not feel like working for a few years.

M : Really? In this case, I think he has a right to be worried.

Directions : Why is Stephanie's father worried about her?

A. She may not be able to graduate.

B. She may not be suitable for the career she chose.

C. She is feeling stressed.

D. She has a poor attitude toward working.

Directions : Conversation 4.

W : Thanks for coming over to help me move house. Have you had breakfast yet?

M : Oh, no. I just got up and came straight here.

W : I see. I'll make you some pancakes. Would you like some bacon and eggs to go along with them?

M : No, thanks. I cannot stomach anything sweet in the morning. And eggs and bacon are too heavy. I usually have a piece of fruit, perhaps some toast and coffee.

W : Well, I can get that ready, if you give me a minute. I already have some coffee on.

M : Thanks. That'd be nice.

Directions : What does the man say about his breakfast preferences?

A. He likes to have something sweet.

B. He prefers something light.

C. He usually skips breakfast.

D. He wants something heavy.

(☆☆○○○○○)

【2】 Directions : Section B.

Please listen to the following two passages. After each passage, two questions will be asked. Four possible responses to each question are listed on the answer sheet. Choose the best one and circle it. Each passage and question will be read only once.

Directions :   Passage 1.

M : Throughout history, a lot of nations have disappeared, often because of conquest or even peaceful unification. However, have nations ever physically vanished before? This vanishing has become a real possibility during the 21st century. Rising sea levels caused by global warming have already threatened several island nations in the Pacific Ocean, including the Marshall Islands. People in the Marshall Islands may have to abandon their native place long before waves sweep over them, because their freshwater wells are becoming polluted with salt water as the sea level rises.

This causes a delicate question. Would the people in the Marshall Islands lose such entitlements as fishing rights? They have fishing rights to 800,000 square miles of ocean surrounding their 29 islands. They sell fishing licenses to foreign fishing companies, and these earnings become their main source of income. No one knows how the laws will change if the islands disappear because of global warming. A decision on their fishing rights may likely rest in the hands of the United Nations.

Directions :   Question 1.   What would be unusual about the vanishing of the Marshall Islands?

A.   It would result from divisions among its people.

B.   It would be approved by its citizens.

C.   It would be caused by the loss of islands.

D.   It would cause further global warming.

Directions : Question 2. According to the speaker, what is one concern of the people in the Marshall Islands?

A. The high costs of saving their country.

B. The loss of their economic livelihood.

C. The high costs of legal issues.

D. The loss of their right to speak at the U. N.

Directions : Passage 2.

M : The thought that girls naturally prefer to play with dolls and boys prefer cars or trains is hotly discussed. A lot of scientists argue that the preference is not inherent but trained. However, new evidence from studies about primates shows that the preference has a strong biological ground. Scientists observed young female chimpanzees in the National Park in Uganda playing with sticks that took the place of simple dolls. This is the first time that wild animals of one gender were observed showing a preference for things not displayed in another gender. Before that, Scientists had observed young female monkeys in the zoo showing a preference for dolls, while young male monkeys preferred boyish toys, such as cars or trains.

The assertion in favor of biology is supported by the fact that wild chimpanzees never see their parents use sticks or other objects as playthings. Scientists believe young female chimpanzees are preparing themselves for motherhood by copying the child-caring behaviors of chimpanzee mothers.

Directions : Question 1. What did scientists observe among young wild chimpanzees?

A. The ability to imagine about males.

B. A gender preference for certain objects.

C. Communication between males and females.

D.   The ability to defend themselves with sticks.

Directions : Question 2.   Why do scientists believe that young female chimpanzees play with stick dolls?

A.   They copy the stick playing of chimpanzee mothers.

B.   They are the most playful of all primate species.

C.   They are lonely without other playmates.

D.   They are practicing for childcare in the future.

(☆☆☆☆○○○○○)

【3】 Directions : Section C.

Please listen to the following two conversations. After each conversation, two questions will be asked. Four possible responses to each question are listed on the answer sheet. Choose the best one and circle it. Each conversation and question will be read only once.

Directions :   Conversation 1.

W : Hi, Tom. You look really tired. Are you OK?

M : Oh, hi, Nancy. Yeah, I stayed up all night finishing a report for my applied psychology class.

W : That doesn't sound like fun. What is the topic about your report?

M : Believe it or not, about optimal study methods. How to understand new texts, how to take notes and how to memorize technical words. Things like that.

W : Well, I suppose it's beneficial, but it doesn't sound very exciting.

M : It's really interesting. There's a lot of research, for example, on how many times we should review new words to learn them most efficiently.

W : You mean, for example, in a biology course?

M : Sure. Or for physics, or chemistry, or any class in which there's a lot of technical words.

57

W : Well, I suppose that's useful for science students.

M : Yeah, but it's also good for other classes.

W : By the way, what is your major, Tom? You've never mentioned it to me.

M : Oh, I'm majoring in sociology, but I need to take an applied psychology course for a general education requirement.

W : So that's why you're taking it.

M : Yeah, and I've got three more classes left before I'm finished with the course.

W : I'm going to the student union. How about a cup of coffee?

M : Thanks, Nancy, but coffee is not the first thing I need. I'm going back to the dormitory to take a nap.

Directions : Question 1. Why is Tom tired?

A. He went to a welcome-party last night.

B. He had a late night meeting.

C. He was up all night writing a paper.

D. He got up early to meet Nancy.

Directions : Question 2. What field do the memorization techniques Tom referred to seem most suitable for?

A. Science.

B. Economics.

C. Sociology.

D. Education.

Directions : Conversation 2.

W : Andy! What are you doing here? It's Sunday today.

M : Oh. hi, Cathy. I'm meeting the other members of my debate team.

W : On Sunday? I thought you lived more than an hour from campus.

M : You're right, but the city debate tournament our university sponsors begins tomorrow morning, and we need all the practice we can get.

W : Oh, I see. I've seen posters up all around campus. Students from all the universities in this city will participate, right?

M : Exactly. And this year our team is going to win it all!

W : You have great confidence, don't you? By the way, who'll make the decision about who wins?

M :Would you believe that there are people who make a livelihood from judging debate contests?

W :You mean professionals? Isn't it expensive to pay people like that?

M :It sure is. In the past we've just asked noted persons of the local community or professors from other schools. But with the reputation our debate tournament has achieved the past couple of years we decided we need professional judges with formal training and experience.

W : What do they base their decision on? The creativity of your arguments and stuff like that?

M : Actually, making an original argument is not nearly as important as how the argument is presented.

W : What does that mean?

M :Well, for example, we get points for our team's delivery style and for how favorably the audience responds to our argument. And we need to organize the argument clearly so that each point follows logically from the next. That's really tough for us to do, because we don't know what the topic is until a few minutes before the debate actually begins.

W : That's why you do need to practice even on Sunday! Good luck, Andy! I hope your team wins.

M : Thanks. We'll do our best.

Directions : Question 1. Who will judge the debate tournament?

A. Students from other schools.

B. Professional debate judges.

C.　Noted persons of the local community.

D.　Professors from area universities.

Directions ：　Question 2.　How will the members of the debate team know which topic to debate?

A.　It will be up to them to choose it by themselves.

B.　It will be chosen by the opposing team members.

C.　It will be given to them the day before the debate.

D.　It will be announced just before the debate.

(☆☆☆○○○○○)

【4】 Directions ：　Section D.

The following article will be read twice. Please write a summary of the contents in Japanese. The summary should be between 150 and 200 characters. You may take notes and begin summarizing while listening. Now, please listen to the article.

M ：Can you imagine how many languages are spoken in the world now? You may be surprised to hear the answer. About 7 thousand! With the present world population of about 7.8 billion people, you could guess that, on average, each language would have more than a million speakers. In fact, however, only 250 languages have more than a million speakers. Half the world's population — that is, about 3.9 billion people — speak one of only 10 major languages, of which Chinese, English and Hindi are the top three.

In contrast, most of the world's languages are spoken by less than six thousand people, and many of these languages are now in danger of extinction. Some linguistic scientists presume that 4.5 percent of all known languages have become extinct during the last 500 years, and the pace of extinction, which is now about ten a year, is accelerated. How many languages will the world have 500 years later? If present trends continue, there may be fewer than a thousand languages spoken by all the human race!

When a language dies out, the sacrifices also include large amounts of knowledge and traditions that generations of native speakers have accumulated and passed on. Unlike the potential of walking, for example, which human babies usually develop on their own, the ability to speak languages does not appear unless babies experience spoken language through their interactions with adults. With decreasing numbers of native speakers of the endangered language, young generations may lose not only their links to their ancestors but also their ethnic identity.

However, there are some language communities which can reverse the trend toward linguistic and cultural extinction. For example, the Maori, the native people of New Zealand, reached the point at which only a fourth of all the native people poke their mother tongue. They decided to take actions to revive their native language. They took the actions in these two ways: by getting Maori adopted as an official language and by enrolling nearly half of their Preschool-aged children in programs which offered total immersion in Maori.

Recently UNESCO has recognized the necessity to preserve the linguistic aspects of culture and has started to promote multilingualism. "Trilingualism" is what UNESCO recommends as the way to rescue the languages from extinction. "Trilingualism" requires people to learn not only their native language but also an international language and then one more "neighbor" language. The "neighbor" language could be any of the world's languages that are now becoming extinct and which must be studied at school if they are to be preserved.

Directions : Stop writing, please. This is the end of the listening test. Thank you.
(☆☆☆☆☆◎◎◎)

【5】次の(1)～(10)の英文の＿＿に入る最も適当な語(句)をア～エの中から それぞれ1つ選び記号で答えなさい。

(1)　Ms. White, chairperson of Lakeside Brewery, wrote the report ＿＿ and printed it on the recycled paper.

　　ア　it　　イ　her　　ウ　herself　　エ　ourselves

(2)　The engineer advised that the equipment is ＿＿ expensive to fix, and that everyone should be very careful to handle it.

　　ア　unbelief　　イ　unbelievable　　ウ　unbelievably

　　エ　unbeliever

(3)　The traffic on the railroad crossing is a little less ＿＿ during the daytime than in the early morning.

　　ア　heaviness　　イ　heavy　　ウ　heavier　　エ　heavily

(4)　You should make a copy of all documents before you ＿＿ it in to the general affairs department.

　　ア　handed　　イ　to hand　　ウ　handing　　エ　hand

(5)　At ICP Insurance Company, a chance of promotion is equally given to ＿＿ male and female employees.

　　ア　both　　イ　either　　ウ　between　　エ　each

(6)　The latest version of the tablet computer was ＿＿ with a variety of convenient features that made it much more popular than the original model.

　　ア　engaged　　イ　encouraged　　ウ　escalated　　エ　enhanced

(7)　The members of the soccer team had a hard training but they failed to win a single game last year. It was so ＿＿ that several teammates quit.

　　ア　discouraging　　イ　distracting　　ウ　engaging

　　エ　enabling

(8)　The woman disliked cockroaches and refused to move into the house until all of them were ＿＿.

　　ア　investigated　　イ　diminished　　ウ　exterminated

　　エ　suspended

(9) After Sarah realized that her driver's license had ＿＿＿, she went to the Driver's License Center to renew it.

ア expired　イ ejected　ウ emerged　エ engaged

(10) The new computer chip delivers five times the processing speed of present chips. It is a ＿＿＿＿ that will revolutionize using computers.

ア sequence　イ migration　ウ breakthrough

エ supplement

(☆☆☆☆○○○○○)

【6】次の(1)～(5)の英文において下線部に最も近い意味の語(句)をア～エの中からそれぞれ1つ選び記号で答えなさい。

(1) Vice-president of operations Josh Grossman has been <u>provisionally</u> appointed as head of North Western Express while the company's board of directors searches for a permanent CEO.

ア increasingly　イ adequately　ウ temporarily

エ eventually

(2) Arman Hotels are a countrywide chain offering convenient, <u>reasonably</u> priced lodging facilities for business travelers.

ア costly　イ moderately　ウ virtually　エ evidently

(3) Since Ms. Smith was hired as plant manager, the factory has drastically increased its <u>output</u>.

ア deadline　イ preparation　ウ location　エ production

(4) Marquette University's commerce program is a great <u>means</u> of obtaining the skills you need to succeed in the business area.

ア technique　イ approach　ウ method　エ knowledge

(5) At the conference, Mr. Robinson presented a convincing <u>logical ground</u> for changing the company's development strategy.

ア cooperation　イ abundance　ウ increase　エ rationale

(☆☆☆☆○○○○)

【7】次の(1)～(5)の英文において不適切な箇所を下線部ア～エの中から
それぞれ1つ選び記号で答え，正しい形，または，適切な語(句)にしな
さい。

(1)　The National Museum of Modern Art has ア<u>traditionally</u> exhibited イ<u>the</u>
best available ウ<u>contemporary</u> works in エ<u>it</u> exhibitions.

(2)　Pennsylvania ア<u>was one</u> of the イ<u>original</u> thirteen ウ<u>colonies</u> エ<u>who</u>
formed the United States in 1776.

(3)　ア<u>Despite of</u> the slim margin of イ<u>his election</u>, John F. Kennedy
ウ<u>became</u> one of the エ<u>most admired</u> presidents in the United States.

(4)　Without ア<u>accurate</u> predictions of future profit, イ<u>a company</u> can expend
its budget such that there ウ<u>was</u> not enough funds エ<u>to cover</u> even fixed
costs.

(5)　A lot of skin ア<u>specialists</u> are イ<u>skeptical</u> of the assertion that diet ウ<u>is</u> the
important factor in skin エ<u>healthy</u>.

(☆☆☆☆○○○○○)

【8】次の(1)～(3)の英文において〔　　〕内の語(句)を正しく並べかえて
文章を完成するとき，〔　　〕内の語(句)の4番目と7番目にくる語をア
～キの中からそれぞれ1つ選び記号で答えなさい。ただし文頭に来る
文字も小文字になっている。

(1)　A: Kevin, did you compile〔ア　the　　イ　to　　ウ　need
エ　give　　オ　all　　カ　documents　　キ　we〕the lawyer?
B : Yes. I'm sure that I got everything we need, but please double-check
it.

(2)　A: The composition of your report on japanese history is confusing. I
suggest〔ア　in　　イ　you　　ウ　historical　　エ　chronological
オ　all　　カ　put　　キ　events〕order, starting with the earliest
ones.
B : OK. I'll do that, Dr. Simons. Thank you.

(3)　A : Why can't I give you a good-bye kiss when I drop you off at school?

B : Because it humiliates me, Mom. 〔ア friends　イ mothers
ウ of　エ let　オ none　カ my　キ their〕kiss
them in front of many students.

(☆☆○○○○○)

【9】次の英文において空欄(1)～(3)に入る最も適当な語(句)をア
～エの中からそれぞれ1つ選び記号で答えなさい。

　The Cornell University Student Union has a special agreement with Ithaca
Books that entitles members to discounts on various items. All of regular
hardcover and paperback fiction is available at 15 percent off the marked
price, (1) non-fiction books are reduced by 25 percent.

　In addition, during August, set books for some classes are available at a 30
percent discount. Students (2) in this limited-time back-to-school offer
should check the details of eligible books on the store's website.

　Please note that it is necessary to have a valid student ID and present it
when you make your purchase. (3), Ithaca Books cannot provide you
with a discount, even if you are a student union member.

(1)　ア　along　　　イ　nevertheless　ウ　including
　　エ　while
(2)　ア　interest　　イ　interested　　ウ　interesting
　　エ　have interested
(3)　ア　Similarly　イ　Incase　　　　ウ　Otherwise
　　エ　Formerly

(☆☆☆○○○○○)

【10】次の英文を読み，以下の各問いに対する答えとして，あるいは問い
の文に続くものとして最も適当なものをア～エの中からそれぞれ1つ
選び記号で答えなさい。

　It has generally been considered that fairy tales were made for children at
first and are mainly the area of children. But nothing could be further from the

truth.

From just the beginning, thousands of years ago when fairy tales were narrated to create bonds for communities in the face of the mighty powers of nature, to the present, when fairy tales are made and told to offer hope in a world seemingly at the moment of catastrophe, grown men and women have been the creators and cultivators of the fairy tale transmission. When fairy tales are introduced, children welcome them generally because they cultivate their vast desire for change and independence. In general, the fairy tale of Western literature has become an established genre within a progress of Western civilization that can be adopted in all ages. Even though a cloud of critics and shamans have mystified and misunderstood the fairy tale because of their spiritual seeking for universal models or their need to save the world through religion, both the oral and the literary forms of the fairy tale are rooted in historical fact: they emerge from inherent struggles to humanize savage and brutal forces which have terrified our minds and ommunities in specific ways, threatening to destroy free will and human consideration. Therefore, the fairy tale attempts to overcome this specific terror mainly through the use of metaphors.

Though it is difficult to specify when the first "literary" fairy tales were made, and also exceedingly difficult to define correctly what a fairy tale is, we do know that oral folk tales, which contain wonderful and surprising elements, have been present for thousands of years and were told mainly by adults for adults. Motifs from these, memorized and passed on in oral transfer, made their way into the Bible and the Western classics. The early oral tales that played a role as the basis for the development of the literary fairy tales were closely tied to the ceremonies and beliefs of tribes, communities, and colleagues. They developed a sense of belonging. They instructed, amused, warned, introduced, and enlightened. They were to be shared and exchanged, and different from the literary tales, after that they were spawned, used and modified according to the necessity of the tellers and listeners.

(1) What is the main topic of the passage?

　ア　The difference between literary and oral folk tales.

　イ　The origin and purpose of fairy tales.

　ウ　The modern need for folk tales.

　エ　The universal topics of fairy tales.

(2) According to the writer, which of the following is the common misunderstanding of fairy tales?

　ア　They were oral before they were written.

　イ　They are an unreliable historical guide.

　ウ　They are intended for children.

　エ　They were passed from generation to generation.

(3) Which of the following is NOT mentioned as one of the purposes of fairy tales?

　ア　To overcome fear of dark, natural powers.

　イ　To create shared human communications.

　ウ　To explain the origin of the physical world.

　エ　To instruct and amuse.

(4) In the third paragraph the writer implies that

　ア　the first folk tales were written down.

　イ　some early fairy tales may be found in the Bible.

　ウ　themes from the earliest folk tales have not been left.

　エ　tellers of folk tales fight over the tales' meanings.

(5) With which of the following statements would the writer most likely agree?

　ア　Fairy tales are a form of the earliest fine art.

　イ　Fairy tales are essential to religious preaching.

　ウ　Fairy tales arise from specific human conditions.

　エ　Folk tales have mainly lost their meaning and value.

(☆☆☆☆○○○○○)

67

【11】次の2つの資料を読み，以下の各問いに対する答えとして最も適当なものをア～エの中から1つ選び記号で答えなさい。

【資料1：求人広告】

Product Manager

Macy's, the leading department store in the U.S., is presently finding a product manager to manage the product development section. The appropriate candidate would manage a product team of developers and coordinators. The product manager should also communicate with vendors to make products that are within the budget.

Position responsibilities:

- Have meetings on a regular basis with other sections to keep product expectations
- Recommend necessary improvements to products to remain competitive
- Supervise development of products
- Attend appropriate meetings to plan new product developments
- Manage the process of production from planning to completion

Competitive salary and other benefits offered. Interested candidates should fax a resume to (516)746-8200. Deadline for application is Aug 31st.

【資料2：ファックス】

TO: Macy's (516)746-8200

FROM: Catlin Murphy (516)811-6126

Pages:3

Dear Sir or Madam,

I'm writing in response to your advertisement about a product manager. I have been looking for this kind of post, and would like to have the opportunity to serve at your company.

I'm quite sure that my career and experience are just what you are looking for. I have over ten years' experience in product development and management. I also have extended experience in product design.

I am a person that learns a lot of knowledge about the latest technology in order to improve products that I have designed and developed. I'm a team player who is thoroughly committed to my work.

Please look through my qualifications and let me know if I would be useful to your company.

Thank you for your time. I look forward to hearing from you.

Sincerely,

Catlin Murphy

(1) Why is Ms. Murphy sending a fax to Macy's?

　ア　To advertise a post.

　イ　To offer a post.

　ウ　To state her post.

　エ　To apply for a post.

(2) Who would the product manager manage?

　ア　A sports team.

　イ　Developers and coordinators.

　ウ　Management from other section.

　エ　Vendors.

(3) What should the manager do with the vendors?

　ア　Communicate with them.

　イ　Criticize them.

　ウ　Confine them.

　エ　Confound them.

(4) What is one of the benefits offered with this position?

　ア　The salary will be low compared with industry standards.

　イ　The candidate will have to pay for benefits.

　　ウ　The salary will be at the same level or higher than what competitors offer.

　　エ　The candidate will have to compete with others to get a salary.

（5）　What kind of a candidate is Ms. Murphy?

　　ア　One who changes jobs often.

　　イ　One who has little experience in product design.

　　ウ　One who works best alone.

　　エ　One who works well with other employees.

（☆☆☆○○○○○）

【12】次の英文を読み，以下の各問いに答えなさい。

　　Several hundred years ago, colonial powers swept throughout Africa in a land plunder that changed the face of the continent forever. It is occurring again, this time in the name of free enterprise system. Countries and companies are purchasing tremendous expanses of arable land, leaving stunned farmers and villagers without work or places to live. The farmers, who cultivated the lands for generations, believed that the land was theirs, until the government sold it from under their feet.

　　The problem is significant. A World Bank study reported that nearly 80 million acres of land was sold during 11 months in 2009 alone. In 2008, only 10 million acres had been sold. Why such a difference? A food crisis in the spring of 2008 showed that food would probably become in short supply in Africa over next several years, setting off conjecture by hedge funds and commodities markets that food prices would go up. As a result, this sparked speculative buying all over Africa.

　　Not everyone is pessimistic about the horseplay of buying arable land. The World Bank, the United Nations, and other distinguished organizations say that forthcoming large-scale agricultural business brings necessary expertise and technology that will increase agricultural production. Jon Anderson, an aid-project manager in U. S., warned that no country can develop economically when a large majority of the nation are small-scale farmers. Those who are struggling should sell their arable land and use the fund to start more successful business.

Critics oppose. Many of the new farm products are exported abroad. About 20 international biofuel companies, for example, have made a purchase of agricultural fields in Ghana, forcing thousands of farmers to leave their land. Though some companies assert they are supporting displaced farmers, the farmers do not make profit in general. Moreover, the biofuel products are exported at a time when about 1.2 million Ghanaians are not provided a sufficient amount of food. Many other investments, made only for speculation, leave large areas of former arable land abandoned and farm product free.

Former U.N. Secretary-General Kofi Annan warned,"The food security of the country concerned should be first and foremost in everyone's mind." However, for many of the investors, financial gain is put before humans.

(1) 次の①～③の問いに対する答えとして，あるいは問いの文に続くものとして最も適当なものをア～エの中から1つ選び記号で答えなさい。

① According to the writer of the passage, what caused the massive land purchases?

ア Former colonial forces that were looking for ways to exercise influence in Africa through the free-market system.

イ Companies that saw Africa as one of the last places where huge arable lands were available.

ウ Struggling farmers who were so desperate that they wanted to sell or give up their lands.

エ A severe food shortage in Africa that attracted attention from overseas investment markets.

② Why do some organizations like the United Nations see the purchases as potentially profitable?

　　ア　Some of the land is not arable, so it is better that farmers on those lands move to more cultivated areas.

　　イ　Large-sized farms are generally more cost efficient and therefore better able to improve agricultural output.

　　ウ　African countries selling arable lands could use benefits to support their people in more productive ways.

　　エ　The free-market system is the best way to sweep struggling farmers who must not continue their hopeless efforts.

③　The biofuel companies mentioned in the passage are an important example of how

　　ア　forthcoming expertise can increase overall agricultural productivity in a country.

　　イ　changing agricultural priorities towards energy production can profit a country.

　　ウ　foreign investment can result in less available food within a country.

　　エ　responsible companies can assist displaced farmers to move to another country.

(2)　次の各英文を，本文中で述べられている順番に並び替え，記号で答えなさい。

　ア　The prediction that food would likely become scarce in Africa.

　イ　Profit is put before people for many of the investors.

　ウ　Purchasing agricultural fields in Ghana by international biofuel companies.

　エ　Purchasing huge expanses of arable land by countries and companies in Africa.

　オ　Large-scale farming enterprises that can boost agricultural production in Africa.

(3)　本文のタイトルとして最も適当なものをア〜エの中から1つ選び記号で答えなさい。

　　ア　Rising of the Food Prices
　　イ　African Farmers Losing Their Farms
　　ウ　Large-scale Farming Enterprises
　　エ　Exporting of the Biofuel Products
　(4)　本文中の下線部 "The food security" について，本文内容と関連付けながら20語程度の英語で説明しなさい。

(☆☆☆☆☆○○○○○)

【13】The Course of Study states that English classes are basically conducted in English. Write an English composition about three or more important points that English teachers need to be aware of using English in the class. The composition should be 60 words or more.

(☆☆☆☆☆○○○)

【14】授業中に生徒が次の(1)と(2)の質問をした。あなたは英語の教員としてどのように説明するか。それぞれについて日本語で答えなさい。(説明の一部に英語を交えても差し支えない)
　(1)　「一生懸命勉強したから，○○高校の入学試験に合格した」という意味で，I studied so hard that I passed the entrance exam for ○○ high school. という英文を作ってALTに見せたところ，strangeと言われました。どうしてstrangeなのですか？
　(2)　「〜がある(いる)」と表現したい場合はThere is (are)〜という英語を使うと習いました。その際，「〜」の部分には「限定できるもの(人)は入らない」と説明されましたが，例外的に「限定できるもの(人)」が入ることはあるのですか？あるならどんな場合ですか？

(☆☆☆☆○○○)

【高等学校】

【 1 】 Read the passage and answer the questions below.

The cult of authenticity

Developing texts for second language students that take into account their lack of linguistic ability and background knowledge is, regrettably, controversial. In language teaching, there is an enduring "cult of authenticity" that originated with the communicative language teaching (CLT) movement of the late 1970s. CLT argued that, for language teaching, authentic materials — those written by and for (　ア　) and not specifically for language teaching — were superior to materials especially written or simplified for (　イ　).

The appeal that authentic texts have for teachers and, as a consequence, for students, and the influence those texts have on students' ideas about reading, can be gauged from the "Introduction to the Student" in Catherine Walter's *Genuine Articles: Authentic Reading Texts for Intermediate Students of American English*:

All of the texts in the book are real samples of written English. . . . None of them was written especially for foreigners. This means that some texts may be easier to understand than others; but *even the easier texts* [italics added] will help you read better. (1986, p.vii)

Part of the cult status of authenticity is the idea that it is the very difficulty of texts that makes them worthwhile as learning tools.

In spite of the widespread acceptance of the use of authentic materials, there is no consensus as to the meaning of *authentic*. Robin Scarcella and Rebecca Oxford note that, "generally, authentic language is considered unedited, unabridged text that is written for native . . . speakers" (1992, p. 98). Catherine Walter, on the other hand, includes texts both "shortened" and "slightly adapted" (1986, p. ix) in her *Genuine Articles* textbook. Yet another

74

view is expressed by Henry Widdowson, who argues that authenticity is not a quality of text at all; instead, "authenticity . . . is achieved when the reader realizes the intentions of the writer" (1976, p. 264). Finally, Eddie Williams says simply that an authentic text is one "written to say something, to convey a message" (1984, p. 25).

Authentic texts — however defined — are used in language teaching because they are considered interesting, engaging, culturally enlightening, relevant, motivating, and the best preparation for reading authentic texts. (This latter reason can presumably be summed up in the axiom "We learn to read authentic texts by reading authentic texts.") As Williams explains, "if the learner is expected eventually to cope with real language (ウ) the classroom, then surely the best way to prepare for this is by looking at real language (エ) the classroom" (1984, p. 25).

But, for many teachers, the most compelling argument for the use of authentic texts is that they are genuine discourse. Christine Nuttall, in the second edition of her influential book *Teaching Reading Skill in a Foreign Language*, elaborates on this point. As she puts it, authentic materials not only motivate students but "exhibit the characteristics of true discourse: having something to say, being coherent and clearly organized" (1996, p. 177).

At the same time, authentic texts, for all their virtues, can actually set back reading development. Williams refers to the paradox that the use of authentic text with learners often has an effect opposite to that intended; instead of helping the reader to read for the meaning of the message, an authentic text at too difficult a level of language forces the reader to focus on the code (1983, p. 175). Wilga Rivers points out that "when average students encounter ungraded material too soon, they are usually forced back into deciphering with the aid of a dictionary, and valuable training in the reading skill is wasted" (1981, pp. 37-38). Nuttall, in her discussion of authentic materials, concedes that "linguistically difficult texts are unlikely to be suitable for developing most reading skills" (1996, p. 177).

In addition, there is the affective toll. Rivers observes that "rushing students too soon into reading material beyond their present capacity for fluent comprehension with occasional contextual guessing . . . destroys confidence" (1981, p. 260).

And yet, in spite of these drawbacks, authentic materials have become, in David Clarke's words, "almost a categorical imperative, a moral *sine qua non* of the language classroom" (1989, p. 73). As a colleague observed to one of us, "All I heard in graduate school ten years ago was the need to use authentic materials, whether in teaching reading or listening or whatever. But at the time, I knew from my own experience both as a second language teacher and learner that simplified materials worked. So I was confused. And ever since then, I have felt guilty using them."

That he and other teachers use simplified materials at all points directly to the fatal flaw of authentic materials. Had Ambrose Bierce been a language teacher, he might well have added the following wonderfully cynical definition, courtesy of Andrew Cohen, to his *Devil's Dictionary*: "Authentic materials are those which are impossible or difficult for language learners to understand."

There was, in fact, some recognition of this problem in the writings of experts from the beginning, but often so indirectly stated that the point was lost. In *Developing Reading Skills*, when Françoise Grellet says "It is important to use authentic texts whenever possible" (1981, p. 7), it is the first part of the statement that makes the impact, not the last two words.

And so it is that teachers and students have come to see authentic materials as preferable to easy, simplified texts. For less-than-fluent second language readers, this is a dangerous view, for it can rob them of the most important source of the reading materials they need to become fluent readers.

The idea that simplified texts are to be avoided and that difficult texts are prestigious is equally pernicious in terms of attitude toward reading. In effect, it associates reading itself with difficulty. Students will *always* be able to find texts that are difficult for them, and they are liable to equate reading and learning to read with struggling through these texts. This is not the way to instill an appreciation for reading.

But the cult of authenticity did not arise in a vacuum. Part of its prominence can be traced to the nature of what may seem to be the only alternative to authentic texts: simplified materials.

1.　Choose the best word for (　ア　) and (　イ　) from among the choices. Write the number of the answer.
　　① 　native speakers 　　　② 　book publishing companies
　　③ 　language learners 　　　④ 　news agencies

2.　Choose the best option which is NOT right for the discussion in the passage about the meaning of authenticity. Write the number of the answer.
　　① 　Scarcella and Oxford have an opinion that differs from Walter.
　　② 　Widdowson thinks that when a writer can convince readers of his/her opinion, it means that his/her text is authentic.
　　③ 　Williams thinks that authentic texts contain writer's message.
　　④ 　There are many arguments about the meaning of authenticity, but we do not have consensus opinion about it.

3.　Choose the best pair of the words from among the choices for (　ウ　) and (　エ　). Write the number of the answer.
　　① 　ウ 　inside 　　　エ 　outside
　　② 　ウ 　across 　　　エ 　outside
　　③ 　ウ 　outside 　　　エ 　across

4.　Choose the best option which is NOT right for the disadvantage of authenticity referred in the passage. Write the number of the answer.
　　① 　Authentic materials sometimes delay development of language learners' reading skill.
　　② 　Finding suitable authentic materials for language learners are often difficult for teachers.

③　If the level of authentic reading materials is not suitable for language learners, they might overuse a dictionary.

④　Authentic materials would destroy language leaners' confidence if their level is beyond learners' comprehension.

5.　As a high school English teacher in Japan, how do you use authentic materials and simplified materials not only for reading but also for other purposes? Write your opinion.

i.　Your essay should consist of 100-150 words.

ii.　You should refer to the information mentioned in the passage.

iii.　You should have specific reasons or details to support your opinion.

(☆☆☆☆○○○○○)

【 2 】 Read the passage and answer the questions below.

Age and second language learning

We now turn to a learner characteristic of a different type: the age at which learning begins. Age is easier to define and measure than personality, (ア)aptitude, or motivation, but the relationship between age and success in second language acquisition is hardly less complex or controversial.

It is frequently observed that most children from immigrant families eventually speak the language of their new community with native-like fluency, while their parents often fall short of such high levels of (イ)proficiency, especially in the spoken language. To be sure, many adult second language learners achieve excellent language skills. One often sees reference to Joseph Conrad, a native speaker of Polish who became a major writer in the English language, and it is not uncommon to find adult second language learners with a rich vocabulary, sophisticated syntax, and effective pragmatic skills, even though there may be subtle differences between their language use and that of those who began learning the language while very young.

The Critical Period Hypothesis is that there is a time in human development

78

when the brain is predisposed for success in language learning. It has been hypothesized that there is a critical period for second language acquisition just as there is for first language acquisition. Developmental changes in the brain, it is argued, affect the nature of language acquisition, and language learning that occurs after the end of the critical period may not be based on the innate biological structures believed to contribute to first language acquisition or second language acquisition in early childhood. Rather, older learners may depend on more general learning abilities — the same ones they might use to acquire other kinds of skills or information. It is argued that these general learning abilities are not as effective for language learning as the more specific, innate capacities that are available to the young child. It is most often claimed that the critical period ends somewhere around puberty, but some researchers suggest it could be even earlier. Others find evidence that there may be multiple critical periods, related to different aspects of language learning. For example, the ability to acquire the pronunciation patterns of a new language may end earlier than the ability to acquire vocabulary.

Of course, it is difficult to compare children and adults as second language learners. In addition to possible biological differences suggested by the Critical Period Hypothesis, the conditions for language learning are often very different. Younger learners in informal language learning environments usually have more time to devote to learning language. They often have more opportunities to hear and use the language in environments where they do not experience strong pressure to speak fluently and accurately from the beginning. Furthermore, their early imperfect efforts are often praised, or at least accepted. Older learners are more likely to find themselves in situations that demand more complex language and the expression of more complicated ideas. Adults are often embarrassed by their lack of mastery of the language and they may develop a sense of inadequacy after experiences of frustration in trying to say exactly what they mean. Such negative feelings may affect their motivation and willingness to place themselves in situations where they will need to use the new language.

Research based on the Critical Period Hypothesis in addition to personal experience or informal observation of adult leaners' difficulties has led some educators and policy makers as well as many parents to conclude that second language instruction is most likely to succeed if it begins when learners are very young. However, some studies of the second language development of older and younger learners learning in similar circumstances have shown that older learners are more efficient than younger learners. By using their metalinguistic knowledge, memory strategies, and problem-solving skills, they make the most of second or foreign language instruction. In educational settings, learners who begin learning a second language at primary school level do not always achieve greater proficiency in the long run than those who begin in adolescence. Furthermore, there are countless anecdotes about older learners (adolescents and adults) who achieve excellence in the second language. Does this mean that there is no critical period for second language acquisition?

Most studies of the relationship between age of acquisition and second language development have concluded that older learners typically have a noticeable 'foreign accent' in the spoken language. But what about other linguistic features? Is syntax (word order, overall sentence structure) as dependent on age of acquisition as phonological development? What about morphology?

Mark Patkowski (1980) studied the relationship between age and the acquisition of features of a second language other than pronunciation. He hypothesized that, even if accent were ignored, only those who had begun learning their second language before the age of 15 could achieve full, native-like mastery of that language. Patkowski studied 67 highly educated immigrants to the United States. They had started to learn English at various ages, but all had lived in the United States for more than five years. He compared them to 15 native-born Americans with a similarly high level of education, whose variety of English could be considered the second language speakers' target language.

The main question in Patkowski's research was: 'Will there be a difference between learners who began to learn English before puberty and those who began learning English later?' However, he also compared learners on the basis of other characteristics and experiences that some people have suggested might be as good as age in predicting or explaining a person's success in mastering a second language. For example, he looked at the total amount of time a speaker had been in the United States as well as the amount of formal ESL instruction each speaker had had.

A lengthy interview with each person was tape-recorded. Because Patkowski wanted to remove the possibility that the results would be affected by accent, he transcribed five-minute samples from the interviews and asked trained native-speaker judges to place each transcript on a scale from 0 (no knowledge of English) to 5 (a level of English expected from an educated native speaker).

The findings were quite dramatic. The transcripts of all native speakers and 32 out of 33 second language speakers who had begun learning English before the age of 15 were rated 4+ or 5. The homogeneity of the pre-puberty learners suggests that, for this group, success in learning a second language was almost inevitable. In contrast, 27 of the 32 post-puberty learners were rated between 3 and 4, but a few learners were rated higher (4+ or 5) and one was rated at 2+. The performance of this group looked like the sort of range one would expect if one were measuring success in learning almost any kind of skill or knowledge: some people did extremely well; some did poorly; most were in the middle.

When Patkowski examined the other factors that might be thought to affect success in second language acquisition, the picture was much less clear. There was, naturally, some relationship between those factors and learning success, but it often turned out that age was so closely related to the other factors that it was not really possible to separate them completely. For example, length of residence in the United States sometimes seemed to be a fairly good predictor. However, it was often the case that those with longer residence had also arrived at an earlier age. Similarly, amount of instruction, when separated from age, did not predict success as well as age of immigration did. Thus, Patkowski found that for learners who acquire a second language primarily in the 'natural' environment, age of acquisition is an important factor in setting limits on the development of native-like mastery of a second language and that this limitation does not apply only to pronunciation.

1. Choose the best definition of the word (ア) from among the choices. Write the number of the answer.

  ① the opinions and feelings that you usually have about something

  ② natural ability or skill, especially in learning

  ③ a desire or liking for a particular activity

  ④ a feeling of being grateful for something someone has done

2. Choose the best definition of the word (イ) from among the choices. Write the number of the answer.

  ① a good standard of ability and skill

  ② having a strong influence or effect

  ③ a job that needs a high level of education and training

  ④ a series of actions that are done in order to achieve a particular result

3. Choose the best statement to describe what "the Critical Period Hypothesis" is. Write the number of the answer.

  ① There are various periods of time when brain is best suitable for language learning.

  ② The critical period of first language acquisition and that of second language acquisition are believed to be different.

  ③ There are various arguments about when the critical period starts or ends, and we do not have consensus.

  ④ Many scholars do not agree that the critical period of learning vocabulary and that of grammar might be different.

4. According to the passage, why is it difficult to compare young language learners and adult learners? Choose the best statement and write the number of the answer.

① Adult learners often have more time to spend language learning, while young learners have less time to do so.

② Young learners often have more opportunities to be exposed to unpressured language learning environment than adult learners.

③ Adult learners are often accused of making mistakes on their language performance but they usually do not care about it.

④ It is often the case that young learners are humiliated when they feel that they do not have a sufficient command of language, while adult learners are not.

5. You are required to make a presentation about the research of Patkowski (1980). Suppose the following is your presentation slide. Read the passage and fill in each blank.

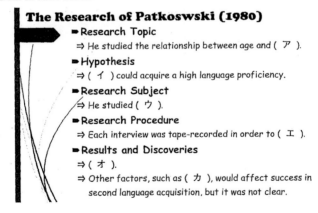

The Research of Patkoswski (1980)

▶**Research Topic**
⇒ He studied the relationship between age and (ア).

▶**Hypothesis**
⇒ (イ) could acquire a high language proficiency.

▶**Research Subject**
⇒ He studied (ウ).

▶**Research Procedure**
⇒ Each interview was tape-recorded in order to (エ).

▶**Results and Discoveries**
⇒ (オ).
⇒ Other factors, such as (カ), would affect success in second language acquisition, but it was not clear.

(1) Choose the best option which is NOT appropriate for (ア). Write the number of the answer.

① grammar　② vocabulary　③ pronunciation
④ writing skill

(2)　Choose the best option for (　イ　). Write the number of the answer.

① Both adult and young learners living in the U.S. and learning their second language more than five years

② Adult learners living in the U.S. more than five years and having a formal ESL instruction

③ Learners who started learning their second language before the age of 15

④ Learners who have a high level of education and whose second language is English

(3)　Choose the best option which is NOT appropriate for (　ウ　). Write the number of the answer.

① immigrants who have a high level of education

② immigrants who started learning their second language at various ages

③ immigrants who lived in the U.S. for more than five years

④ immigrants whose age was 15 years old

(4)　Choose the best option for (　エ　). Write the number of the answer.

① examine the relationship between pronunciation and success in language learning

② transcribe five-minute samples from the interviews for the untrained judges

③ evaluate the results without the affection of accent

④ place each transcript on five-point scale so that examinees can improve their performances

(5)　Choose the best option for (　オ　). Write the number of the answer.

① Success in learning a second language depends on when to start it

② The Critical Period Hypothesis is not always true

③ Adult learners need to have an appropriate ESL instruction to master their second language

④ The relationship between pronunciation and age is critical

(6)　Choose the best option for (　カ　). Write the number of the answer.

　　①　nationality　　②　motivation　　③　first language

　　④　length of residency

6.　Do you think that we should start learning a second language as early as possible based on the Critical Period Hypothesis? Write your opinion.

　i.　Your essay should consist of 100-150 words.

　ii.　You should refer to the information mentioned in the passage.

　iii.　You should have specific reasons, your experiences or details to support your opinion.

(☆☆☆☆☆◎◎◎◎)

解答・解説

【中高共通】

【１】Conversation 1　C　　Conversation 2　A　　Conversation 3　D

　　Conversation 4　B

〈解説〉4つの会話と，それぞれの内容に関する質問を聞き，読み上げられる各4つの選択肢から正しいものを選ぶ。放送は1回のみ。選択肢は印字されていないので，音声のみの情報で解答しなければならない。Conversation 1　健康診断に来た女性と診断結果を伝えている男性の会話。市の病院にワクチンを打ってもらうために紹介状を書いてもらうこととなる。I'll write a letter of reference for you now.とあることから，男性が次にすることは書類の準備であると考えられる。　Conversation 2　今日の午後の委員会でプレゼンテーションがあるにも関わらずパソコンにログインできない男性が，女性に対して電話で助けを求めている会話。Could you come here and take a look right now? とあることから，パソコンの補助を求めていることが分かる。　Conversation 3　卒業の2カ月前で就職が決まっていない女性とそれを元気付ける男性の

85

会話。女性は父親に，職を得るモチベーションがなく，数年働ける気がしないと伝えており，父親が心配になるのも無理はないと男性は返している。このことから，父親が女性を心配しているのはhave a poor attitude toward working「働くことに対して態度が悪い」ことであると考えられる。　Conversation 4　引っ越しの手伝いに来た男性と，男性の朝食を用意しようとする女性の会話。女性はベーコンエッグとパンケーキの朝食を提案しているが，男性は朝食に甘いものや重いメニューは胃が受け付けないと返し，いつもはフルーツとトースト，コーヒーを摂ると言っている。このことから，男性の朝食のpreferences(好み)は軽いものであると考えられる。

【２】Passage 1　Question 1　C　　Question 2　B　　Passage 2　Question 1　B　　Question 2　D
〈解説〉2つのパッセージと，それぞれ2つの質問が読み上げられる。放送は1回のみであるが，解答の選択肢は解答用紙に印字されている。Passage 1　海抜の上昇により物理的に消滅の危険性があるMarshall Islandsについての内容。塩害による影響で漁業権を周辺国家に販売して収入を得ているが，地球温暖化によって物理的に国がなくなってしまった場合には法的にどうなるのか疑問を述べている。　Question 1 Marshall Islandsの消失について特異なことはRising sea levels caused by global warming have already threatened several island nationsと述べられている。なお，実際に島が海の中に沈むのではなく，真水の井戸が海水に汚染されてしまうことが原因であることが述べられている。Question 2　Marshall Islandsの住人が心配していることはNo one knows how the laws will change if the islands disappear because of global warming.と述べられている。この法律とは直前で述べられている漁業権の売買に関することであり，国の主要な収入になっているため，経済的な生計を心配していると分かる。　Passage 2　女の子は人形，男の子は車や電車などのおもちゃで遊ぶという傾向は人間だけでなく，チンパンジーにも見られる。UgandaのNational Parkでは棒人形で遊ぶメスのチ

ンパンジーの子どもと，車や電車で遊ぶオスのチンパンジーの子ども
がおり，ジェンダーによる違いが見られた。　Question 1　野性のチン
パンジーに関して見られた傾向は，ジェンダーにより遊ぶおもちゃの
嗜好が異なることである。　Question 2　メスの子どものチンパンジー
が棒人形で遊ぶのはScientists believe young female chimpanzees are
preparing themselves for motherhood by copying the child-caring behaviors
of chimpanzee mothers.と述べており，子どもを将来育てる練習をして
いると考えられる。

【3】Conversation 1　Question 1　C　　Question 2　A　　Conversation 2
Question 1　B　　Question 2　D
〈解説〉2つの会話と，それぞれ2つの質問が読み上げられる。放送は1回
のみ。設問【2】と同様に，解答の選択肢は解答用紙に印字されてい
る。　Conversation 1　応用心理学の授業のレポートを終わらせるため
に徹夜をしていたTomとNancyの会話。レポートの内容は専門用語を
記憶する際やノートの取り方などに関する最適な学習方法に関するも
のであった。　Question 1　Tomが疲れている理由はI stayed up all night
finishing a reportと述べているため，a reportをa paperで置き換えたCが
適切。　Question 2　Tomが言及した専門用語の記憶方法が適切な分野
として例が挙げられていたのはbiology, physics, chemistryである。選
択肢の中でこれらの分野の上位語として適切なのはscienceである。
Conversation 2　日曜日にディベートのチームと会うAndyとそれを応援
するCathyの会話。CathyがディベートについてAndyに気になる点をい
くつか尋ねる形式である。　Question 1　ディベートでの勝利を決定す
る人はwe decided we need professional judges with formal training and
experienceと述べられていることから，選択肢Bが適切。　Question 2
ディベートのトピックについてはwe don't know what the topic is until a
few minutes before the debate actually beginsと述べられていることから，
選択肢Dが適切。

【4】世界で話されている言語は約7,000語存在するが，世界人口の半分は10の主要言語の話者である。7,000人以下の話者しか持たない言語は，大半が消滅の危機に晒されている。1つの言語が消滅することは，民族の伝統やアイデンティティーの消失につながる。マオリ族は，公用語化と教育により，マオリ語をよみがえらせる活動を進めている。ユネスコは存続の危機に瀕している言語を「隣人語」として学習することを推奨している。(199字)

〈解説〉読み上げられる記事の内容を日本語150～200字で要約する問題。記事は約400語であり，放送は2回ある。記事の内容は言語消失に関するものである。パラグラフが5つあり，それぞれにトピックが異なる。第1パラグラフでは現代の世界で使われている言語の数と話者人口，第2パラグラフでは500年後の世界で話されている言語の数の予測，第3パラグラフでは積み重ねられてきた知識と文化が消失すること，第4パラグラフではニュージーランドのマオリ族の取り組み，第5パラグラフではUNESCOの取り組みについてそれぞれ述べている。解答例では，パラグラフの順に沿って内容を簡潔にまとめている。なお，要約の際には，例示されている複数の下位語を上位語で置き換える方法(例：tennis, baseball, soccer→sport)や，詳細すぎる情報をカットする方法(例：ベッドに横たわったまま，目を開け，その後に体を起こした→起床した)などがある。

【5】(1)　ウ　　(2)　ウ　　(3)　イ　　(4)　エ　　(5)　ア　　(6)　エ　(7)　ア　　(8)　ウ　　(9)　ア　　(10)　ウ

〈解説〉(1)　the report oneself「出勤，出頭」は出勤した際の証明を表す。主語がMs. Whiteであり，単数形のherselfが適切。　(2)　空所の直後にあるexpensiveは形容詞であることから，形容詞を修飾する副詞のunbelievablyが適切。　(3)　2者の程度をless 原形 thanで比較する構文は劣勢比較と呼ばれ，not so[as] 原形 asで表すことができる。空所の後ろにthanが登場していることから，比較級のheavierを選ばないように注意。なお，a littleは肯定的な意味，lessが否定的な意味をそれぞれ表

している。　(4)　時を表す副詞節では現在時制が用いられる。句動詞hand in A to B「AをBに提出する」の目的語が代名詞の場合にはhand it in to Bのように，本動詞と副詞inの間に挟まれる語順になることにも注意。　(5)　相関接続詞としてのbothはA and Bを補部に選択する。この種にはeither A or B，neither A nor B，not A but B，not only A but(also)Bなどがある。なお，eachは単数形が後続する。　(6)　コンピュータ分野で使われる語彙として適切なのはenhance A「A(ソフト・ハード)の性能を高める」である。engage A「A(注意・関心・人)を引きつける」，encourage A「Aを励ます」，escalate A「Aを段階的に拡大させる」。　(7)　サッカーの練習を一生懸命にしたけれども初戦で敗退してしまったことがdiscouraging「(人を)がっかりさせるような」であったため，チームの何名かがやめてしまったという意味。distracting「気を逸らす，紛わらす」，engaging「人を引きつける，愛嬌のある」，enabling「権能を与える，授権的な」。　(8)　女性はゴキブリを嫌い，exterminate A「A(害虫など)を完全駆除する」までその家に引っ越すことを拒否したという意味。terminate Aは「Aを終結させる」という意味であり，強調を表す接頭辞ex-が付いて「完全駆除する」という意味になる。investigate A「Aを調査する」，diminish A「Aを減らす」，suspend A「Aを一時中断する」。　(9)　免許証がexpire「有効期限が切れる」したことに気づいたため，再発行に行くという意味。eject from A「(CDなどが)A(機器)から出てくる」，emerge from/out of A into B「A(水中・暗闇など)からBへ現れる」。engage in A「Aに従事する」。(10)　新しいコンピュータチップは現在のチップの5倍の処理速度であり，コンピュータ使用に革命をもたらすという意味。空所はrevolutionizeを動詞として選択していることから，a breakthrough「飛躍的な進歩」であると推測できる。a sequence of A「一連のA」，migration「移住，転居」，a supplement to A「Aの補足」。

【6】(1)　ウ　　(2)　イ　　(3)　エ　　(4)　ウ　　(5)　エ

〈解説〉(1)　副社長のJosh Grossmanがprovisionally(仮に，暫定的に)North Western Express社のトップとして任命されたが，会社の取締役の委員会では任期のないChief Executive Officer(CEO)を探している。increasingly「ますます，だんだん」，adequately「十分に，適切に」，temporarily「一時的に，仮に」，eventually「結局，最後に」。

(2)　Arman Hotelはビジネスでの旅行者に対して便利で，reasonably(適度な)価格帯の宿泊施設を提供している全国的なチェーンである。costly「高価な」，moderately「適度に」，virtually「実質的には，ほとんど」，evidently「明らかに，間違いなく」。　　(3)　Ms. Smithが工場管理者として雇用されてから，その工場のoutput(生産高，産出量)が劇的に増加した。a deadline「締切，期限」，preparation「準備すること」，a location「場所，位置」，production「製造，生産」。　　(4)　Marquette Universityのコマース・プログラムは，ビジネスの分野において成功するために必要なスキルを得るmeans(方法)として優れている。a technique「(実務的専門)技術」，an approach to A「Aへの取り組み」，a method for A「Aのための(組織的な)方法」，knowledge「知識」。

(5)　Mr. Robinsonは会議において，会社の成長戦略を変えるような説得力のあるa logical ground(論理的根拠)を提示した。cooperation with A「Aとの協力」，abundance「大量，豊富」，increase「増加，増強」，a rationale for A「Aの理論的根拠」。

【7】(1)　記号…エ　　語…its　　(2)　記号…エ　　語…which(that)

(3)　記号…ア　　語…Despite　　(4)　記号…ウ　　語…is

(5)　記号…エ　　語…health

〈解説〉(1)　エは前置詞inの目的語であることから，itのままではexhibitionsが不要となってしまい非文法的である。目的語をexhibitionsとするためにitを所有格のitsにする。　　(2)　colonies「植民地」は人ではなくモノであるため，関係代名詞はwhoではなくwhichもしくはthatが適切。なお，coloniesはone of the 複数名詞の構文の一部であるため

複数形である。 (3) despiteは「…にもかかわらず」という意味の前置詞であり，in spite ofよりも堅い語である。前置詞のofが使われてしまうと二重に前置詞が登場するため不適切。 (4) 文意は「将来の利益を正確に予測できなければ，固定費すら賄えないほど予算を消費してしまう」である。such A that「とても…なので」の異形であるsuch thatが使われている。that節の主語として使われているthereは仮主語であり，存在を表すthere構文とは異なるため，複数形のfundsと一致してare/wereになるわけではない。that節の意味上の主語は主節のexpendの目的語であるits budgetであり，時制は主節と一致することから，現在形のisが適切。 (5) 前置詞inの目的語は名詞である必要があるため，形容詞のhealthyは不適切。

【8】 (1) 4番目…キ 7番目…エ (2) 4番目…ウ 7番目…エ
(3) 4番目…ア 7番目…イ

〈解説〉 (1) 正しい順番はall the documents we need to giveである。空所の直前には他動詞compile A「(編集のために)Aをまとめる」があるため，空所では最初に目的語が必要となる。allは定冠詞や指示代名詞，人称代名詞の所有格などに限定される単数名詞の直前に置かれる。普通名詞documentsには定冠詞が必要であるから，all the documentsとなる。あとは「書類」を「私たちが弁護士に渡す必要のある～」と修飾すればよい。関係代名詞が省略された形である。 (2) 正しい順番はyou put all historical events in chronologicalである。suggest that A(should)do は「Aは～してはどうかと提案する」。shouldが省略されているため，putは原形であり，put B in chronological order「Bを時系列で並べる」というコロケーションをなす。目的語はall historical eventsとなる。
(3) 学校に送って行った母が子どもに行ってきますのキスができない理由を尋ねると，恥ずかしいからであると答えている。空所ではその理由が述べられる。正しい順番はNone of my friends let their mothersである。noneはnoの代名詞用法に相当し，none of the＋複数名詞で「何一つ…ない，誰一人…ない」という意味となる。使役動詞letは目的語

と原形不定詞を取る。

【9】(1)　エ　　(2)　イ　　(3)　ウ

〈解説〉(1)　フィクションは15％オフ，ノンフィクションは25％オフという対立関係が述べられているため，whileが適切。neverthelessも対立関係を示すが，こちらは文修飾の副詞であるため節をつなぐ接続詞としての機能はない。文をつなぐ場合にはbutやalthoughを伴う。　(2)　過去分詞の後置修飾用法の問題。後置修飾は関係代名詞とbe動詞(who is)が省略された形である。interest A in B「AにBへの興味を持たせる」は他動詞であり，主語が興味を持つ人であることから，受動の意味を表す過去分詞が使われている。　(3)　購入の際には学生証を提示しなければ割引が得られないことが述べられている。前述の内容が起こらなかった際に予想されるよくない結果を導くotherwise「さもなければ，もしそうでなければ」が適切。なお，otherwiseはif notで置き換えることができる。

【10】(1)　イ　　(2)　ウ　　(3)　ウ　　(4)　イ　　(5)　ウ

〈解説〉(1)　英文のトピックについて答える問題。第2パラグラフの冒頭ではfairly tales「おとぎ話」の起源や歴史についての言及があり，最後には目的が述べられていることから，イが適切。　(2)　第1パラグラフにておとぎ話が子ども向けであると広くみなされているが，決して真実ではないと述べられている。このことから，よくある誤解についてはウが適切。他のはいずれも真実であるため不適切。　(3)　おとぎ話の起源は第2パラグラフにて述べられているが，ウの現実世界の起源を説明する記述はない。to create bonds for communities in the face of the mighty powers of natureとあるため，アおよびイは適切。また，エについては，第2パラグラフにてchildren welcome them generally because they cultivate their vast desire for change and independence，第3パラグラフにてThey instructed, amused, warned, introduced, and enlightened.とそれぞれ述べられており，教育と娯楽目的であることがわかる。　(4)　第

3パラグラフではfairy talesとoral folk talesの違いや宗教・文化との関わり，口頭伝承の違いによる所属意識などが述べられている。アはit is difficult to specify when the first "literary" fairy tales were madeと述べられているため不適切。イはMotifs from these, memorized and passed on in oral transfer, made their way into the Bible and the Western classics.と述べられているため適切。ウはThe early oral tales that played a role as the basis for the development of the literary fairy tales were closely tied to the ceremonies and belief of tribes, communities, and colleagues.と述べられているため，テーマや内容は現代にも引き継がれていることが読み取れることから不適切。エはmodified according to the necessity of the tellers and listenersと述べられているため，対立しているわけではないから不適切。 (5) classic「古典」やplay「劇」などの語が登場しているがartに関する言及がないため，アは不適切。Bible「聖書」やreligionなどの語が登場しているがpreaching「伝道」に関する言及がないため，イは不適切。ウは第2パラグラフにて，they emerge from inherent struggles to humanize savage and brutal forces which have terrified our minds and communities in specific ways, threatening to destroy free will and human considerationと述べられているため適切。folk talesのテーマが現代にも引き継がれていることが示されていることから，エは不適切。

【11】(1) エ　(2) イ　(3) ア　(4) ウ　(5) エ

〈解説〉(1) 資料1にはInterested candidates should fax a resumeとあり，仕事への応募のためにファックスを送ったと考えられる。advertise A「Aを宣伝する」，offer A「Aを申し出る」，state A「Aを述べる」，apply to A for B「AにBを出願する」。 (2) 資料1にはThe appropriate candidate would manage a product team of developers and coordinators.と述べられているため，イが適切。 (3) 資料1にはThe product manager should also communicate with vendors to make products that are within the budget.と述べられているため，アが適切。 (4) 資料1にはCompetitive salary and other benefits offered.と述べられていることから，企業側から割のいい

給与が与えられることを表したウが適切。　(5)　Ms. Murphyについての特徴は資料2にまとめられている。アはI have over ten years' experience in product development and management.と述べられているため不適切。イはI also have extended experience in product design.と述べられているため不適切。I'm a team player who is thoroughly committed to my work.と述べられているためウは不適切であるが，エは適切である。

【12】(1)　①　エ　　②　イ　　③　ウ　　(2)　エ→ア→オ→ウ→イ
(3)　イ　　(4)　The fact that a place is able to produce or obtain enough food to feed its population. (17 words)

〈解説〉(1)　①　大規模な耕作地買収が生じたことについて，第2パラグラフにA food crisis in the spring of 2008 showed that food would probably become in short supply in Africa over next several years, setting off conjecture by hedge funds and commodities markets that food prices would go up. As a result, this sparked speculative buying all over Africa.と述べられている。in short supply「供給が不足した」，conjecture「推論，推測」，hedge funds「ヘッジファンド(先物やオプション取引などの金融派生商品を運用して収益を得ようとする投資信託)」，commodities「日用品」，food prices go up「食品価格が上昇する」，spark A「Aを引き起こす」，speculative「投機的な(市場の変動による差額を得るために行う取引のような)」。このことから，企業がアフリカの土地を買ったのは，アフリカが将来的に食料危機に陥るため，耕作地を購入して利益を得ようとしていたためであるとわかる。　②　国連に関する記述は，第3パラグラフにThe World Bank, the United Nations, and other distinguished organizations say that forthcoming large-scale agricultural business brings necessary expertise and technology that will increase agricultural production.とある。ここでは専門性と技術を有する企業がアフリカの広大な耕作地を開拓することで，地元の農家が農業をするよりも効率的であることを述べている。なお，小規模農業では国の経済発展が望めないとして農民に農地売却を推奨するのは，Jon Andersonという人物の意見で

あり，国連などの組織の意見ではないので，ウは不適切。　③　バイオ燃料(食物を発酵させた油やガスを使った燃料)に関しては，第4パラグラフにthe biofuel products are exported at a time when about 1.2 million Ghanaians are not provided a sufficient amount of foodと述べられている。ガーナ国内で十分な量の食料がないにもかかわらず，バイオ燃料として食料が輸出されている。企業がアフリカの耕作地を購入して効率的に農作物を栽培したとしても，それがアフリカの国内で消費されることはない例であるため，ウが適切。　(2)　示されている5つの選択肢は本文の5つのパラグラフを表している。第1パラグラフでは植民地時代と同様に，自由競争の名の下にアフリカの耕作地が大規模に買収されていることを述べている。第2パラグラフでは起こりうる食料危機に目をつけた企業が耕作地を買収すること，第3パラグラフでは世界銀行や国連が企業の耕作地買いに悲観的でない理由として，大規模農耕の技術があることを述べている。第4パラグラフではバイオ燃料の企業は結局のところアフリカ国内に対して食料を提供せずに輸出していること，第5パラグラフでは前国連事務局長のKofi Annanが経済的な利益よりも人間を重視するべきだと主張していることと，投資家は人間よりも経済的な利益を重視していることが述べられている。

(3)　選択肢はいずれも本文にて述べられている内容である。本文のタイトルとしてはより包括的な情報もしくは著者が伝えたいメッセージである必要がある。本文の内容としてアフリカの耕作地買いが取り上げられているが，第5パラグラフにあるように，アフリカの住民にメッセージの焦点が当てられると考えられる。そのため，アフリカの農家が耕作地を失っていることを表したイが適切。　(4)　下線部food securityは「食料安全保障」のことを指し，国連食糧農業機関(FAO)によると「全ての人が，いかなる時にも，活動的で健康的な生活に必要な食生活上のニーズと嗜好を満たすために，十分で安全かつ栄養ある食料を，物理的，社会的及び経済的にも入手可能であるときに達成される状況」と定義される。本文ではアフリカの耕作地が海外企業によって買収され，その耕作地で栽培された作物がバイオ燃料として国外

に輸出されてしまい，国内では十分な食料が国民のために確保できないという事例が示されていた。このことをふまえ，「耕作地があり，国民に十分な量の食料を確保できる状態」を英語でまとめるとよい。

【13】 We, English teachers should keep the following three attention points in mind when we conduct classes based on the use of English. The first one is to increase the opportunities for students to come into contact with English. The second is to make classes the places of communication. The third is to try to use English according to the level of understanding of the students. (65 words)

〈解説〉英語を使って英語の授業を実施するにあたっての注意点について，60語以上の英語で3つ以上の注意点を述べる自由英作文問題。解答例の他にも，難しい語彙はジェスチャーやイラストなどを使って表現したり，文法の解説などを日本語で説明した方が効果的な場合には，全てを英語で説明しないようにしたりすることが挙げられる。

【14】(1)　「so～that…」の表現は，「ある程度極端な，普通では考えにくい意味内容」を表す場合や，soの後に望ましくない意味を表す語が用いられ，thatの後に否定的な内容が来る場合かの，どちらかで用いられるのが一般的です。この文は内容的にどちらにも当てはまりませんので，ALTはstrangeと感じたのだと思います。I studied very hard, and I passed the entrance exam for ○○ high school.と表現するほうがいいでしょう。　(2)　「There is(are)～」の表現は，聞き手・読み手にとって新情報である内容を伝えるときに用いるのが一般的です。通例a, an, someなど「特定されないもの」が主語として用いられます。ただ，theを用いて「特定できる」ものであっても，それが「新情報」である場合に限り主語として用いることが可能です。具体的には「the＋名詞(句)」が後置修飾を伴う場合や，「the＋最上級の形容詞＋名詞(句)」の場合などが挙げられます。

〈解説〉生徒から質問される可能性のある文法事項について，教員として

どのように返答するかを日本語で説明する問題。 (1)「so～that…」の表現の解説は解答例の通り。辞書に記載されている例文を参照すると，望ましくない意味を表す形容詞としてtired, hungry, weakなどが使われている。なお，書き換えの案として接続詞andを使って時系列通りに示しているが，becauseを使って因果関係として表すこともできる。 (2) there構文は新情報・旧情報の概念を使うことにより説明される。生徒に説明することを想定すると解答例のように具体例を示しながら説明するとよい。

【高等学校】

【 1 】 1 （ア） ① （イ） ③ 2 ② 3 ① 4 ② 5 I think that high school English teachers should use authentic materials, because the goal of English education is to give students an adequate command of English. After graduating from high school, students will read and write English academic papers in college. In the company, they will talk with business partners in foreign countries and negotiate with them. Therefore, English teachers should give students many opportunities to use authentic English. However, at the same time, I believe that English teachers should be careful about using authentic materials in class. As Rivers and Nutall say, unless English teachers prepare appropriate materials, students cannot understand them and will lose confidence and motivation for English learning. There are many kinds of authentic materials on the Internet, and we can find good authentic materials for novice-level learners. English teachers should observe their students before choosing what kind of authentic materials they use. (147 words)

〈解説〉オーセンティックなテキストを言語指導で使うべきかについて論じた英文の読解問題。 1 空所に入る適語を選択肢から選ぶ問題。 （ア） 空所は，authentic materialsについての説明文の中の，ダッシュで囲まれた箇所に位置している。Communicative Language Teaching(CLT)は，赤ちゃんが母語を習得するのと同じように，コミュニケーション

を通して第2言語も習得されるという理念に基づいたアプローチである。オーセンティックなテキストとは，言語指導を目的としていない母語話者向けに作られたもので，具体的には，ネイティブがネイティブ向けに放映・制作・執筆したニュースや映画，小説などである。したがって，(ア)にはnative speakerが入る。CLTではオーセンティック教材との比較対象として，言語学習者向けに書かれて単純化されたテキストが挙げられる。したがって，空所(イ)にはnative speakerと対比関係にあるlanguage learnersが入る。　2　「オーセンティック」に関する議論は，第3パラグラフにある。Scarcella and Oxfordは"generally, authentic language is considered unedited, unabridged text that is written for native…speakers"と述べ，WalterはCatherine Walter, on the other hand, includes texts both "shortened" and "slightly adapted"と述べられている。①　第3パラグラフ2文目でOxfordの説が述べられ，続く3文目にはon the other handとともに，Walterの説が述べられている。on the other handは対立関係のディスコースマーカーであるため，両者の考えは異なると分かる。よって正しい。　②　同パラグラフ4文目でWidowsonはauthenticity is not a quality of text at all; instead, "authenticity…is achieved when the reader realizes the intentions of the writer"と述べられている。したがって，選択肢にあるように，書き手が読み手をconvince「説得する」ものではないため誤り。　③　同パラグラフ5文目にWilliamsはan authentic text is one "written to say something, to convey a message"とある。よって「オーセンティックなテキストには書き手のメッセージが込められている」は正しい。　④　パラグラフの冒頭でIn spite of the widespread acceptance of the use of authentic materials, there is no consensus as to the meaning of authentic.と述べられているため正しい。　3　空所ウ及びエに当てはまる組み合わせを選ぶ問題。空所では教室の言語とreal languageが対比されて述べられている。オーセンティックなテキストがreal languageであることを踏まえ，教室外で使われる言語がreal languageであると分かる。このことから，学習者が最終的にreal languageを使うため，その準備としてオーセンティックな教材を教室

内で使うべきであるという論調ができあがる。したがって，公式解答では①が正答となっているが，空所ウにはoutside，空所エにはinsideが入るのが適切であると思われる。 4 オーセンティックな教材のデメリットについては第6パラグラフ以降に列挙されている。 ① Williams, Rivers, Nuttallは，難易度の高いテキストは辞書を繰り返し引くこととなり，読解スキルを発達させるために向いていないと述べているので正しい。 ② 教師にとっての難易度については言及されていないので誤り。 ③ Riversの主張と一致するので正しい。 ④ 第7パラグラフでRivers が "rushing students too soon into reading material beyond their present capacity for fluent comprehension with occasional contextual guessing … destroys confidence" と述べているので正しい。 5 オーセンティックなテキスト及び言語学習者用に単純化されたテキストをどのような目的で使用するかについて，100〜150語の英語で述べる自由英作文問題。設問の前提条件として，高校の英語教員であると想定して書くこと，パッセージの情報に言及すること，具体例を入れることが指定されており，これらをクリアして指定の語数でまとめなければならない。パッセージの中で言及された文献に触れ，主張を裏付けるような具体的な理由や詳細情報を述べる必要がある。解答例では，高校卒業後に英語を使った具体的な場面に出合うため，オーセンティックなテキストを高校で使うべきであるという肯定的な主張を述べている。また，RiversやNutallが主張するように，レベルに合わない難しい教材ではモチベーションを下げてしまう危険性があることについても言及している。オーセンティックな教材に対して否定的であるという立場の別解としては，高校生でも熟達度に大きな差が開いている場合には，言語学習者向けに教育的な立場から作成されたテキストの方が適切であることを述べ，引用としてはRiversの辞書を頻繁に引いて流暢な読解を妨げることを言及するとよい。

【２】1　②　　2　①　　3　③　　4　②　　5　(1)　③　　(2)　③
(3)　④　　(4)③　　(5)　①　　(6)　④　　6　I agree with the idea that we should start learning a second language as early as possible. However, I would like to claim that we can acquire an adequate command of a foreign language even if we start learning it after we become an adult. As the author says, I believe that adult learners have their learning strategies and they can use them to learn a foreign language effectively, which younger learners cannot. In addition, I think that a good command of the first language is the most important thing to learn a foreign language. If we cannot think logically or do not have a rich vocabulary in our first language, it is impossible to do so in a second language. As a high school English teacher, I would like to focus on how to make use of students' learning strategies effectively. (141 words)

〈解説〉英語の学習開始年齢に関する長文読解問題。　1　aptitude「適性，素質」の定義を選ぶ問題。英語の定義は英英辞典を参照することで確認できる。aptitudeも日本語の対訳だけでは何かを学習する際の能力であることは分からないため，積極的に学習者用の英英辞典を引くことをお勧めする。　2　proficiency「熟達，熟練」の定義として適切なのは①「能力やスキルが優れた基準であること」。　3　the Critical Period Hypothesis「臨界期仮説」についての記述として適切なものを選ぶ問題。臨界期仮説については，第3パラグラフで，人間の発達段階では言語習得に成功する脳の時期があること，音素，形態素，構文などの言語レベルによって臨界期が異なることなどが述べられている。

①　第3パラグラフの最後の2文に，言語の下位区分である発音などには別の臨界期があることが述べられているが，言語習得の臨界期は小児期であり，「脳が言語習得に最適な時期は多数ある」と包括的に述べることはできないため不適切。　②　母語と第2言語における臨界期の関係について述べられていないため不適切。　③　「若いほど第2言語指導が成功する」と主張する研究と，「大人は方略的な能力やメタ言語知識を使うことができるため効率的な第2言語学習に成功する」という研究があり，総意は得られていないため適切。　④　語彙と文

法の臨界期は異なることに多くの研究者が賛成しているため不適切。
4　子どもと大人の言語習得を比較することが難しい理由についての問題。第4パラグラフに述べられている。　①　学習時間に関してはパッセージに言及がないため不適切。　②　They often have more opportunities to hear and use the language in environments where they do not experience strong pressure to speak fluently and accurately from the beginning.と述べられているため適切。　③　大人の場合はミスをすると恥ずかしいと思うことがあると述べられているため不適切。

④　young learnersとadultの説明が逆であるため不適切。　5　第7パラグラフに述べられているMark Patkowskiの研究についてまとめる問題。

(1)　冒頭にMark Patkowski(1980) studied the relationship between age and the acquisition of features of a second language other than pronunciation.と述べられているため，研究対象となっていないのは「発音」である。

(2)　同パラグラフ2文目に，15歳以前に学習を始めた子どもが高い言語熟達度に至ることができると仮説を立てたことが述べられている。

(3)　研究対象となった協力者の特徴については，同パラグラフ3文目及び4文目に述べられている。5年以上アメリカに住んでいたことと，15歳以前に学習を始めている子どもについての研究であることを踏まえると，協力者は全員少なくとも20歳以上であることが分かる。この条件に当てはまらないのは，④「15歳の移民」である。　(4)　インタビューを記録した理由は，第9パラグラフ2文目より，③の「アクセントの影響を除外すること」が適切。　(5)　①　第11パラグラフ最終文で，第2言語をネイティブ並みに習得するには，言語の習得年齢が重要な要因であると述べられていることから適切。　②　年齢要因が言語学習に影響する結果と矛盾するため不適切。　③　English as a Second Language (ESL)環境について言及がないため不適切。　④　発音を対象としていないことと矛盾するため不適切。　(6)　第11パラグラフ3文目及び5文目より，空所カの候補はlength of residence in the United States及びamount of instructionであるので，④が適切。　6　臨界期仮説に基づいて，第2言語学習を早くに実施するべきかについて，

100〜150語の英語で自由に作文する問題。なお，パッセージで言及されている情報に触れ，自分の意見を支持する具体的な理由や経験，詳細情報などを述べなければならない。解答例では賛成派の立場であり，大人の学習者が学習方略を用いた効率的な学習について触れている。さらに，高校の英語教師としての考えを述べて締めくくっている。反対派の別解として，ESL環境(インドやシンガポールのように，日常的生活に英語が密接な環境)で得られている研究結果を，日本のような外国語としての英語(English as a foreign language; EFL)を学ぶ環境に直接当てはめて考えることは不適切であると主張できる。

2022年度　実施問題

【中高共通】

Script

[There are three speaking roles for this test: Directions , Man(M), and Woman(W).]

Directions : Please turn the test paper over. The Listening Comprehension Test will now begin. You may take notes while listening.

【1】 Directions : Section A.

Please listen to the following conversations. After each conversation, a question will be asked, and four possible answers will be read. Choose the best answer and circle the corresponding letter on your answer sheet. Each conversation, the question, and the answers will be read only once.

Directions : Conversation 1.

M : Hello, I'm calling from Boston College. I placed an order for 50 textbooks from your store last month. I have just gotten the delivery, but 15 of the books have torn covers. I was hoping you would be able to replace all of them.

W : I'm very sorry about that, sir. They may have been damaged during delivery. I can send you 15 good copies instead.

M : I need the textbooks for a course that starts next Wednesday. How soon can you get them to us?

W : I'll make a special note to send them by express delivery. Therefore, they should arrive by Monday morning at the latest.

Directions : Where does the woman work?

A. A shipping company.

B. A bookstore.

C. An office supply firm.

D. A bank.

Directions : Conversation 2.

M : Hi, I bought this electric toothbrush at your store last Sunday, but it's not working normally. I tried changing the battery, but that didn't work.

W : It must be a trouble with the mechanism. If you leave it here, I can ask someone to repair it. It will perhaps take a few days.

M : OK. I'll come back on Tuesday, then.

W : In fact, we're no longer open on Tuesdays. Why don't you come to us on Wednesday morning? If we're not able to repair the electric toothbrush, I can replace it with a new one, since it's guaranteed by the manufacturer's warranty. In that case, I'll need a receipt, so please bring that with you.

Directions : What does the clerk suggest?

A. Going to another store.

B. Contacting the manufacturer.

C. Using a different battery.

D. Bringing a proof of purchase.

Directions : Conversation 3.

W : Hi, Mark. Is that a new tie?

M : Exactly. You are the first to notice. I have seen over twenty people so far, but no one said anything.

W : I really like it. You look more authoritative with the color.

M : I don't usually choose red, but the sales clerk gave a convincing pitch.

W : You mean you bought it because she was fascinating?

|M| : How did you guess?

|W| : Come on! How long do you think we've known each other?

|Directions| :　Why did Mark buy the new tie?

A.　He liked the sales clerk.

B.　He liked the color.

C.　He thought it was fascinating.

D.　He could save money on it.

|Directions| :　Conversation 4.

|W| : Excuse me. I seem to have lost my way, a little bit. I'm wondering if you could help me.

|M| : No problem. So, is this your first time in D.C.?

|W| : Yes, I just arrived here this morning and I'm supposed to be at the convention center in twenty minutes. I don't think I'll make it.

|M| : You've still got some time.

|W| : I guess I am a typical traveler who loses their way.

|M| : No need to worry. You are not the first one. That's what the information office is for.

|Directions| :　What do we learn from the man?

A.　The woman will be late for her meeting.

B.　The convention center is far away.

C.　Other people have gotten lost.

D.　There are not so many tourists in D.C.

(☆☆○○○○○)

【2】 |Directions| :　Section B.

　　Please listen to the following two passages. After each passage, two questions will be asked. Four possible responses to each question are listed on the answer sheet. Choose the best one and circle it. Each passage and question will be read only once.

Directions : Passage 1.

M : Shogi and chess, having originated from a similar ancient game, of course have similarities. Both are games in which two players move some pieces on the board, take the opponent's pieces, and try to put the opponent in check to win. Shogi pieces can move almost the same ways as chess pieces.

The two games also have different characteristics. While a chess board has 8 by 8 (that is, 64) squares painted in white and black, a shogi board has 9 by 9 (that is, 81) squares in a woody color. Each chess player begins with 16 black or white pieces in 6 different three dimensional forms. Each shogi player, on the other hand, starts with 20 pieces in 8 pentagonal varieties of various sizes, and can also use captured pieces as their own, which is the most outstanding difference between these two games. This special rule enables shogi players to use many kinds of offensive tactics while arranging several pieces to defend the king. On the other hand, at chess, few pieces remain on the board at the end of the game, so that a chess player moves all the pieces including the kings offensively.

Directions : Question 1. What is the most important difference between chess and shogi?

A. The size of the board the game is played on.

B. The treatment of captured pieces.

C. The number of pieces given to players before the game.

D. The shape and the dimension of pieces.

Directions : Question 2. What do chess players have to do in the final stage of a game?

A. Use their remaining pieces for exclusively defensive strategies.

B. Move the kings as far back as possible.

C. Engage in offensive movements with the pieces that are left.

D. Accurately grasp how many pieces the opponent has.

Directions : Passage 2.

M : Every year, more than 60 million people in the U.S. — or 25 percent of the total population — volunteer in all kinds of community projects, from taking care of the homeless and cleaning up streets and highways to fixing up ruined houses. Specialists say that volunteering helps establish strong, healthy communities, reduces problems like crime, and even makes a contribution to the mental health of the volunteers themselves.

Although all kinds of people participate in volunteer work in the U.S., in fact those who are more educated and wealthy are more likely to volunteer than those less-educated and poorer. Reports explain that volunteering rates fall, however, when there are problems with volunteering — such as long drives to volunteer sites. Also, volunteering rates fall when volunteers are given "too much" work to do. This is one reason why institutions that depend on volunteers try to make it more appealing for them to spare their time by offering incentives. For example, they may have shuttle buses to take volunteers to volunteer sites or events, or give out snacks or T-shirts to them.

Directions : Question 1. Which group of people is more likely to volunteer?

A. People who enjoy fixing houses.

B. Poor citizens of rundown communities.

C. People who have a past record of crime.

D. Those with higher levels of schooling.

Directions : Question 2. How are some institutions increasing volunteering rates?

A. By providing free transportation to volunteers.

B. By giving volunteers work challenging enough to do.

C. By asking volunteers to invite their friends.

D. By varying the types of volunteering events available.

(☆☆☆☆○○○○○)

【3】 Directions : Section C.

Please listen to the following two conversations. After each conversation, two questions will be asked. Four possible responses to each question are listed on the answer sheet. Choose the best one and circle it. Each conversation and question will be read only once.

Directions : Conversation 1.

W : Excuse me, Professor Robinson, may I speak with you for a while?

M : Sure, come on in, Becky. I have a few minutes before my next class.

W : Well, the reason I came here is that I'm not satisfied at all with the grade I got for my essay.

M : Oh, really? Why do you think so?

W : Well, I did my best for it. I believed that I was a better writer.

M : If I recall correctly, you got a B minus. That's not bad!

W : I know, but I was really expecting an A.

M : Well, the paper was generally well-organized and I can say that you shaped your ideas in it. But you didn't use enough supporting details and you made some careless grammar errors.

W : I know, but…

M : Becky, you have the capacity to make an A paper. When did you write it? The night before the deadline?

W : Right.

108

M : Well, I suggest you give yourself more time. Write your next essay earlier and work on it over a week. You'll be able to find out your weak points and fix your grammar errors.

W : OK, I'll do my best.

M : Good luck, Becky. I hope you'll do better next time.

Directions : Question 1. Why did the woman want to talk with the professor?

A. She was unhappy with her grade.

B. She had some questions about grammar.

C. She wanted to thank him for his help.

D. She wanted to research the topic of her next essay.

Directions : Question 2. What does the professor think of the woman's potential to write an essay?

A. She has no potential.

B. She was idle.

C. She is careless.

D. She could improve as a writer.

Directions : Conversation 2.

W : John, long time no see!

M : Hi, Cathy. It's been about half a year, hasn't it?

W : Maybe. So why did you drop out of sight for an entire semester?

M : Well, I had this really great internship at the city planning department for all this semester. I actually worked with the urban designers and architects — looking at a lot of proposed developments, like where new parks should be located, how they should be designed, the size and scope of the buildings, and so on.

W : Sounds great!

$\boxed{\text{M}}$: Yeah, and the best thing for me was not only getting course credit for it but also getting paid.

$\boxed{\text{W}}$: Are you kidding? You got paid to go to school?

$\boxed{\text{M}}$: Exactly. Of course, almost all internships are unpaid, but there are some rare cases that you can get a salary or scholarship. The city planning program that I'm in has some great connections in government and companies, so they can place students in some great situations. You get course credit plus a salary. The cash was useful. But, frankly, I learned about ten times more working in the city planning department than I'd have learned in a classroom.

$\boxed{\text{W}}$: Boy, that sounds like a pretty good program. So how do you feel to be back to the university?

$\boxed{\text{M}}$: Not so bad, actually. Anyway, I'm going to graduate at the end of this year.

$\boxed{\text{Directions}}$:　Question 1.　Where has the man been working?

A.　A construction company.

B.　A university planning department.

C.　A government office.

D.　An urban studies program.

$\boxed{\text{Directions}}$:　Question 2.　What was an unusual point about the man's internship?

A.　It lasted all of the year.

B.　He received money for doing it.

C.　It was unrelated to his major.

D.　He obtained it after his graduation.

(☆☆☆◎◎◎◎)

110

【4】 Section D.

The following article will be read twice. Please write a summary of the contents in Japanese. The summary should be between 150 and 200 characters. You may take notes and begin summarizing while listening. Now, please listen to the article.

M : There is a common belief that human beings use "only 10 percent" of their brains. A steady believer of this opinion says that if ordinary people could activate the other 90 percent, they could cultivate special, even extraordinary competence, like memorizing 200 different words in five minutes and then reciting them in alphabetical order without making any mistakes, or using psychic force to make a cup float in the air without even touching it! Though it sounds attractive, the "10 percent" myth is so wrong that for brain experts it seems almost ridiculous.

The source for the "10 percent" myth is uncertain, but some brain experts believe it is connected with the 19th century psychologist and philosopher William James in the U.S., who claimed that most people use only a small section of their mental and physical resources.

The strengthening of the myth seems to come from people's groundless conceptions about their own brains: they regard their own weakness as proof of the existence of idle parts of their brains. This is a false prejudice.

Certainly, while people are completely sleeping, they might be using only 10 percent of their brains. But the other times, we make much greater use of our brains. "Specialists agree that people use effectively every part of their brain, and that most of the brain is active almost all the time," says one brain expert in the U.S. "Actually, the brain accounts for only three percent of the body's weight but consumes twenty percent of the body's energy."

The human brain is composed of three parts. The largest part conducts all higher cognitive functions like understanding, reasoning, memorizing, calculating, and so on; another takes charge of motor functions, such as the coordination of movement and balance; and the third consists of involuntary functions like breathing. Most of the energy consumed by the brain enables millions of neurons in these three portions to interact with each other. Specialists claim that it is such interactions that make all of the brain's higher functions possible.

Although it is generally accepted that, at any time, not all of the brain's parts are activated simultaneously, brain experts have shown that, like the body's muscles, most of them are active during a 24-hour period; even in sleep, some parts of the brain are actively functioning. Scientific proof shows that everyone makes use of nearly 100 percent of their brain during a day.

Directions : Stop writing, please. This is the end of the listening test. Thank you.

参考文献(すべて全面的に加筆修正)
・『DAILY　30日間　英検準1級集中ゼミ』(旺文社・2009年)
・『TOEFL　ITP　TEST　実戦問題集』(語研・2011年)
・『英検準1級　頻出度別問題集』(高橋書店・2016年)
・『TOEICテスト超リアル模試600問』(コスモピア株式会社・2011年)
・『完全攻略！TOEFL ITPテストリスニング』(株式会社アルク・2016年)

(☆☆☆☆☆○○○○○)

【5】次の(1)～(10)の英文の_____に入る最も適切な語(句)を，ア～エの中からそれぞれ1つ選び記号で答えなさい。

(1) The participants honored firefighters in the city, _____ have been dedicating their lives to saving citizens.

ア who　　イ which　　ウ whose　　エ whom

(2) The application of the benefit is required to be submitted _____ September 10th.

ア in　　イ by　　ウ at　　エ until

(3) Public transportation, essential services, and government offices kept _____ during the emergency declaration.

ア to operate　　イ operate　　ウ operated　　エ operating

(4) Mr. Hopkins was impressed by the management strategy and wanted to know _____ idea it was.

ア how　　イ whether　　ウ who　　エ whose

(5) It _____ for a long time that there is a risk of MWC's drugs causing inflammation in the stomach.

ア has known　　イ has been knowing　　ウ had known

エ has been known

(6) Mr. Dickens _____ his friendship with Ms. Yoshida, the ex-ambassador to his country. Every year he invites her to his residence and shows her his respect for her country.

ア cherishes　　イ afflicts　　ウ constitutes　　エ dooms

(7) The foreign employee didn't try hard to defeat the language barrier, which was one of the major _____ to communicating with him.

ア rituals　　イ obstacles　　ウ amnesties　　エ comfirmations

(8) Tom tried to _____ his lost time with his daughter when he met her again after ten years of separation.

ア catch up wih　　イ come down with　　ウ make up for

エ keep up with

(9) The kids are staying in their own room _____ with video games

113

throughout the day instead of going out and visiting their friends.

　ア　devoted　　イ　lenient　　ウ　obsessed　　エ　subtle

(10)　The superior remarked on her clothes _____. His words were terribly mean. It was as if he had intended to hurt her feelings from the beginning.

　ア　sarcastically　　イ　inconsequentially　　ウ　amiably

　エ　unwittingly

(☆☆☆○○○○○)

【6】次の(1)〜(5)の英文において下線部に最も近い意味の語(句)を，ア〜エの中からそれぞれ1つ選び記号で答えなさい。

(1)　The personnel department supports moved employees and helps them make an unimpeded <u>transition</u> to their new office.

　ア　migration　　イ　integration　　ウ　interaction　　エ　arrival

(2)　Mid-American Tour takes every <u>precaution</u> needed to assure customers' health and safety throughout the tour.

　ア　advice　　イ　carefulness　　ウ　rule　　エ　idea

(3)　Farmers <u>all over</u> the state are concerned that this year's harvest will not meet expectations as a result of the cold weather in summer.

　ア　over all　　イ　wherever　　ウ　anywhere　　エ　throughout

(4)　In the factory, maintaining a safe and clean working environment takes <u>priority</u> over all other matters.

　ア　precedence　　イ　issue　　ウ　concern　　エ　importance

(5)　<u>Many</u> of the client feedback survey respondents described that they were satisfied with City Bank's services.

　ア　Every　　イ　Much　　ウ　Most　　エ　Almost

(☆☆○○○○○)

【7】 次の(1)～(5)の英文において不適切な箇所を，下線部ア～エの中か
らそれぞれ1つ選び記号で答え，正しい形，または，適切な語(句)にし
なさい。

(1) ア<u>Although</u> the paintings of Morris Louis don't イ<u>recognizably</u> feature
figures, landscapes, or objects, ウ<u>their</u> form and vigor have a エ<u>power</u> effect
on people.

(2) ア<u>Generally</u>, the weaker the immune function of イ<u>a</u> living creature is,
the ウ<u>great</u> its susceptibility to エ<u>infection</u>.

(3) ア<u>From</u> 1978 to 1981 the Einstein telescope イ<u>made</u> remarkable
discoveries by using a complicated set of reflecting mirrors ウ<u>to form</u> an
image of the heavenly body and send エ<u>them</u> back to Earth.

(4) ア<u>By</u> the end of 1980's, the CPI (consumer price index) had イ<u>climbed</u>
ウ<u>from</u> a value of 100 in 1970 to more than 300, エ<u>raising</u> more than 200
percent.

(5) ア<u>As</u> a result of the experiments using radiation, Madame Curie was
イ<u>the first</u> to identify the distinction ウ<u>among</u> a non-radioactive element
エ<u>and</u> a radioactive isotope.

(☆☆○○○○)

【8】 次の(1)～(3)の英文において〔 〕内の語(句)を正しく並べかえて
文章を完成するとき，〔 〕内の語(句)の4番目と7番目にくる語(句)
を，ア～キの中からそれぞれ1つ選び記号で答えなさい。ただし文頭に
来る文字も小文字になっている。

(1) A : Why don't we make use of the information in this research report to
draw up our own?
B : No, I think that's plagiarism. The 〔ア told イ to only
ウ own エ us オ our カ professor キ use〕
ideas.

(2) A : Thanks so much for your kindness in this study team.
B : That's OK. I couldn't just 〔ア you イ a ウ and let

エ　stand　　オ　poor　　カ　by　　キ　get〕result!

(3)　A : I'm sorry, but I don't think I'll be able to drive you home tonight.

　　　B : I〔ア　of　　イ　can't　　ウ　out　　エ　backing

　　　　　オ　believe　　カ　your promise　　キ　you're〕. I was looking

　　　　　to you for help.

(☆☆○○○○○)

【９】次の英文において空欄1～3に入る最も適切な語(句)を，ア～エの中からそれぞれ1つ選び記号で答えなさい。

　The Ohio State Film Fair kicks off this weekend with an exciting line-up of movies. The opening film (Friday, 6 P.M.) is The Missing Link, a local production directed by William Robert about a young woman who sets out on an emotional journey

　(　1　) her missing father. It is recommended for fans of heartwarming drama.

　The Cinnamon Buyer, which plays on Saturday (3 P.M.), is set in 1890s Denmark. Mixing drama and mystery, it is an imaginative but somewhat difficult movie. Fans of director Adam Nelson's previous films should enjoy it, but others may be (　2　) by its difficult storyline.

　The Fiesta (Sunday, 2 P.M.), on the other hand, is a (　3　) tale of small Spanish town's attempts to prepare an annual festival. With its interesting characters and amusing script, it's a suitable choice for those seeking light entertainment.

1　ア　finds　　　　　イ　to find　　　ウ　has found

　　エ　finding

2　ア　confused　　　イ　confusion　　ウ　confusing

　　エ　confuses

3　ア　controversial　イ　humorous　　ウ　disappointing

　　エ　fearful

(☆☆○○○○○)

【10】 次の英文を読み，以下の各問いの英文を完成させるのに，本文の内容と最も適するものを，ア～エの中からそれぞれ1つ選び記号で答えなさい。

As opposed to the planets which revolve around the sun counter-clockwise almost in a circular orbit on the same level, comets approach the sun in slender elliptical orbits from every direction. Furthermore, they have pretty small masses. Each comet has a nucleus that is supposedly like a large ball of ice mixed with dust and small pieces of solid objects. Although most comets are small, the icy nucleus of a large comet may be as wide as 500 miles (800km).

As a comet comes near the sun, the heated material on the surface of its nucleus evaporates and forms a coma and tail. Some of the material—for instance, carbonates and silicates in the form of small particles and soil—does not evaporate, however, but keeps moving along in company with the comet's main part. When the earth passes through a location of small cometary particles of this material, we can observe a meteor shower. More than 100,000 "shooting stars" may be observed lighting up the sky during a few hours.

This reduction of particles by a comet, with the loss of gas involved in forming a tail at the same time, slowly reduces the comet's main part. After many orbits around the sun, the comet is likely to change to a stream of tiny particles. The fact that new comets are discovered every year, and probably have been appearing since the days that the solar system appeared, indicates that somewhere there must be a huge supply source of their cometary material. This supply source is thought to exist on the outer edges of the solar system, past the orbit of the farthest planet, because most of the comets have orbits that take them beyond the further side of Neptune.

(1) It can be inferred about planets from paragraph 1 that

　ア　they orbit around the sun in a clockwise direction.

　イ　they were created in the same period as the sun.

　ウ　their orbits are much more irregular than those of comets.

エ　they have larger mass than comets.

(2)　Paragraph 1 implies that the nucleus of a comet can best be described
like

ア　a dirty snowball.

イ　an inflated tire.

ウ　an erupting volcano.

エ　a falling round stone.

(3)　It can be inferred from paragraphs 2 and 3 that at the end of a comet's
life it

ア　burns up in the sun.

イ　gradually disintegrates.

ウ　crashes into the planets.

エ　becomes denser and colder.

(4)　According to paragraph 3, comets probably originate

ア　at the outer limits of the solar system.

イ　in the asteroid belt.

ウ　just inside the solar system.

エ　near the sun.

(5)　The tone of this passage could best be described as

ア　anxious.

イ　cynical.

ウ　objective.

エ　speculative.

(☆☆☆○○○)

【11】 次の2つの資料を読み，以下の各問いに対する答えとして最も適切
なものを，ア～エの中から1つ選び記号で答えなさい。

【資料1 : INVOICE】

INVOICE   Shipment Date : Oct. 7th

Natural Beauty INC.

Description of articles	Charges
Premium make-up kit	$150.00
Tax	7.50
Surcharge	25.00
Total	$182.50

Card number: 7845-651-0209

Thank you for your payment

*Payments remitted by credit card will show up on your statement as
N. B. Inc. Personal Checks are not accepted*

Natural Beauty Customer Service ;

PO Box 22573

Lansing, MI 48901

service@naturalbeauty.com

For bill or product inquiries only

【資料2 : E-mail】

To: Linsey William＜lwill@mwa.com＞
From: T. Clark＜tclark@naturalbeauty.com＞
Subject: Your inquiry

Dear Ms. William,

Thank you very much for your inquiry to our customer service department regarding the surcharge added to your online order of our premium make-up kit.

We regrettably had to require $25.00 as a surcharge for shipping and handling because you are at an overseas address. We require this charge to ensure that your order gets there safely.

We are very sorry for the inconvenience and thank you for your understanding in this case.

We would also like to offer you 10 percent off your next purchase at Natural Beauty as our way of saying "thank you." Just reply to this mail to receive a 10 percent off coupon.

Sincerely yours,

Tayler Clark
Customer Service Representative, Natural Beauty Inc.

(1)　Why did Ms. William send a message to the customer service department?

　　ア　She wanted to find out why $25.00 was subtracted from her order.

　　イ　She wanted to inquire about a fee that was added to her order.

ウ　She wanted to find out why her order had not been shipped.

エ　She wanted to inquire how to use her make-up kit

(2)　What was the surcharge added for?

ア　Manufacturing the product.

イ　Handling at the warehouse.

ウ　Sending by ship.

エ　Shipping overseas.

(3)　Who can contact Natural Beauty's customer service?

ア　Anyone who wants to contact Natural Beauty's management.

イ　Anyone looking for a job.

ウ　Anyone who has a question about a product.

エ　Anyone who wants to know more about Natural Beauty.

(4)　How was the bill paid?

ア　By bank remittance.

イ　By personal check.

ウ　In cash.

エ　By credit card.

(5)　What did Natural Beauty do to make up for the inconvenience?

ア　They offered her their condolences and gratitude.

イ　They offered her a reduction in the price of her next order.

ウ　They offered her a discount on the shipping charge.

エ　They offered her a discount on the shipping surcharge of her next order.

(☆☆☆○○○)

【12】次の英文を読み，以下の各問いに答えなさい。

　　The human brain is by far the most complicated computer known to us, but at the same time, it is the least understood. That is why, as yet, (　あ　) if part of it breaks down. According to scientists in the field of bionics, however, repairing brain damage and other troubles in neutral systems may require little more than the replacement of broken neurons with implants in the near future. In fact, bionic research is presently making progress in several fields.

One of those is the creation of equipment that can accept information from the brain of a disabled person and send it to a computer or an artificial limb. Although this technology is still in an early stage, a company called Neural Signals in the US has already constructed a system that enables a person who has been paralyzed completely to spell words by operating a virtual computer keyboard through transmitters connected to the brain. Professor Richard Anderson of Caltech is now developing more advanced implants that can "read the minds" of paralyzed patients quickly. The patients think of specific words or signals, and then the implant receives these signals from the parts of the brain responsible for language. Anderson says the process would not be automatic, likening it to mastering to ride a bicycle, because the implant and the patient would have to "learn" how to work together to ensure that signals were transformed into the suitable words and signs.

Other bionic implants are also developed to transplant or enhance improperly working sense organs. Maybe the most well-known neural prosthesis today is the cochlear implant, used by more than 80,000 hearing-impaired people all over the world to convert sound waves to electrical signals that are wired directly to the auditory nerve of the brain. This gives people just about 80 percent hearing functionality. This astonishing breakthrough has been a great encouragement to researchers at the Dobelle Institute based in the U.S., who are now developing "a bionic eye." This is actually a camera mounted on a pair of glasses that sends signals to a computer placed on the user's belt. Then the computer processes and reroutes the signals to 68 electrodes connected to the visual cortex of the brain. The result achieved so far is the equivalent of 20/400 vision, narrowly enough to allow blind people to navigate large obstructions by sight.

Though still in its early stages, bionics promises to give a solution for many hard-to-treat injuries and diseases, as well as the possibility of artificial human enhancement. However, not everybody feels happy with the prospect of the latter possibility. Science fiction has already made a clear image of a dark future populated by cyborgs enslaving people through the use of bionic technology. Could today's bionic implants lead finally to X-ray vision or even psychic powers? Somehow or other, <u>this Pandora's box</u> has already been opened, and now human beings have the ability to develop every kind of technology to enhance human powers. Only time will tell whether the potential of this technology will be used in a responsible way.

(1)　Choose the best phrase from among the four choices to complete the sentences below.

① It is stated about the implants being developed by Richard Anderson that

ア　they will be sufficiently sophisticated to allow communication with unconscious patients.

イ　they will automatically send definite messages to the part of the brain that is responsible for speech.

ウ　patients will require a certain amount of practice in order to use the devices effectively.

エ　patients with major physical impairments will not likely benefit from the enhanced abilities the implants provide.

② The difference between the cochlear implant and the Dobelle Institute's "bionic eye" is that

ア　while the cochlear implant includes some external components, the bionic eye is entirely internal.

イ　the bionic eye is more advanced and more closely approximates a functioning sense organ.

ウ　the cochlear implant has already proven its value in real life, whereas the bionic eye remains at the developmental stage.

エ　the bionic eye has less practical appeal than the cochlear implant because of its higher cost needed in developing.

③　The author concluded about bionics that

ア　the claims of researchers are often exaggerated, as breakdowns invariably occur during the development of pragmatic devices.

イ　since bionic enhancements pose a threat to our society, we should strictly control research into their development.

ウ　the threats that bionic developments create will most likely be overcome though science fiction paints a black picture of the future.

エ　the technology is not without risk, but its continued development seems to be inevitable.

(2)　Complete the sentence in (　あ　) so that the passage will make sense. Fill in the blank with about 10 words.

(3)　Choose the most appropriate title of this passage from the phrases below.

ア　Bionic Implants

イ　Repairing Brain Damage

ウ　The Potentiality of Artificial Human Enhancement

エ　The Cochlear Implant

(4)　Explain the underlined phrase "this Pandora's box," related to this passage. (about 20 words, in English)

(☆☆☆☆☆○○○○○)

【13】 According to the new curriculum guidelines, we have to give lessons which take into consideration the content learned in other subjects. Write a composition about one example of an effective idea of this in English, including a description of its effectiveness for students. The composition should be 80 words or more.

(☆☆☆☆☆○○○)

【14】授業中に生徒が次の(1)と(2)の質問をした。あなたは英語の教員と
してどのように説明するか。それぞれについて日本語で答えなさい。
(説明の一部に英語を交えても差し支えない)

(1)　期間を表す言葉として「for」と「during」がありますが，使い方
の違いについて教えてください。

(2)　何かをしようと試みる，ということを表現したいとき，「try to do」
を用いるのか「try doing」を用いるのか，どちらが正しいのでしょ
うか？

(☆☆☆○○○)

【高等学校】

【 1 】 Read the passage and answer the questions below.

Assessment in Second Language Classrooms

(前略)

Productive skills: Speaking and writing

Speaking and writing are often called productive skills because they require
students to produce language and, in doing so, to create meaning. Unlike the
receptive skills, language output is an (　ア　) behavior, at least in terms of
student products such as spoken responses or pieces of writing, and so lends
itself to being assessed through direct measures, particularly at more
advanced, levels of language proficiency. Additional attention is also often
paid to the processes inherent in producing these outputs, and like the
receptive skills, these processes require more indirect methods of assessment.
Figure 9 sets out sample language performances in speaking and writing along
with selected tasks for assessing students' proficiency in using those skills. (中
略)

Sample Speaking Performances	Sample Assessment Tasks	Sample Writing Performances	Sample Assessment Tasks
Learners produce comprehensible words or phrases.	· Repetition of words and phrases provided by a teacher · Recitation of rhymes and poems · Picture cued items	Learners produce letters, words, punctuation, and brief texts.	· Copying letters or words · Spelling tests · Picture cued items · Multiple choice
Learners produce utterances in response to short stretches of language.	· Dialogue completion · Picture cued narratives or descriptions · Pair/group structured tasks	Learners produce guided writing.	· Picture-cued narratives, sequences, or descriptions · Reordering mixed-up words into a sentence or out-of-sequence sentences into a paragraph · Short answer or sentence completion
Learners produce longer interactive stretches of discourse.	· Role play · Information gap · Interview	Learners produce texts.	· Paragraphs · Texts in various genres (e.g., summaries, book reports, essays)
Learners produce monologues.	· Oral presentation · Debate · Retelling stories	Learners engage in the writing process.	· Comments on other students' drafts, focusing initially on ideas rather than each grammatical error · Writing conferences

Figure 9. Sample language competencies and tasks for speaking and writing.

Once students move away from more (　イ　) language production and begin generating (　ウ　) texts either in spoken or written performances, teachers are faced with the problem of how to capture and make sense of the language that students are generating. In addition to the assessment task itself — for example, producing a paragraph or engaging in a debate — a consistent means of scoring student performances is needed.

Performance assessments such as these consist of two components: (1) a prompt that sets the task for the assignment; and (2) a way of scoring the language that students produce. Well-crafted prompts do more than instruct the student to write 150 words or take one side of an issue for a debate. They specify the amount or type of information necessary to meet teacher expectations for a satisfactory performance and to generate the desired type of speaking or writing. Additional useful features in a prompt include the identification of an audience, a purpose, and a context for generating

126

language. Here's an example of a prompt for a piece of writing: [　エ　]
Scoring guides are generally used in assessing the language that students produce. They provide consistency in scoring as well as a clear picture of the criteria that will be used in judging a language performance. In this way, teachers and students can develop a shared understanding of learning aims embodied in the criteria found in the guides and identify what will count as a satisfactory performance. Following are several commonly used types of scoring guides. As with all assessments, there are advantages and shortcomings to each one.

Checklists are one type of assessment tool used in documenting speaking and writing performances. As the name suggests, ①*checklists* are made up of lists of features of a language performance with a space for noting whether or not that feature is present in a specific performance. Table 1 provides an example of a checklist for a writing assignment. ②Checklists are simple to use and can be easily adapted to observations of language production during class activities. However, ③they provide much information about the quality of a performance.

A frequently used scoring guide is a *rating scale*, in which the performance is scored or rated according to a list of features. Some rating scales include only numbers and a brief statement of what the rater should focus on. ④Ones designed for younger learners may display a range of graphic "faces" (e.g., from faces with smiles to ones with frowns) that can be circled. Table 2 is an example of a rating scale for assessing the quality of oral participation in a discussion task. ⑤Rating scales cannot offer more scoring choices than checklists or the opportunity to give more points to some features than others, and ⑥the lack of detailed descriptions for each scoring point can lead to differences in scoring the same language performance.

Table 1. Writing Checklist

Rating Criteria	Assessment Yes	No
Is the writer's purpose clear?	____	____
Is there a beginning, middle, and end?	____	____
Does each paragraph have a main idea?	____	____
Is each main idea developed?	____	____
Are all the sentences complete?	____	____
Is newly learned vocabulary used appropriately?	____	____

Table 2. Oral Participation Rating Scale

Rating Criteria	Assessment
Interacts with all members of the group during the task	1 2 3 4
Maintains rapport with other members of the group	1 2 3 4
Uses a range of targeted structures	1 2 3 4
Uses a range of learned vocabulary	1 2 3 4
Pronunciation of learned vocabulary is comprehensible	1 2 3 4
Key: 1 = lowest score; 4 = highest score	

Two additional types of scoring guides are *holistic* and *analytic rubrics*. Unlike the previous scoring guides, both types of rubrics include specific criteria related to various qualities of language proficiency that are aligned with a scale or range of levels. Each score is tied to a set of descriptors. Because of these descriptors, such tools are particularly useful in assessing complex performances such as extended writing or speaking. They also help to ensure more consistency in scoring across performances and across raters by focusing attention on specific aspects of a performance.

Holistic scoring draws on a rater's response to an entire performance produced by a language user. Holistic rubrics generate a single score for a performance. An example of a holistic writing rubric can be found in [　A　]. (中略) Holistic tools are useful for quick scoring of a language performance and are used extensively, for example, when assessing numerous writing samples at the end of a marking period or during a placement procedure. They do not, however, provide specific information about individual components or subskills.

Analytic scales rate the various components of a language performance and provide scores for each one. An example of an analytic writing rubric can be found in [　B　]. (中略) Analytic tools provide specific information about each component of a language performance since each component receives its own score. While it takes more time to use an analytic tool than a holistic one, analytic tools provide information that is useful for _オdiscerning a learner's strengths and pinpointing areas for continued efforts. (後略)

(1)　Choose the best word from among the choices for (　ア　). Write the number of the answer.

①　ambiguous　　②　observable　　③　unnoticeable

(2)　Choose the best pair of the words from among the choices for (　イ　) and (　ウ　). Write the number of the answer.

①　イ　　abstract　　　　ウ　　concrete

②　イ　　controlled　　　ウ　　extended

③　イ　　specific　　　　ウ　　uncertain

(3)　Choose the best example of a prompt from among the choices for ［　　エ　　］. Write the number of the answer.

①　Write a one-page letter to another student in the class about one of the books we've read this year. In your letter, describe what the book is about and why you have chosen to write about this book.

②　Write a report consisting of 3 parts on one of the sustainable development goals you are most interested in.

③　Write a 300-word summary of one book you read last year. You should add a short biography of the author of the book to your summary.

(4)   Part of one of the underlined sentences ①～③ has been changed so that the sentence won't fit in the context. Choose that sentence and write the number of the answer.

(5)   Part of one of the underlined sentences ④～⑥ has been changed so that the sentence won't fit in the context. Choose that sentence and write the number of the answer.

(6)   Choose the best statement to describe the meaning of the underlined word ォ discerning from among the choices. Write the number of the answer.

①   to know, recognize or understand something

②   to pay no attention to something

③   to succeed in reaching a particular goal, or standard

(7)   Choose the appropriate sample writing rubric from among the choices for [　A　] and [　B　]. Write the number (①/②) of the answer.

①

Assessment	Topic Sentence	Supporting Sentences	Concluding Sentence
4	Presents the main point clearly. Sentence is complete. There are no grammar or spelling errors.	There are three or more complete supporting sentences, with ideas that stick to the main idea presented in the topic sentence. There are no grammar or spelling errors.	There is a concluding sentence that reaffirms the main idea presented in the topic sentence and summarizes the ideas in the supporting sentences. There are no grammar or spelling errors.
3	Presents the main point clearly. Sentence is complete. There are a few grammar and/or spelling errors.	There are a couple of complete supporting sentences, with ideas that stick to the main idea presented in the topic sentence. There are a few grammar and/or spelling errors.	There is a concluding sentence that reaffirms the main idea presented in the topic sentence. There are a few grammar and/or spelling errors.
2	The main point is presented in an incomplete sentence. There are a few grammar and/or spelling errors.	There are a couple of supporting ideas presented. There are a few grammar and/or spelling errors.	The concluding sentence is presented in an incomplete sentence. There are a few grammar and/or spelling errors.
1	Grammar and spelling errors make it almost impossible to understand the main point.	Grammar and spelling errors make it almost impossible to identify supporting sentences.	Grammar and spelling errors make it almost impossible to identify the concluding sentence.
0	There is no topic sentence.	There are no supporting sentences.	There is no concluding sentence.

This rubric was developed by Adriana Scheidegger as part of the requirement for the Learner Assessment course at The New School. Used with permission.

②

5	Well organized with very few errors in grammar to impede comprehension. A wide and appropriate use of vocabulary. Fully comprehensible.
4	Minor problems in content and/or organization. Some errors in grammar and lexical choice that require attention. Generally comprehensible.
3	While some problems in content and/or organization are evident, the paper is comprehensible for the most part. There are obvious errors in grammar and lexical choice that indicate a need for further language development.
2	There are serious problems in content and/or organization. The paper is difficult to understand at times. Errors in grammar and lexical choice are frequent and distracting. Not easy to understand.
1	Unclear content and organization. Overwhelming problems with grammar and lexical choice that make comprehension very difficult.

(8)   Which type of assessment tool would you use to evaluate the following performance? Choose one from among the choices (①～④) and write the number of your choice. Also, explain in English the reason(s) why you have chosen it. Note that you should write <u>more than 30 words</u> and refer to the characteristics of the tool(s) mentioned in the passage.

Class / English Level: 40 1st-year-senior high students / Lower-intermediate

Performance: [In the last lesson before summer vacation] Each student wiil make a two-minute-speech in front of the class about the most ideal place in Japan to spend summer, followed by some questions by a teacher. Students must try to make as many classmates as possible actually feel like going there in summer.

①   Checklist   ②   Rating Scale   ③   Holistic Rubric

④   Analytic Rubric

(☆☆☆☆☆◎◎◎◎◎)

【2】 Read the passage and answer the questions below.

[Notes]   TBLT: task-based language teaching / L2: second language / L1: first language

CF: corrective feedback / ESL: English as a second language

GJT: grammaticality judgement test

Task-Based Interaction in Small Group Work

All the research we have considered to date has examined interaction in tasks performed in a teacher-class participatory structure. In some ways this runs contrary to a general understanding of what TBLT* entails. Mainstream accounts of TBLT assume that tasks will be largely carried out in small group work. We need to ask, therefore, whether the interactions that arise in small groups when tasks are performed manifest focus on form similar to that found in teacher-led lessons and whether learning results.

Group work is generally seen as advantageous for language learning. In an early study, Long et al. (1976) reported that students working in small groups produced a greater quantity of language and also better quality language than students in a teacher-fronted, lockstep classroom setting. Small group work provided more opportunities for language production and greater variety of language use in (　ア　), asking for clarification, (　イ　), competing for the floor and joking.

Group work has been found to result in more interactional adjustments than in teacher-class interaction but only if the task is of the required information exchange type (Pica and Doughty, 1985a, 1985b). In an often-cited article, Long and Porter (1985) pointed to a number of advantages of group work:

1.　Quantity of practice (i.e. there is more opportunity for language practice in group work than in lockstep lessons).

2.　Variety of practice (i.e. in group work learners can perform a wide range of language functions).

3.　Accuracy of student production (i.e. learners have been shown to use the L2* just as accurately in group work as in lockstep lessons).

4.　Correction (i.e. students engage in self- and other corrections to a greater extent in group work than in lockstep teaching).

5.　Negotiation (i.e. students engage in more negotiation of meaning sequences when performing communicative tasks in group work than in teacher-led lessons).

132

6. Task (i.e. group work lends itself to the performance of two-way tasks that elicit negotiation of meaning sequences).

(中略)

However, not all researchers provide such a favourable account of group work. Researchers have noted that learners sometimes overuse their L1* when performing tasks in groups (Carless, 2004). Adams, Nuevo and Egi (2011) observed that the studies vary in how frequently CF* occurs in learner-learner interactions, with some showing that it is very (　ウ　). Toth (2008) noted that learners in groups tend to use a (　エ　) range of feedback strategies and, in contrast to teachers, they tend to focus on a wide range of linguistic features.

Few studies have actually investigated whether group work interaction results in acquisition. Adams et al. (2011) investigated whether the implicit and explicit feedback in learner-learner interactions was related to acquisition. Learners in high-intermediate classes in an adult ESL* school in the United States worked in pairs to complete tasks designed to elicit the use of past tense and locatives. They were not instructed to provide CF. The interactions were coded for all instances of feedback, whether the feedback was implicit or explicit, and whether the learners modified their output when they were corrected. Acquisition was measured by means of a GJT* and an oral production test. Adams et al. reported that a third of the feedback was non-target-like and that there was relatively little output-prompting feedback. There was no evidence that either implicit or explicit corrections promoted acquisition of past tense but recasts were related to scores for the locative in the delayed post-test. They concluded 'it seems likely that feedback may not play as important role in learner-learner interactions as it plays in NS-learner interactions [native speaker-learner interactions].' They suggested that the widely focused nature of the feedback may have made it less salient and that the learners may have been hesitant in accepting that the feedback they received was correct.

133

The difference in the accounts of group work interaction found in these studies is not so surprising as its effectiveness must surely depend on the particular learners involved. What may be crucial is the mindset of the learners. Sato (2017) defined mindset as 'a disposition toward the task and/or interlocutor prior to and/or during the interaction.' His study indicated that learners with a positive mindset engaged in more correction, language-related collaboration and collaborative sentence completion than learners with a more negative mindset. One way of inducing a positive mindset is through training. Sato and Lyster (2012) reported that training Japanese university students to make use of CF during group work led to them providing both more and more effective CF (prompts) and also to more repair work. For group work to deliver on its promises in TBLT, then, learners may require guidance in the behaviours that are needed to ensure that it is effective for acquisition.

(1)　Choose <u>TWO</u> activities from among the choices for (　ア　) and (　イ　). Write the numbers of the answers. The order does not matter.

①　initiating discussion　②　interrupting　③　reading aloud
④　reciting

(2)　Choose the best pair of the words from among the choices for (　ウ　) and (　エ　). Write the number of the answer.

①　ウ　frequent　　エ　diverse

②　ウ　infrequent　エ　limited

③　ウ　rare　　　　エ　wide

(3)　Write your opinion about having Japanese senior high students work in small groups in English classes and why you think it is suitable/not suitable for Japanese students.

ⅰ.　Your essay should consist of <u>150-250 words</u>.

ⅱ.　You should refer to the information mentioned in the passage.

ⅲ.　You should have specific reasons or details to support your opinion.

(☆☆☆☆☆○○○○)

解答・解説

【中高共通】

【1】Conversation 1　B　　Conversation 2　D　　Conversation 3　A
Conversation 4　C

〈解説〉男女の会話を聞き，質問に対する適切な解答を4つの選択肢の中から1つ選ぶ問題。質問と選択肢は問題用紙に印刷されていない。スクリプトは比較的短く，難易度も高くはないが，スクリプトが読まれるのは1回のみである。　Conversation 1　女性の職場はどこかを問う問題。大学教員の男性が教科書を注文した内容であることから，女性は書店で働いていると推測できる。　Conversation 2　店員は何を勧めているのかを問う問題。故障した電動歯ブラシを持ってきた客に対し，店員は①修理をすること，②休業日の次の日の朝に来ること，③修理できなかった場合のためにレシートを持ってくることを勧めている。receiptを言い換えているa proof of purchase「購入の証拠」が適切。Conversation 3　Markが新しくネクタイを買った理由について問う問題。Markが購入したのは，店員に勧められた普段は身につけない赤のネクタイであった。女性の発言からsales clerkが魅力的であったことが示されているため，Aが適切。　Conversation 4　ワシントンを初めて訪れた女性と案内所の男性の会話であり，男性の発言から分かることを問う問題。You are not the first one. から，他にもたくさんの人が道に迷っていることが分かる。

【2】Passage 1　Question 1　B　　Question 2　C
Passage 2　Question 1　D　　Question 2　A

〈解説〉パッセージが2つと，質問が各2問読み上げられる。問題用紙には各4つの選択肢が印刷されている。パッセージと質問が読まれるのは1回のみである。　Passage 1　将棋とチェスに関する内容のパッセージである。概要は以下の通り。将棋もチェスも似たような駒の動きをす

るが，その駒の数や盤面の数が異なる。最も際立った違いは，将棋では相手の取った駒を使うことができる点である。さらに，将棋では王将を守る駒が存在する一方で，チェスではキングが攻撃的に動くこととなる。　Question 1　将棋とチェスの最も重要な違いは，can also use captured pieces as their own, which is the most outstanding differenceと述べられている。　Question 2　チェスの対局の最後は，お互いに駒を取り合うことから盤上に残る駒が少なく，キングを含めて駒を動かし，互いに攻撃的な戦術を取ることとなる。　Passage 2　アメリカのボランティアに関する内容のパッセージである。概要は以下の通り。アメリカでは道路の掃除や壊れた家屋の修理など様々な種類で，年間6,000万人の人々がボランティアに参加する。なお，学歴が高く裕福な人の方が参加率は高い。ボランティアでは社会的なつながりを形成し，精神的な健康にもよいが，近年は参加者が減少しつつある。理由としてはボランティアの実施場所まで遠かったり，ボランティアの時間が長かったりすることが挙げられる。この対策としてバスの送迎やTシャツなどの配布が行われている。　Question 1　ボランティアに参加する可能性がより高いグループは，those who are more educated and wealthy are more likely to volunteerから，Dが適切。　Question 2　ボランティアへの参加率を高めるための方策としてthey may have shuttle buses to take volunteers to volunteer sitesと言っていることから，Aが適切。

【３】Conversation 1　Question 1　A　　Question 2　D

Conversation 2　Question 1　C　　Question 2　B

〈解説〉男女の会話が2つと，質問が各2問読み上げられる。選択肢は問題用紙に印刷されている。会話と質問が読まれるのは1回のみである。Conversation 1　Robinson教授とレポートの成績に不満を持つBeckyの会話である。概要は以下の通り。レポートの構成はよかったが，詳細情報の欠如と文法ミスがいくつか見られた。レポートに取り掛かったのは締切前日の夜であったことから，Robinson教授は時間に余裕を持ってレポート執筆にあたるように指導した。　Question 1　Beckyが

Robinson教授に話しかけたのはthe reason I came here is that I'm not satisfied at all with the grade I got for my essayから，Aが適切。

Question 2　Robinson教授がBマイナスの評価であったBeckyの可能性について考えていることは，you have the capacity to make an A paperからDが適切。　Conversation 2　半年ぶりに会うJohnとCathyの会話である。Johnは今学期に都市計画に関する長期の有給インターンシッププログラムに参加し，都会の公園のデザインなどを学んだ。さらに，インターンで単位を取得して今年卒業する予定である。　Question 1　都市開発で公園の位置などを調整することへの言及があることから，Johnの働いていたところは，Cであると推論できる。　Question 2　通常のインターンとは異なる点は，almost all internships are unpaid, but there are some rare cases that you can get a salary or scholarshipから，Bが適切。

【4】人間は脳の10％しか活用していないとよく言われるが，これは誤りだと専門家は指摘している。脳はエネルギーの20％以上を使用しており，ほぼ1日中活動していることが判明している。脳は認知や記憶を司る部分，運動機能を司る部分，呼吸のような不随意機能を司る部分の3つに分かれており，消費するエネルギーの大半が使われている。科学的な根拠によって，1日のうちに誰もが脳のほぼ100％を使っていることは明らかである。(200字)

〈解説〉400語程度の雑誌記事が2回読まれ，その内容を日本語150～200字で要約する問題である。リスニングとライティングとの技能統合テストであること，脳科学という専門的なトピックであることから，難易度が高い。

【5】(1)　ア　　(2)　イ　　(3)　エ　　(4)　エ　　(5)　エ　　(6)　ア　(7)　イ　　(8)　ウ　　(9)　ウ　　(10)　ア

〈解説〉(1)　「関係者は市民を救うために命を捧げている市内の消防隊員に敬意を表した」。関係代名詞whoはthe cityではなく，firefightersを修飾している。先行詞と関係代名詞の間に前置詞句が挿入されていること

とに惑わされてwhichを選ばないように注意。　(2)　「補助金の申し込みは9月10日までに提出されることが求められている」。期限を表すbyが適切。untilは一定期間継続する動作の継続を表すため，submit A「Aを提出する」とは共起しないと考えられる。　(3)　「緊急事態宣言の間，公共交通機関や必要不可欠なサービスや政府機関は稼働を続けた」。keep doing「〜し続ける」。essential servicesとは，医療機関のように，政府からストライキを禁止されているサービスのことである。emergency declaration「緊急事態宣言」。　(4)　「ホプキンス氏は，その経営戦略に感銘を受け，誰のアイデアなのか知りたがっていた」。knowの目的語であるideaの直前に空所があることから，所有格関係代名詞whoseが適切。howとwhetherもknowの目的語となり得るが，節が後続しなければならないため，本問では不適切。be impressed by A「Aに感動する」。　(5)　「MWCの薬が胃に炎症を起こすリスクがあることは以前から知られていた」。仮主語itが用いられているのは，knowの目的語のthat節が長いためである。for a long timeと現在まで続く期間を表す語句が用いられていることから，現在完了形を用いることとなる。

(6)　「ディケンズ氏は，元駐在大使の吉田さんとの友情を大切にしている。毎年，吉田さんを私邸に招き，彼女の祖国へ敬意を表している」。cherish A「Aを大切にする」。接辞ex-は「前の」という意味。

(7)　「その外国人従業員は，コミュニケーションを図る際の大きな困難の1つである言語の壁を，懸命に打破しようとしなかった」。

(8)　「トムは離れ離れになった娘と10年ぶりに再会し，娘との失った時間を取り戻そうとした」。catch up with A「Aに追いつく」。

(9)　「その子どもたちは，外出して友達の家へ遊びに行くかわりに，1日中部屋にこもってビデオゲームに夢中になっている」。obsessed with「(他のことが目に入らないほど)〜に取り憑かれている」。　(10)　「その上司は彼女の服について皮肉たっぷりに感想を述べた。彼の言葉はひどく意地悪だった。まるで，最初から彼女の気持ちを傷つけるつもりだったかのようだ」。sarcastically「嫌味に，皮肉を込めて」。remark on A「Aの感想を述べる」，mean「(形容詞で)意地悪な」。

【6】 (1) ア　　(2) イ　　(3) エ　　(4) ア　　(5) ウ

〈解説〉(1) 「人事部では，異動した社員をサポートし，彼らの新しい職場へのtransitionを支障なくできるように支援する」。下線部はtransition「移行，移り変わり」。migration「移住，移動」，integration「統合」，interaction「やりとり」，arrival「到着」。　　(2) 「Mid-American Tourは，ツアー中のお客様の健康と安全を確保するために必要なあらゆるprecautionを講じます」。下線部はprecaution「予防措置」。advice「忠告」，carefulness「慎重」，rule「規則」，idea「考え」。　　(3) 「州のall overの農家は，夏の低温の影響で今年の収穫が期待通りにならないことを懸念しています」。下線部はall over A「Aの至る所で」であり，throughoutが適切。　　(4) 「工場では，安全で清潔な作業環境を維持することが何よりもpriorityを持つ」。下線部priority over A「Aよりも優先であること」。最も近い意味はprecedence「優先，先行」である。issue「問題」，concern「懸念，関心事」，importance「重要性」。　　(5) 「City Bankのサービスに満足しているとの記述がお客様の声アンケートにて多く見られました」。a respondent「(アンケートの)回答者」が複数形となっていることから，量を表すMuchは不適切。EveryおよびAlmostは代名詞としての用法はないため不適切。

【7】 (記号／語(語句)の順) (1) エ／powerful　　(2) ウ／greater
(3) エ／it　　(4) エ／rising　　(5) ウ／between

〈解説〉(1) 「モーリス・ルイスの絵画では人物，風景，物体などを認識できるように描写していないが，その形と力強さが人々に強い影響を及ぼしている」。although節の述語はdon't featureであり，recognizablyは副詞として正しい。theirはfigures, landscapes, or objectsを指す。powerはeffectを修飾するため，形容詞powerfulが適切である。　　(2) 「一般に，生物の免疫機能は弱くなればなるほど，感染症にかかりやすくなる」。前半の節ではthe＋比較級の形を取っていることから，後半のgreatは比較級となる。　　(3) 「1978年から1981年にかけて，アインシュタイン望遠鏡は，複雑な反射鏡を使って天体の像を作り，地球に送ることに

よって，驚くべき発見をした」。from A to B「AからBまで」，make a discovery「発見をする」。下線部エの代名詞は単数形のa complicated set of reflecting mirrorsを指すことからthemではなくitである。 (4) 「1980年代末までには，1970年に100だったCPI(消費者物価指数)が300以上になり，200％以上も上昇した」。by the end of A「Aの終わりまでに」，climb from A to B「AからBまで上昇する」。主語がthe CPIであり，上昇するものであることから他動詞のraiseは不適切であり，自動詞のriseを分詞構文の形にする。 (5) 「放射線を使った実験の結果，キュリー夫人は非放射性元素と放射性同位元素の区別を初めて明らかにした」。as a result of A「Aの結果」，the first「最初の人物」，the distinction between A and B「AとBの区別」。amongは3つ以上の関係性について言及する際に用いられるため，2者間について言及するbetweenが適切。

【8】(1) 4番目…イ 7番目…ウ (2) 4番目…ア 7番目…オ
(3) 4番目…エ 7番目…カ
〈解説〉(1) 正しい順番はThe professor told us to only use our own ideas.である。tell A to do「Aに～するように言う」。「A自身のB」は所有格人称代名詞＋own＋名詞の形を取る。 (2) 正しい順序はI couldn't just stand by and let you get a poor result!である。stand byは自動詞で「傍観する，待機する」という意味。get a poor result「悪い結果となる」。(3) 正しい順番はI can't believe you're backing out of your promise.である。back out of A「A(約束・契約など)を破棄する」。

【9】1 イ 2 ア 3 イ
〈解説〉1 空所1はan emotional journeyを修飾していることから，本動詞であるアとウは不適切である。「父を探すための旅」という意味となるto findが適切。現在分詞は「～しているA」という意味であり，「父を探している旅」となってしまうことから不適切。 2 受動態はbe動詞＋過去分詞の形を取るので，be confused by A「Aに困惑する」が適切。 3 第3パラグラフ2文目のit's a suitable choice for those seeking

light entertainment「軽いエンタテインメントを求める人に向いている」という記述から，humorous「ユーモアのある」が適切。controversial「論争を呼ぶ」，disappointing「がっかりするような」，fearful「恐れている」。

【10】(1)　エ　　(2)　ア　　(3)　イ　　(4)　ア　　(5)　ウ
〈解説〉第1パラグラフでは彗星の特徴を述べている。通常の天体は反時計回りの円形の軌道であるが，彗星は細長い楕円形の軌道であり，質量がとても小さい。さらに，チリと固形の細粒とで構成された大きな氷玉のような核を持つ。第2パラグラフでは彗星が太陽に近づくにつれて表面が蒸発する点，地球が彗星粒子の近くを通るとき流星群が見られることが述べられている。第3パラグラフでは，尾を引く彗星が太陽系の外から毎年やって来ていることから，太陽系の外に巨大な彗星粒子の供給源があると考えられることを示している。　(1)　第1パラグラフの3文目より，彗星が惑星より小さいとわかる。　(2)　彗星の核はチリと細粒でできていることから，dirty snowball「汚い雪玉」が適切。　(3)　彗星は最終的に蒸発したり，非常に細かい流星群となったりすることから，gradually disintegrates「次第に分解する」が適切。(4)　第3パラグラフの4文目に，彗星は太陽系の外縁部で生まれると考えられることが述べられている。　(5)　英文の文体は，事実だけを淡々と述べたobjective「客観的」なものである。anxious「心配している」，cynical「皮肉な」，speculative「推測的な」。

【11】(1)　イ　　(2)　エ　　(3)　ウ　　(4)　エ　　(5)　イ
〈解説〉(1)　Williamさんがメールをした理由は資料2にregarding the surcharge added to your online order of our premium make-up kit「プレミアムメイクアップキットのオンライン注文における追加料金について」という記述からイが適切。アはsubtract A form B「AからBを引く」とあることから25ドルの追加料金の内容に反する。　(2)　追加料金の説明は資料2にWe regrettably had to require $25.00 as a surcharge for shipping

and handling because you are at an overseas address.「ご住所が海外であることから，送料として25ドルが必要となってしまいます」とあるため，エが適切。　(3)　お客様サービスへ連絡ができるのは，資料1にFor bill or product inquiries only「請求，製品に関するお問い合わせのみ」とあることから，ウが適切。　(4)　金額支払い方法は資料1にPayments remitted by credit card will show up on your statement「クレジットカードで送金された支払いは明細に表示されます」とあり，クレジットカードの番号が記載されていることから，エが適切。　(5)　追加料金への補償として資料2にはWe would also like to offer you 10 percent off your next purchase at Natural Beauty「Natural Beautyでの次回のお買い物を10％OFFにさせていただきます」とあることから，イが適切。

【12】(1)　①　ウ　　②　ウ　　③　エ　　(2)　we have few repair manuals to tell us what to do (11 words)　　(3)　ア　　(4)　Bionic research is currently making progress in several areas and promises to provide the possibility of artificial human enhancement.(19 words)

〈解説〉bionic implants「バイオニックインプラント(身体器官を電子装置で機能強化し，それを身体内部に埋め込むこと)」に関する英文である。(1)　設問に続く英文を選択肢の中から選ぶこととなる。　①　Richard Andersonによって開発されたインプラントは第2パラグラフ5文目にて，自転車を乗りこなすように自動的ではなく練習が必要であることが述べられている。このことから選択肢ウが適切。　②　cochlear implant「人口内耳」とbionic eyeの違いは第3パラグラフ2文目および4文目にて述べられている。cochlear implantは耳が聞こえない80,000人に使用されているが，bionic eyeはDobelle Instituteの研究者によって開発中である。このことからウが適切。　③　著者による結論は第4パラグラフから推論する必要がある。bionicsは多くの人にとって解決策を提供する一方で，サイボーグが人間を支配する暗い未来を描いているSFのように，全ての人が好ましく思っているわけではない。しかしながら，5文目および6文目で，この研究がすでに始まっており，どのように使

われるかわかるのは時間の問題であると述べている。よって，テクノロジーにリスクはつきものだが，発展は止められないとしているエが適切。　(2)　空所(あ)のある第1パラグラフでは人間の脳が複雑で未解明の点が多いことを述べている。空所の直前ではthat is whyとあることから，脳の一部が損傷した際に元の機能が回復する方法がまだ見つかっていない理由を述べる。　(3)　文章中のトピックとなっていることから，アのbionic implantsが適切。脳の損傷の修復については述べられておらず，イは不適切。ウは最後に言及されているが，全体としてのタイトルとしては相応しくない。エはbionic implantsの1例である。(4)　Pandora's box「パンドラの箱」とは，さまざまな災いを引き起こす原因となるもののたとえ。科学技術によって人間生来の能力を超えた人工的な人間を生み出してしまう懸念を英語でまとめればよい。

【13】In the unit related to World Heritage Sites, it is possible to make students interested in the subject by confirming what they have learned in the geographical field of social studies with the social studies teacher before the class. We can introduce it according to the degree of understanding of the students. In particular, by utilizing the photographs and materials used in the social studies class, it is possible for students to focus on the "use of English" and how to describe the World Heritage Sites.(86 words)

〈解説〉新学習指導要領にて述べられている，英語以外の教科で学んだことを取り入れることについて，具体例を1つ含めた効果的な指導のアイデアを英語80語以上で述べる問題。解答例では社会科の授業で学習した世界遺産について英語で説明するというアイデアを挙げている。他にも家庭科の調理実習を英語で行ったり，国語で学んだ文学作品のあらすじを英語で紹介したりする活動なども考えられる。

【14】(1)　「for」の後には期間を表す名詞がつきます。それに対し，「during」の後には期間を表す名詞以外に「出来事」を表す名詞もつきます。また「for」にはその期間中ずっと継続しているというニュアン

スがありますが，「during」にはどちらかというと「その期間のある一部，又は特定の時」というニュアンスがあります。　　(2)　「try to do」は一般的に「～しようと努力する」の意味で使うことが多く，「try doing」は「試しに～してみる」の意味で使うことが多いです。ただ，「try to do」は「実際にはできなかった」という文脈で使われることが多く，「実際に試みた」という文脈では「try doing」を用いることになります。

〈解説〉文法に関する生徒からの質問にどのように解答するかを述べる問題。深く文法を理解している必要がある。生徒には正しい情報を示すべきであるため，授業中に解答できない場合は「先生の宿題にさせてください」のように対処するとよいかもしれない。　　(1)　forとduringのような似た意味の違いについては文法書よりも辞書の記述を参考にするとよい。期間を表す類語にはinやthroughもあるが，例文とともに詳しい記述がある。　　(2)　to不定詞と動名詞で意味が異なる動詞はtry以外にも，forget，remember，regretなどがある。

【高等学校】

【１】(1)　②　　(2)　②　　(3)　①　　(4)　③　　(5)　⑤　　(6)　①　　(7)　A　②　　B　①　　(8)　選んだ方法…②　　理由…A rating scale with brief statements would make it easy for students with lower proficiency to understand and be useful for teacher(s) to quickly and effectively evaluate performances, while at the same time, let each student know to what extent his/her perfomance is satisfactory depending on each feature. (48 words)

〈解説〉パフォーマンス評価に関する英文を読み，内容に適切な選択肢を選ぶ問題。　　(1)　スピーキングとライティングは産出技能と呼ばれ，アウトプットとして生徒が産出したものを直接的に評価することとなる。よって，observable「観察可能な」が適切。ambiguous「曖昧な」，unnoticeable「目立たない」。　　(2)　①～③の選択肢は，それぞれ反意語のペアとなる。　　①　abstract「抽象的な」，concrete「具体的な」。　　②　controlled「制限された」，extended「派生的な」。　　③　specific

「具体的な」，uncertain「不確かな」。　空所を含む文では，生徒がイの言語産出からウの言語産出へと至る際，教師は生徒が生み出した言語の意味を理解する際に困難を抱えると述べられている。指導の流れは，「制限的なもの→自由なもの」となることから，②が適切。　(3)　空所を含むパラグラフでは，ライティングやスピーキングのようなパフォーマンス評価では課題の内容と採点方法が重要であること，課題を達成するために必要な情報量を組み込むことで教師が望む量のパフォーマンスが得られること，話す・書く相手や目的，言語を産出する文脈などを明確にすることが必要であることなどが述べられている。これらを満たす例としては，①「今年読んだ本の中から一冊選び，本の内容となぜその本を選んだかについて，クラスの友達に1ページ分の手紙を書くこと」が適切。　(4)　下線①～③のうち，文脈に不適切な文を選ぶ問題。ライティング・スピーキングのパフォーマンスを採点する際に用いられるチェックリストについて述べた文脈である。文脈に適切かどうかを判断する際にはディスコースマーカーを頼りにするとよい。②と③の間に逆接のhoweverが用いられていることから，②と③は逆の内容となっていなければならない。本文を見てみると，②は肯定的な内容，③にも肯定的なことが述べられている。よって③が不適切。　(5)　下線④～⑥のうち文脈に不適切な文を選ぶ問題。評価尺度について述べた文脈である。直前のパラグラフで取り上げられていたのは，Yes/Noで採点するチェックリストについてであったが，評価尺度では各観点を段階別(1～4段階など)に評定するため，チェックリストよりも情報量は多くなると言える。このことから，⑤が不適切。(6)　discern「～を見定める，見極める」なので，①「何かを知ること，識別あるいは理解すること」が適切。難易度の高い語彙は自分の使える簡単な語彙を使って説明できるように普段からトレーニングをしておくとよい。　(7)　Aはholistic scoring「全体的な評価」(パフォーマンスを全体で採点し1つの評価を下す)，Bはanalytic scoring「分析的評価」(パフォーマンスをいくつかの構成要素に分割してそれぞれに評価を下す)をそれぞれ表している。①は，ルーブリック(観点と尺度)に複数の

観点があるので分析的評価，②は単一の観点であるので全体的評価である。　(8)　低～中程度のレベルの高校1年生40名のクラスで，日本の夏を過ごす最も理想的な場所はどこかについて，2分間でスピーチを行う。これを評価するにあたって，①～④の中から評価方法を選び，その理由を述べ，本文で触れた評価方法の特徴に言及するという問題。英作文で求められている理由と本文の特徴をそれぞれ記述する必要があることに注意。1つのクラス，40名という人数，2分でのパフォーマンスであることから，解答例ではRating Scaleが挙げられているが，評価者がクラス間で異なったり，生徒の数が多かったりした際にはチェックリストやHolistic Rubricも有用である。

【2】 (1) ①, ②　　(2) ②　　(3) We should provide Japanese senior high students with as much opportunity to work in small groups in English as possible. Given that in Japan, students rarely speak English outside the classroom, it is really important for them to actually use the language as much as possible, at least in English lessons. If they speak English only when they are asked a question by a teacher or if their opportunity to "speak" English in class is only when they read the textbook aloud, they will never be able to learn how to use it in real life. However, by having them work on a task or do an activity in English in groups, all the students in the class will have to use it to communicate with their group members. In addition, having students work in small groups can help remove one of the obstacles many of them often have when speaking English: "shyness." The group members in the lessons at school are more or less familiar with each other and less likely to have a large gap in English proficiency. So, it seems it would be easier for both students and teachers to create a safe learning environment, especially in making students feel comfortable speaking English even if they make some mistakes. That will help students become more and more motivated to learn English, which is surely important to acquire English skills. For these reasons, I strongly suggest giving Japanese senior high students more chances to work in small groups. (250 words)

〈解説〉(1)　少人数でタスクベースの言語活動を行うときの利点について述べたパラグラフである。①のinitiating discussion「議論を開始すること」，②のinterrupting「(相手の発言を)遮ること」の2つは相手がいなければ成立しないが，③のreading aloud「音読」，④のreciting「暗唱」は1人でもできる。よって，グループ活動としては①および②が適切。

(2)　空所ウおよびエに適切な組み合わせを選ぶ問題。空所のあるパラグラフは逆接のhoweverから始まっており，グループワークの利点を述べていた前の内容とは逆のことを述べることが示唆されている。グループワークでは母語を多用し過ぎてしまう点，研究によってCorrective Feedback(訂正フィードバック；ペアの英語が誤っている場合にはそれを指摘するフィードバック)の頻度が異なる点が，デメリットとして述べられている。否定的な内容であることから，空所ウはCFの頻度が低く(infrequent)，空所エはフィードバックの方略の幅も限定的(limited)と判断できる。　(3)　日本の高校生が英語の授業において，少人数のグループで活動することについての意見を，「①150〜250語の英語で」，「②英文で言及された情報について触れ」，「③自身の意見を裏付ける具体的な理由や詳細情報を述べる」問題。解答例では賛成の立場から意見を述べているが，反対の立場から意見を述べる場合は，本文に記載されている通り，学習者同士で文法の誤りについて言及する可能性が低いこと，そもそも英語を使わずに日本語で話してしまうことなどを問題点として記述することができる。

2021年度　実施問題

【中高共通】

Script

[There are three speaking roles for this test: Directions , Man(M), and Woman(W).]

Directions : Please turn the test paper over. The Listening Comprehension Test will now begin. You may take notes while listening.

【1】 Directions :　Section A.

Please listen to the following conversations. After each conversation, a question will be asked, and four possible answers will be read. Choose the best answer and circle the corresponding letter on your answer sheet. Each conversation, the question, and the answers will be read only once.

Directions :　Conversation 1.

W : Excuse me, could you tell me if this T-shirt is available in any other colors?

M : I'm afraid we only have that item in blue.

W : I really like the design, but I was looking for a brighter color. Do you have anything similar in the same price range?

M : Yes, I think we have something that might suit you. Let me show you. I'll help choose several T-shirts for you.

Directions :　What does the man offer to do?

A.　Show the woman other items.

B.　Provide the woman with a discount.

C. Give directions to another store.

D. Order a similar T-shirt.

Directions : Conversation 2.

W : Hi, I understand that the city community center provides free Chinese classes. I'm interested in signing up for one.

M : We have three different levels of class, from beginner to advanced. What is your ability level?

W : To tell the truth, I'm not sure. I took three years of Chinese in college, but that was eight years ago and I haven't even opened my textbooks since then.

M : Well, you probably won't want to start at the beginner level, but you should talk to the instructor first. She can evaluate your level and make sure you're put in the appropriate class.

Directions : What does the man suggest?

A. Starting at the low level.

B. Talking to the instructor.

C. Filling out an evaluation form.

D. Changing to a different class.

Directions : Conversation 3.

W : Oh my god! Is it 7:00 already? I got up so late.

M : Why are you in such a hurry? You haven't had your breakfast yet.

W : I have a meeting with my professor at 8:00 a.m. today.

M : Are you going to meet him this early?

W : Yeah, he has classes all day today, so that is the only time he is available.

W : OK, I'll talk to you later.

Directions : Why can't the woman meet the professor later?

A.　He will be busy teaching.

B.　He won't be on campus.

C.　He has other meetings.

D.　He is sick today.

Directions : 　Conversation 4.

W : What are our choices for summer vacation? A casino tour in Las Vegas or scuba diving in Miami?

M : No, this website also has choices abroad.

W : Let's go somewhere domestic this time. I don't want to take any chance of getting stuck abroad and missing the big department meeting after the vacation.

M : All right then. So what's your choice?

W : Either Las Vegas or Miami will be OK, but I would prefer not to go through Detroit. Air traffic in Detroit is terrible.

M : Well, it is hard to avoid Detroit while flying to Las Vegas from here.

W : Then you know my answer!

Directions : 　What are they most likely to do during their vacation?

A.　Go gambling in Las Vegas.

B.　Go on an overseas cruise.

C.　Go to the sea in Miami.

D.　Go to a museum in Chicago.

(☆☆☆○○○○○)

【２】 Directions : 　Section B.

　　Please listen to the following two passages. After each passage, two questions will be asked. Four possible responses to each question are listed on the answer sheet. Choose the best one and circle it. Each passage and question will be read only once.

Directions : Passage 1.

M : Housing values are watched by nearly everyone. People who already have their own houses generally hope for higher prices. When that happens, they can get the possibility of selling the home for a profit later — regardless of their real personal earnings. Also, Governments tend to favor generally rising housing prices: higher home prices are a leading index that an economy is robust. New home construction also offers well paying jobs for construction workers.

Home values represent the greater part of normal peaple's wealth in many countries. House owners are further inclined to see homes as safe investments that only rise in value, However, this is not true at all time. When an economy is embroiled in trouble, home prices tend to go down as well — sometimes rapidly. This may wipe out home value profits. This happened in Japan in the beginning of the 1990s, during the long recession. It has also oceurred in America and Britain about ten years ago, as both countries have been damaged by economic crises. Governments around the world are spending billions of dollars to boost a housing sector which aggears to be in great difficulty.

Directions : Question 1.   What do increasing home prices signal?

A.   Personal incomes are rising.

B.   Ordinary people are seeking safety.

C.   Leading indicators are changing.

D.   Economies are performing well.

Directions : Question 2.   What do we learn about investing in real estate?

A.   There is a high risk of loss.

B.   It is frequently undervalued by owners.

C. It reduces the impact of serious recessions.

D. There are more profits in Western countries.

Directions : Passage 2.

M : Parents use their implicit daily beliefs to make a lot of family decisions, including who sleeps where and how. In cultures where the leading parental goal is to integrate children with the household and society, babies sleep in their arms, even during the night. In contrast to this case, babies and children sleep by themselves in such Western societies as the United States that value independence and self-support. There is a basic assumption based on such an unconscious societal goal. Those are the ways they turn out as adults.

In other words, family sleeping arrangements may have a moral significance, and the foundation of that morality is culturally constructed. Parents in Western countries believe it is morally "correct" for babies to sleep alone, so they can learn to be independent. They consider child-parent co-sleeping as mentally unhealthy, even sinful. On the other hand, those in co-sleeping cultures such as Japan think the Western practice of placing a baby alone is wrong, close to child neglect. Parents in both kinds of cultures may be convinced that only their moral structure is "correct".

Directions : Question 1.　What effects are parental treatments of their children believed to have on the children?

A. How fast they will learn a language.

B. How they communicate with other children at school.

C. What kind of people they will grow up to become.

D. What kind of childhood dream they will have.

Directions : Question 2.　What is a Japanese mother's likely reaction towards a 6-month baby sleeping in his own bed in his own room?

A.　She will adopt the practice herself.

B.　She will suspect that the parents do not take a good care of him.

C.　She will immediately report the child abuse to the police.

D.　She will have more respect towards his parents than before.

(☆☆☆◎◎◎◎)

【3】 Directions ：　Section C.

　　Please listen to the following two conversations. After each conversation, two questions will be asked. Four possible responses to each question are listed on the answer sheet. Choose the best one and circle it. Each conversation and question will be read only once.

Directions ：　Conversation 1.

W ：Dr. Martinez, do you have some time?

M ：Sure, Lindsey. Come on in. What's the matter?

W ：I'm having difficulty with my term report. I'm really interested in the role women played during the western reclamation era in the 19th century. So I started out trying to find resources on what women did in wagon trains that crossed the Great Plains during the period. But, even though I've spent so much time in the library looking for books and searching various databases, I can't find very much.

M ：I'm surprised to hear that, Lindsey. Usually the students in my history classes face the opposite problem. They choose topics that are too wide, so they can't really focus or write well about them. But in your case, you should broaden your topic. Maybe it's better for you to focus on something like the role of women in frontier life. Depending upon your resources, you can narrow your focus to the Midwest in the 1850's, or even a particular state such as Kansas.

W ：All right, I now understand your suggestion. You're saying I should open my topic up a little, like to frontier women, and then depending on what resource materials I found, focus on something particular.

M : Exactly. Also, when you start making some progress in writing, don't be afraid to drop in and see me during my office hours. I'd be happy to give you some feedback on your construction, introduction and conclusion, and so on.

Directions : Question 1.　Why is the woman talking to the man?

A.　To discuss a presentation topic.

B.　To ask about a missed assignment.

C.　To request an introduction.

D.　To receive help on an essay.

Directions : Question 2.　What initial problem did the woman have in researching her topic?

A.　She didn't know what to focus on.

B.　She could not find many resources.

C.　She chose a theme that was too broad.

D.　She could not use the library databases.

Directions : Conversation 2.

M : Hi, Diana. By the way, how about your scholarship applications? Last time we met, you were gathering a lot of information on all the different national subsidies and scholarships available to students.

W : Things have changed. I found I had to do a lot of paperwork required with those scholarship applications, and I checked out how many students apply for them and how few scholarships are really awarded. So I decided just to obtain an additional loan.

M : I'm sorry to hear that. It's going to be terrible for you to graduate with so much debt. Also, I know you have a high scholastic performance, and your professors evaluate you so well.

$\boxed{\text{W}}$: It's nice that you say that, Eliot. But, I did a careful cost-benefit analysis, and when I estimated how much work the applications would demand, and how small my chances were to earn a substantive sum of money, it just seemed that my efforts were better put into studying for my courses and graduating on schedule. That's why I decided to use a bank loan.

$\boxed{\text{M}}$: I see your point. But I have one recommendation for you. You should talk to your advisor and also maybe some of the professors you are close to in your department. They have some scholarships within the university that departments can award to prominent students. In those cases, there's no application process at all.

$\boxed{\text{W}}$: I hadn't heard about them.

$\boxed{\text{M}}$: Yes, they're called endowment scholarships. Each department may have one or two. I don't know if they include a lot of money, but I'm sure a little bit would help.

$\boxed{\text{W}}$: You've said it! Anyway, I was on my way to talk to my advisor right now. Of course I'm going to ask him about this.

$\boxed{\text{Directions}}$: Question 1.　How will the woman obtain the money she needs?

A.　She will ask her parents.

B.　She will borrow it.

C.　She will win a scholarship.

D.　She will work overtime.

$\boxed{\text{Directions}}$: Question 2.　What does the woman plan to do next?

A.　Apply for a job.

B.　Go to the bank.

C.　Meet with her advisor.

D.　Study at the library.

(☆☆☆○○○○)

155

【4】 Directions ： Section D.

The following article will be read twice. Please write a summary of the contents in Japanese. The summary should be between 150 and 200 characters. You may take notes and begin summarizing while listening. Now, please listen to the article.

M ： Though robots were formerly imaginary characters in science fiction books and films, they are now stimulating great interest among engineers and senior levels of companies. For nearly a century, carmakers have tried to automate their factories, but machines performed only limited steps in the assembly process until about half a century ago, when IC chips appeared along with the IT revolution. Since then, engineers have developed smaller industrial robots that can perform many functions with greater speed and precision than before. They were impossible under the older human / machine system.

Robots can be divided into two groups, depending on the way of interaction with humans. One group consists of robots that assist people directly. The other group is comprised of robots that work far away from us. It would be preferable for robots in the first group to resemble humans, show sensitivity, and communicate in human language. In contrast, robots in the second group need not look or act like humans but should be adjusted to specific and, in some cases, dangerous environments. They should also be substantially more durable to complete their missions.

Examples of the first group are the world-famous robots ASIMO by Honda and AIBO by Sony. ASIMO looks like a child astronaut wearing a space suit and can stand, walk, and run while keeping its balance by moving its waist joint. People who saw this robot were highly impressed and felt that the robot age had finally arrived. While ASIMO was not intended for sale, AIBO, the dog-shaped robot, was developed for the consumer market. When it was released, a number of people rushed to get one even though it was quite expensive. Owners of an AIBO enjoyed its reactions to their directions in human language and its ability to learn from experience. As the population ages in Japanese society, the demand for such robots will increase dramatically.

Designers of robots in the second group want to develop robots based on the movements of living creatures other than human beings. The field of science that explores such thought is called biomimesis. For example, as taller buildings are increasingly constructed in the metropolis, a need will grow for robots that can climb the glass walls of skyscrapers. To move up the smooth surface of glass walls, robots have to make use of inter-molecular attraction, between their feet and the wall. One Chinese scientist has developed an "insect-robot" whose feet release a sticky mixture of honey and water to make liquid bridges between the surface of the glass and its feet. Taking another approach, an American roboticist has adapted the climbing method used by the reptilian gecko, which can hold on to the surface of the glass by means of millions of hairs on the underside of its feet. Using such new technologies, scientists, engineers and industrial designers will develop future robots that will make life more comfortable for human beings — that is, of course, unless the robots take over the world and make us do their work for them.

Directions : Stop writing, please. This is the end of the listening test. Thank you.

参考文献(すべて全面的に加筆修正)
・『DAILY 30日間 英検準1級集中ゼミ』(旺文社・2009年)
・『TOEFL ITP TEST 実戦問題集』(語研・2011年)
・『英検準1級 頻出度別問題集』(高橋書店・2016年)

(☆☆☆☆☆◎◎◎)

【5】次の(1)～(10)の英文の＿＿＿＿に入る最も適当な語(句)を，ア～エの中からそれぞれ1つ選び記号で答えなさい。

(1) Ms. Collins started her business about 5 years ago at a time when ＿＿＿＿＿＿ wanted to find a job immediately.

　　ア　it　　イ　she　　ウ　he　　エ　one

(2) The identity card plan ＿＿＿＿＿＿ more than $2.8 billion to establish and run over the next 5 years.

　　ア　will cost　　イ　is cost　　ウ　cost　　エ　costing

(3) Complicated heart surgery was ＿＿＿＿＿＿ performed on a four-year-old boy at the National Circulatory Organ Medical Center recently.

　　ア　success　　イ　successful　　ウ　successfully　　エ　succeed

(4) Unless the common people and the scientists respect our research, ＿＿＿＿＿＿ will be difficult for us to get government support.

　　ア　there　　イ　what　　ウ　this　　エ　it

(5) Due to a lack of experience, new operators cannot treat information as ＿＿＿＿＿＿ as superiors.

　　ア　less　　イ　efficient　　ウ　possible　　エ　effectively

(6) To behave ＿＿＿＿＿＿ is one of the characteristics of Japanese culture. If we do not boast of our achievements in Japan, everything goes well.

　　ア　purposefully　　イ　unconsciously　　ウ　humbly
　　エ　recklessly

(7) The party's subcommittee has been held for thirty-six hours consecutively because none of its members have ＿＿＿＿＿＿ a draft bill that can be agreed upon.

　　ア　come up with　　イ　given some help　　ウ　gotten away with
　　エ　jumped our of

(8) Although Roy believed most of his ancestors were German, he found out that he's actually a direct ＿＿＿＿＿＿ of a Norwegian political figure.

　　ア　celebrity　　イ　correspondence　　ウ　descendant
　　エ　beggar

(9) Lucy wants her work to be _____ objectively by someone from the outside, but it is difficult. Few can comprehend her work well.

ア refined イ appraised ウ pronounced

エ appropriated

(10) Ms. William's radical argument about an economic reform caused a serious problem to her party. She persisted in saying that it was her conviction, but finally she had to _____ her statement.

ア overdraw イ impose ウ displace エ withdraw

(☆☆☆○○○○)

【6】次の(1)～(5)の英文において下線部に最も近い意味の語(句)をア～エの中からそれぞれ1つ選び記号で答えなさい。

(1) Some psychologists believe that classical music is <u>soothing</u> for infants and can prompt their brain development.

ア comforting イ amiable ウ obedient エ courteous

(2) Dr.Anderson <u>imposed</u> a strict diet on Mr. Green, because he had become seoriously overweight.

ア interfered イ enforced ウ opposed エ transposed

(3) The board of directors will have a conference to discuss whether the extension is <u>practicable</u>.

ア potential イ capable ウ feasible エ upcoming

(4) Further information <u>about</u> the Donald's Foundation can be found on the association's homepage.

ア connecting イ concerning ウ referring エ stating

(5) Made completely with natural <u>materials</u>, Mini-Meal bars are a delicious and nutritious food option at any time of day.

ア amounts イ functions ウ aspects エ ingredients

(☆☆☆○○○○)

【7】次の(1)～(5)の英文において不適切な箇所を，下線部ア～エの中か
らそれぞれ1つ選び記号で答え，正しい形，または，適切な語(句)にし
なさい。

(1)　One of the conspicuous ₇characteristic of the Hudson River School of
Painting ₄was its focus on ₉vast landscapes, ₑespecially hills and rivers.

(2)　The market ₇price of germanium, like ₄those of gold or silver, is
determined by a combination of elements ₉including present supply, future
production, and expected ₑdemand.

(3)　Throughout the history of the United States, immigrants ₇have
generally been able to support ₄them only ₉by taking the ₑlowest paying
jobs.

(4)　At the ₇end of the 1940's, ₄the number of American composers began
experimenting ₉with non-musical sounds in ₑtheir compositions.

(5)　Graphite, ₇widely used in pencils, ₄it is a kind of carbon that ₉is soft
enough to draw a line ₑon paper.

(☆☆☆○○○○)

【8】次の(1)～(3)の英文において〔　　〕内の語(句)を正しく並べかえて
文章を完成させるとき，〔　　〕内の4番目と7番目にくる語(句)を，そ
れぞれ1つ選び記号で答えなさい。ただし，文頭に来る文字も小文字
になっている。

(1)　A : I'm going to spend a month in Spain next week on vacation.

B : Really?〔ア　practice　　イ　I　　ウ　you
エ　that opportunity　　オ　to　　カ　recommend
キ　exploit〕your Spanish as much as you can.

(2)　A : Are you sure Cathy can deal with the next client presentation?

B : I'm certain it won't be a problem〔ア　she
イ　an excellent reputation　　ウ　because　　エ　for
オ　public　　カ　speaking　　キ　has〕.

(3)　A : You're here so late every night! What's your incentive for working so

160

hard?

B : Apart from job satisfaction, 〔ア　the year　　イ　if
ウ　I hope　　エ　at the end of　　オ　I do　　カ　a bonus
キ　to get〕my job well.

(☆☆☆○○○○)

【9】次の英文において空欄(　1　)～(　3　)に入る最も適当な語(句)を,
ア～エの中からそれぞれ1つ選び記号で答えなさい。

Commuters in the Stanley area will soon be able to use the Internet while riding the bus. The city is now preparing to introduce free Wi-Fi access on all its vehicles. The service has been available on select buses on a trial basis for the (　1　) few weeks. City Transportation Bureau spokeswoman Stephanie Nicole reports (　2　) it has been a success to date and the response from passengers has been positive. "There have been no serious technical problems, and (　3　) have told us they were able to get a reliable Wi-Fi connection," says Stephanie. "We anticipate the service will be operational on the rest of the fleet by the end of this year."

1　ア　distant　　　　イ　next　　　　　ウ　more
　　エ　past
2　ア　if　　　　　　イ　then　　　　　ウ　that
　　エ　on
3　ア　programmers　イ　receptionists　ウ　passengers
　　エ　illustrators

(☆☆☆○○○○)

【10】次の英文を読み,あとの各問いの英文を完成させるのに,本文の内容と最も適するものを,ア～エの中からそれぞれ1つ選び記号で答えなさい。

A lot of physical phenomena have their own rhythms, patterns, and timing. There are day-night cycles, cycles of the moon, cycles of the seasons, and so on. Living organisms frequently display the same rhythmic activities. Among animals there are a lot of physiological and behavioral processes that occur on a periodic cycle. One of the most obvious examples of a remarkably timed behavior is the sleep-wakefulness cycle of mammals, reptiles, and birds. Another example is the return of hunting animals to a particular place 24 hours after a successful hunt there. There are also more slight physiological processes that have their own cyclical changes. For example, the pulse, blood pressure, and temperature of the body show day-night changes in humans as well as in many other animals. These are all examples of a circadian rhythm, which originates from the Latin *circa*, meaning "approximately," and *dies*, meaning "day." Thus, a circadian rhythm is one that varies with a cycle of nearly 24 hours.

So much rhythmic activity in behavior suggests management by some internal biological clock. The existence of such an internal time-keeping mechanism has been proved experimentally. If it were correct that these repetitive 24-hour changes are only a function of the ordinary changes in light and temperature that occur in a regular day-night cycle, then an environment with constant light or constant dark should confuse basic behavior cycles, such as sleep-wake cycles, because there would be no changing signals in the amount of light to indicate the passing of time. However, in numbers of studies both animal and human subjects have been found to adjust comparatively quickly to an artificial environment with constant light or darkness; they soon begin to live a day-night cycle that is roughly 25 hours long.

Yet, if the internal biological clock is set for about 25 hours, why do our internal and behavioral rhythms keep on a 24-hour cycle? Why doesn't our daily activity cycle stick out of phase with local time? The answer is because there is a mechanism that synchronizes the internal timer with local time. From the behavioral point of view, the most remarkable aspect of local time is the alternation of light and dark cycles. For there to be an accurate reference

162

against local time, an internal biological clock must be synchronized with the external and local day-night cycle and it must have a steady period that is comparatively free of unpredictable environment change. This stage of synchronization is called "entrainment." This is, of course, what occurs when a person takes a trip by air through several time zones. At first, the internal clock is still set according to the time at the place the person departed from. But for most people this jet lag is gradually resolved at a rate of 1/2 to 1 hour per day through the synchronization of the biological clock to the local day-night cycle, though some people can adjust twice as quickly.

(1) The writer mentions cycles of the moon as an example of

　ア　a pattern of natural phenomena.

　イ　a day-night cycle.

　ウ　seasonal cycles.

　エ　physiological process.

(2) The writer mentions hunting animals in paragraph 1 to

　ア　demonstrate that all animals are capable of learning.

　イ　argue that animals must eat at regular intervals.

　ウ　show the necessity of food in animal survival.

　エ　offer an example of a circadian behavior.

(3) It can be inferred from paragraph 2 that, if animals possessed no internal timing mechanism and were kept in the dark,

　ア　they eventually would be unable to fall asleep.

　イ　their normal activities would be greatly reduced.

　ウ　they would have irregular periods of activity and rest.

　エ　their body temperatures would fluctuate wildly.

(4) Paragraph 3 implies that for the process of entrainment to operate effectively a person needs

　ア　a steady interval free from erratic environmental changes.

　イ　extensive experience adjusting to different time zones.

　ウ　an objective awareness of daily routines.

エ　equal periods of night and day in the local time zone.

(5)　It can be inferred from paragraph 3 that the quickest that an individual could overcome jet lag associated with traveling through four time zones is

ア　one day.

イ　two days.

ウ　four days.

エ　eight days.

(☆☆☆○○○○○)

【11】次の英文を読み，あとの各問いに対する答えとして最も適当なものを1つ選び記号で答えなさい。

Worker's Manual for the Janitorial Staff

1.　Training New Janitors

①　Training must be carried out safely.

　　a.　Proper equipment must be provided.

　　b.　Workers must put on the proper shoes and uniforms.

　　c.　Rubber gloves must be always worn.

2.　Handling Cleaning Materials

①　Materials must be delivered to the workplace where they will be used.

②　Caution must be observed when handling hazardous materials.

③　Hazardous materials must be stored in locked warehouses.

④　Rotate shifts when stocking items on the shelves.

⑤　Store cleaning agents in smaller or lighter containers or drums.

3.　Cleaning Equipment Operation

①　Follow instructions on the accurate way to operate equipment.

②　Rotate shifts on heavy equipment to avoid employee tiredness.

③　Make sure all equipment is maintained on a regular basis.

④　Use all equipment in a proper way.

To: George Quincy, HR Director

From: Carol Perez

Subject: The manual for the janitorial staff

Hi, George

I have revised the current manual for the janitorial staff and am sending it along for agreement. Considering the accident that occurred last month, I have added an extra clause to part 3 of the manual. That accident would have never occurred if the janitor at work had not been fatigued. Therefore, I believe it is indispensable for the janitorial staff to change shifts frequently. This ensures that they will be able to use all of the equipment properly.

I have added a similar clause to part 2 of the manual, too. I've done this so that the janitors can avoid accidents when stocking the shelves. I'm sure you'll agree that a fatigued employee performing this work could have a tragic result.

Please run your eyes over the new additions to the manual and give me your thoughts on them. I would like to give it to the janitorial staff by early next month.

Thanks very much.

Regards,

Carol

(1) What has Carol done?

ア She has had an accident.

イ She has written an entire manual.

ウ She has changed the janitor's manual.

エ She has given a new manual to the staff.

(2) Which clauses has Carol added to the manual?

ア Part 3, number ② only.

イ　Part 2, number ④ and part 3, number ②.

ウ　Part 2, number ② and part 3, number ④.

エ　Part 2, number ③ and part 3, number ②.

(3)　What must janitors do at all times?

　ア　Stock the shelves.

　イ　Wear gloves.

　ウ　Provide proper equipment.

　エ　Deliver materials.

(4)　What must be done before using the equipment?

　ア　The janitors must have proper manners.

　イ　The janitors must wash their hands.

　ウ　The janitors must be fatigued.

　エ　The janitors must read the operation instructions.

(5)　What would Carol like George to do?

　ア　Make some changes to the current manual.

　イ　Give the new manual to the employees.

　ウ　Meet with her about the matter next month.

　エ　Tell her what he thinks of the manual.

(☆☆☆○○○○)

【12】次の英文を読み，あとの各問いに答えなさい。

For a long time, psychologists have studied how those with exceptional skills obtained them, trying to determine whether innate ability or intense practice was the key. Research into chess players has discovered evidence that chess masters create an intricately detailed mental structure of the various moves, the development of which relies more on intense training than innate talent. Actually, chess grand masters score no better on typical memory tests than average people. Nor do chess novices possess an essentially inferior ability to analyze than chess masters. Yet when facing a difficult move, less experienced players may take 30 minutes to consider their best move and still miss the best choice, while a masterplayer would be able to visualize their best move immediately without having to analyze it particularly. It is believed that other experts also have this ability to visualize potentialities.

But where, you may ask, do such visualizations come from? K. Anders Ericsson of Florida State University points out that physicians are able to keep information into their long-term memory and remember it much later to make diagnoses. Long-term memory seems to be an important thing to high levels of skill. Brain imaging studies carried out at the University of Konstanz in Germany supported Ericsson's discovery. They found that expert chess players activate long-term memory more often than beginners.

With one consent, theorists conclude that it takes great effort to build these intricate memory structures. Herbert Simon at Carnegie Mellon University developed a model that postulates it takes about 10 years of intense study to become a master of any field. Such child prodigies as Mozart in music and Bobby Fischer in chess became child masters of their respective fields by starting earlier and packing in more intensive studies in shorter periods.

Ericsson postulates that "effortful study," is conclusive. The majority of us who play games such as chess or golf for hundreds or even thousands of hours never progress over the average, while the serious youth properly trained can break us in a comparatively short time frame. Most novices advance rather quickly during the beginning because any skilled task or game requires effortful study at first. But as we become competent at playing within our circle of friends and colleagues, we relax and lose our competitive spirits. We put in less effort to move ahead of our circle, while the experts in training are incessantly absorbing new information and critically analyzing their abilities in comparison to that of leaders in their game or field.

It's interesting to note that we are experiencing a proliferation of chess prodigies for several decades. In 1958, Bobby Fischer stunned the chess world when he became a grand master as a 15-year-old boy. More recently, Ukrainian Sergey Karjakin achieved his grand master title when he was 12 years old. This proliferation can be attributed at least in part to computer-based training methods that enable children to play against master-level software programs, training that few could make use of in former decades.

With access to greater information, and with more opportunities to (あ), it is small wonder that young people today (い). Records keep getting broken, and the marvel of young prodigies continues to amaze us again and again.

(1) Choose the best phrase from among the four choices to complete the sentence below;

① Studies of chess experts revealed that

ア the physical structures of the brains of chess masters were naturally different from those who were not as accomplished.

イ chess masters were not intrinsically better at either analysis or memory performance than lower-level players.

ウ chess masters are able to analyze complex moves in greater detail and in far less time than amateurs.

エ the ability to visualize better moves was actually no worse among novices than advanced players.

② Chess experts can visualize the correct move more often than novices, because

ア they have developed a sophisticated memory system that enables them to store and retrieve useful information over long periods.

イ they have an intuitive sense that, combined with superior analysis, enables them to foresee the best possible move.

ウ they have a more developed sense of visual thought as opposed to verbal thought, providing them with a huge advantage.

エ brain scans give evidence that experts naturally have a more acute long-term memory from the beginning.

③ One difference between the theories of Ericsson and Simon is that

ア Ericsson believes that those who want to advance quickly must take on tasks that is just beyond their abilities, while Simon focuses more on hard effort over the long-term.

イ   Ericsson argues that innate ability paired with intense effort is the key, while Simon says that anyone can become highly skilled with sufficient effort.

ウ   Ericsson argues that developing long-term memory is critical, while Simon believes it is more important to expand one's ability to analyze and conceptualize.

エ   Ericsson postulates that anyone who is highly motivated can become a master, while Simon believes that only those with the right kind of training can progress.

(2)   Complete the sentence in (あ   ) and (い   ) so that the passage will make sense. Fill in each blank within 10 words.

(3)   Choose the most appropriate title of this passage from the phrases below.

ア   Child Masters of Their Respective Fields

イ   How to Visualize the Strongest Move on Chess

ウ   Activating Our Long-Term Memory

エ   Experts in the Making

(4)   Explain the underlined phrase "effortful study," related to this passage. (within 30 words, in English)

(☆☆☆☆○○○○○)

【13】 ALTs (Assistant Language Teachers) are very effective for teaching students in their English lessons. Write a composition in English about one example of effective use of an ALT in a lessen, including a description of its effectiveness for students. The composition should be 80 words or more.

(☆☆☆☆☆○○○○)

【14】授業中に生徒が次の(1)と(2)の質問をした。あなたは英語の先生としてどのように説明するか，それぞれについて日本語で答えなさい。(説明の一部に英語を交えても差し支えない。)

(1)　書籍を紹介する英文を考え，The book became the best seller in the world. という英文を作りALTに見せたところ，in the world の代わりにall over the world を使う方がいいよ，とアドバイスされました。in the world とall over the world は，どのように使い分ければいいのですか？

(2)　同じように「いくつか」という意味を表す表現として，some, several, a fewの3つを習いました。3つの表現の違いは何ですか？

(☆☆☆◎◎)

【高等学校】

【 1 】 Read the passage and answer the questions below.

◆An Options-based Approach to Doing Task-based Language Teaching

(中略)

What is a 'Task'?

For a language teaching activity to be considered a task it must satisfy the following four criteria:

(1)　The primary focus should be on 'meaning', i.e. learners should be mainly concerned with processing the semantic and pragmatic meaning of utterances.

(2)　There should be some kind of 'gap', i.e. a need to convey information, to express an opinion or to infer meaning.

(3)　Learners should largely have to rely on their own resources — linguistic and non-linguistic — in order to complete the activity, i.e. the task materials do not dictate what linguistic forms are to be used.

(4)　There is a clearly defined outcome other than the use of language, i.e. the language serves as the means for achieving the outcome, not as end in its own right.

These criteria effectively distinguish a 'task' from an 'exercise'. By way of example consider these two language teaching activities.

Activity 1: Dialogue

Students are given a script of a dialogue and put into pairs. Each student is allocated a part in the dialogue and asked to memorize the lines for this part. The students then act out the dialogue.

Activity 2: Spot the Difference

Students are placed in pairs. Each student is given a picture and told that the two pictures are basically the same but there are five small differences. Without looking at each other's picture, they talk together to locate and write down the five differences.

Table 11.1   Comparing an 'exercise' and a 'task'

Criteria	Dialogue	Spot the Difference
1. Primary focus on meaning	No	Yes
2. Gap	No	Yes(information)
3. Own linguistic resources	No	Yes
4. Communicative outcome	No	Yes

Table 11.1 describes these two activities in terms of the four criteria above. In 'Dialogue' the focus is not primarily on meaning as students can perform it without even having to understand what is being said. There is no gap because both students can see the whole dialogue. They do not have to use their own linguistic resources — just memorize and reproduce the text they are given. There is no communicative outcome — the only outcome is the performance of the dialogue — language practice for its own sake. In 'Spot the Difference', the focus is clearly on meaning (i.e. the students have to make themselves understood to each other), there is an information gap (i.e. each student has a

171

different picture), they have to use their own linguistic resources (i.e. they are not given any language to use), and there is a communicative outcome (i.e. a list of the differences in the two pictures).

The type of discourse that arises from these two activities is likely to be very different. In the case of 'Dialogue', the language use is likely to be mechanical — focused on an accurate ₁rendition of the script. In the case of 'Spot the Difference', the discourse is likely to be interactionally authentic. That is, ①it will resemble the kind of language use that occurs outside the classroom where the aim is to encode and decode real messages. For example, it is probable that ②communication problems will arise leading to attempts by the students to resolve them with the result that there is attention to form.

My purpose, however, is not to suggest that exercises such as 'Dialogue' are pedagogically worthless and tasks such as 'Spot the Difference' are worthy. ③Both may have a place in a language course as they cater to different aspects of language learning. However, ④a course that consists only of exercises is likely to develop the kinds of communicative skills that students need in order to cope with the exigencies of real-life communication outside the classroom. To achieve this, most of some of the teaching time will need to be based on tasks.

In previous chapters, we have seen that there are many different types of tasks and many ways of classifying them. Nunan (1989) distinguished 'real-world tasks', i.e. tasks that ₇replicated situations that occur in the real-world, and 'pedagogic tasks', i.e. tasks that seek to achieve interactional authenticity but not situational authenticity. A second distinction of importance is that between input-based and production-based tasks. The former consist of oral or written input and require listening or reading on the part of the learner. The latter require oral or written output from the learner. In a third distinction common in the TBLT literature, tasks are distinguished in terms of whether the gap involves information-providing or opinion-making. A fourth distinction is between unfocused and focused tasks. The difference here

consists of whether the task has been designed to elicit language use in general or the use of some specific linguistic feature such as a grammatical structure. 'Spot the Difference' is a pedagogic task, it is (エ), it involves an information gap and it is (オ). 'Candidates for a Job' (see Table 11.2) is also a pedagogic task (but perhaps for some learners could have elements of a real-world task), it is production-based, it involves an opinion-gap, and it is focused, i.e. it was designed to provide learners with the opportunity to practise their use of the present-perfect tense. Of course, there is no guarantee that learners will try to use this tense when they perform the task. Learners are
カ adept at avoiding the use of grammatical structures that are difficult for them. It is extremely difficult to design tasks that might make the production of a predetermined grammatical structure 'essential' (Loschky & Bley-Vroman, 1993) although, as we will see, it is possible to induce attention to the target form methodologically (e.g. through focus-on-form techniques).

(中略)

Table 11.2 'Candidates for a Job' task (based on Ur, 1988)

Candidates for a job

Imagine you are a student in a private language school. Consider the following four applications for a job as a teacher in your school. Which of the applicants would you hope would be chosen for the job? Discuss with the other students in your group.

▶ JOCK, aged 30

B.A. in social studies.

Has spent a year working his way round the world.

Has spent six years teaching economics in state school.

Has written a highly successful novel about teachers.

Has lived in a back-to-nature commune for two years.

Has been married twice — now divorced. Two children.

Has been running local youth group for three years.

▶ BETTY, aged 45

Has been married for 24 years, three children.

Has not worked most of that time.

Has done evening courses in youth guidance.

Has spent the last year teaching pupils privately for state exams ― with good results.

Has been constantly active in local government ― has been elected to local council twice.

▶ ROBERT, aged 27

(中略)

▶ CLAIRE, aged 60

(中略)

(1)　Choose the best statement to describe the meaning of each of the underlined words イ, ウ, and カ from among the choices for each word. Write the numbers of the answer.

イ rendition

① the performance of something, especially a song or piece of music

② the process of changing something that is written or spoken into another language

③ the way in which a language or a particular word or sound is pronounced

ウ replicated

① to copy something exactly

② to recognize or show that two things are not the same

③ to think of and plan a system, a way of doing something, etc.

カ adept

① good at doing something that is quite difficult

② likely to do something that quite difficult

③ poor at doing something that is quite easy

(2)   Part of one of the underlined sentences ①〜④ has been changed so that the sentence won't fit in the context. Choose that sentence and write the number of the answer.

(3)   Choose the best pair of the words from among the choices for (エ) and (オ). Write the number of the answer.

  ①   エ   input-based   オ   unfocused

  ②   エ   production-based   オ   focused

  ③   エ   production-based   オ   unfocused

(4)   As for ァActivity 1: Dialogue, explain in Japanese how you can redesign this activity and make it into 'task'. Note that you must cover the four criteria mentioned in the passage.

(☆☆☆☆○○○○)

【2】 Read the passage and answer the questions below.

◆Cooperative Language Learning

introduction

Language teaching is sometimes discussed as if it existed independently of the teaching of other subjects and of trends in teaching generally. [A] However, like teachers in other areas of a school curriculum, language teachers too have to create a positive environment for learning in the classroom. They have to find ways of engaging students in their lessons, to use learning arrangements that encourage active student participation in lessons, to acknowledge the diversity of motivations and interests learners bring to the classroom, and to use strategies that enable the class to function as a cohesive group that collaborates to help make the lesson a positive learning experience. [B] Cooperative Language Learning (CLL) is one such example. CLL is part of a more general instructional approach, known as Collaborative or Cooperative Learning (CL), which originated in mainstream education and emphasizes peer support and coaching. CL is an approach to teaching that makes maximum use of cooperative activities involving pairs

175

and small groups of learners in the classroom. It has been defined as follows:

Cooperative learning is group learning activity organized so that learning is dependent on the socially structured exchange of information between learners in groups and in which each learner is held accountable for his or her own learning and is motivated to increase the learning of others.

(Olsen and Kagan 1992: 8)

Cooperative Learning has antecedents in proposals for peer-tutoring and peer-monitoring that go back hundreds of years and longer. [　C　] The early-twentieth-century US educator John Dewey is usually credited with promoting the idea of building cooperation in learning into regular classrooms on a regular and systematic basis (Rodgers 1988). It was more generally promoted and developed in the United States in the 1960s and 1970s as a response to the forced integration of public schools and has been substantially refined and developed since then. Educators were concerned that traditional models of classroom learning were teacher-fronted, fostered (　ア　) rather than (　イ　), and favored majority students. [　D　] They believed that minority students might fall behind higher-achieving students in this kind of learning environment. CL in this context sought to do the following:

- raise the achievement of all students, including those who are gifted or academically handicapped
- help the teacher build positive relationships among students
- give students the experiences they need for healthy social, psychological, and cognitive development
- replace the competitive organizational structure of most classrooms and schools with a team-based, high-performance organizational structure

(Johnson, Johnson, and Holubec 1994: 2)

In second language teaching, CL (where, as noted above, it is often referred to as Cooperative Language Learning ─ CLL) has been embraced as a way of promoting communicative interaction in the classroom and is seen as an

176

extension of the principles of Communicative Language Teaching. It is viewed as a (ウ) approach to teaching that is held to offer advantages over (エ) classroom methods. In language teaching its goals are:

- to provide opportunities for naturalistic second language acquisition through the use of interactive pair and group activities;
- to provide teachers with a methodology to enable them to achieve this goal and one that can be applied in a variety of curriculum settings (e.g., content-based, foreign language classrooms; mainstreaming);
- to enable focused attention to particular lexical items, language structures, and communicative functions through the use of interactive tasks;
- to provide opportunities for learners to develop successful learning and communication strategies;
- to enhance learner motivation and reduce learner stress and to create a positive affective classroom climate.

[E] CLL is thus an approach that crosses both mainstream education and second and foreign language teaching. (中略) The word *cooperative* in Cooperative Learning emphasizes another important dimension of CLL: it seeks to develop classrooms that foster cooperation rather than competition in learning. Advocates of CLL in general education stress the benefits of cooperation in promoting learning:

Cooperation is working together to accomplish shared goals. Within cooperative situations, individuals seek outcomes beneficial to themselves and all other group members. Cooperative learning is the instructional use of small groups through which students work together to maximize their own and each other's learning. It may be contrasted with competitive learning in which students work against each other to achieve an academic goal such as a grade of "A."

(Johnson et al. 1994: 4)

From the perspective of second language teaching, McGroarty (1989) offers _オ six learning advantages for ESL students in CLL classrooms.

(1) Among the choices [A] to [E] throughout the passage, choose the best place where the following statement should be put.

In dealing with issues such as these, language teachers can learn much from considering approaches that have been used in mainstream education.

(2) Choose the best pair of the words from among the choices for (　ア　) and (　イ　). Write the number of the answer.

① 　ア　collaboration 　　イ　competition

② 　ア　competition 　　　イ　cooperation

③ 　ア　motivation 　　　　イ　skills

(3) Choose the best pair of the words from among the choices for (　ウ　) and (　エ　). Write the number of the answer.

① 　ウ　competency-based 　　エ　content-based

② 　ウ　learner-centered 　　　エ　teacher-fronted

③ 　ウ　teacher-fronted 　　　　エ　student-centered

(4) As for ₊six learning advantages, among the following six choices, choose the **TWO** statements that are **NOT** appropriate for those six learning advantages. Write the numbers of the answer.

① Freedom for teachers to master new professional skills, particularly those emphasizing communication

② Increased frequency and variety of second language practice through competitive interaction

③ Opportunities for teachers to act as resources for each other, thus assuming a more active role in their learning

④ Opportunities to include a greater variety of curricular materials to stimulate language as well as concept learning

⑤ Opportunities to integrate language with Content-Based Instruction

⑥ Possibility for development or use of language in ways that support cognitive development and increased language skills

(5) Referring to Table 13.1 below, write the pros and cons of Cooperative Language Learning (CLL) and traditional approaches.

178

i.   Your essay should consist of <u>150-250 words</u>.

ii.   You should refer to the characteristics shown in Table 13.1.

iii.   You should have specific reasons or details to support your opinion.

Comparison of Cooperative Language Learning and traditional approaches

Zhang compares CLL and traditional approaches in Table 13.1. In practice, many classrooms may fall somewhere between CLL and traditional approaches, where teaching is not necessarily teacher-fronted and elements of CLL are incorporated, but where the approach does not form the basis for the organization of the course.

179

Table 13.1   Comparison of Cooperative Language Learning and traditional language teaching (from Yan Zhang 2010)

	Traditional language teaching	Cooperative Language Learning
Independence	None or negative	Positive
Learner roles	Passive receiver and performer	Active participator, autonomous learners
Teacher roles	The center of the classroom, controller of teaching pace and direction, judge of students' right or wrong, the major source of assistance, feedback, reinforcement and support	Organizer and counselor of group work, facilitator of the communication tasks, intervener to teach collaborative skills
Materials	Complete set of materials for each student	Materials are arranged according to purpose of lesson. Usually one group shares a complete set of materials.
Types of activities	Knowledge recall and review, phrasal or sentence pattern practice, role play, translation, listening, etc.	Any instructional activity, mainly group work to engage learners in communication, involving processes like information sharing, negotiation of meaning, and interaction
Interaction	Some talking among students, mainly teacher-student interaction	Intense interaction among students, a few teacher-student interactions
Room arrangement	Separate desks or students placed in pairs	Collaborative small groups
Student expectations	Take a major part in evaluating own progress and the quality of own efforts toward learning. Be a winner or loser.	All members in some way contribute to success of group. The one who makes progress is the winner.
Teacher-student relationship	Superior, inferior or equal	Cooperating and equal

(☆☆☆☆☆○○○○)

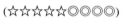

解答・解説

【中高共通】

【1】Conversation 1　A　　　Conversation 2　B　　　Conversation 3　A
Conversation 4　C

〈解説〉男女の短い会話と，その内容に関する質問を聞き，4つの選択肢から適切な答えを選ぶ問題。選択肢は問題用紙に印刷されておらず，読み上げられる。放送は1度のみである。　Conversation 1　店員の男性が2番目の発話で，買い物客の女性が最初に見つけたのと似たようなTシャツを見せると言っている。　Conversation 2　市民センターの職員と思われる男性が，2番目の発話で講座のクラスはレベルが3つあると言い，4番目の発話で講師と話してどのレベルか決めてもらうことを勧めている。　Conversation 3　学生と思われる女性が3番目の発話で，教授は1日中授業があって忙しいと言っている。　Conversation 4　女性は3番目の発話で，ラスベガスとマイアミのどちらでもよいが，デトロイトを経由したくないと言っている。それに対し男性は，デトロイトを経由せずにラスベガスに行くことは難しいと言っている。したがって，女性はマイアミに行きたいと間接的に言っていることがわかる。

【2】Passage 1　Question 1　D　　　Question 2　A
Passage 2　Question 1　C　　Question 2　B

〈解説〉パッセージと，その内容に関する質問が2問放送される。4択問題で，解答の選択肢は問題冊子に印刷されている。パッセージは2つあり，放送は1度のみである。　Passage 1　Question 1　第1パラグラフの4文目に，家の価格が高いことは経済が好調な指標であると述べている。　Question 2　第2パラグラフの2～3文目に，家を持っている人は家のことを価値が上がる安全な投資対象であると捉える傾向にあるが，必ずしもそうでないと述べられている。　Passage 2　Question 1

第1パラグラフの4～5文目に該当の記述があり，家庭での教育方針が，子どもが大人になった時の姿に影響するのである。　Question 2　第2パラグラフの4文目に該当の記述がある。子どもを一人で寝かせるという西洋人の習慣は，日本人にとっては育児放棄に近いように捉えられる。

【3】Conversation 1　Question 1　D　　Question 2　B
　　　Conversation 2　　Question 1　B　　Question 2　C
〈解説〉男女の会話と，その内容についての質問が2問放送される。放送は1度のみ。4択問題で，解答の選択肢は問題用紙に印刷されている。会話は2つあり，放送は1度のみである。
　Conversation 1　Question 1　女性は2番目の発話の1文目で期末レポートのことで困っていると言っている。それを受けて男性は，レポートのトピックを広げて資料を探し，手に入った資料の中の何かに焦点を当ててみてはどうかと具体的なアドバイスをしている。　Question 2　女性は2番目の発話の4文目で，レポートに必要な資料が図書館で見つからないと言っている。　Conversation 2　Question 1　女性の1番目の発話の3文目，または2番目の発話の3文目に該当の記述がある。女性は奨学金を申請しようとしていたが，銀行から学生ローンを借りることに決めたと言っている。　Question 2　女性の4番目の発話の2～3文目に該当の記述があり，アドバイザーの先生と話をすると言っている。

【4】ICチップ発明後，技術者は速く精密で多機能の小型の産業用ロボットを開発してきた。言葉でコミュニケーションをとれ，人間を直接的に助けるロボットのグループと，危険な環境に適応する，人間から遠く離れて働くロボットの2つのグループがある。1つ目の例はアシモとアイボであり，人間との共感が大きな特徴である。生体模倣のような新技術を用いて，科学者たちはより快適な生活を可能にする2つ目のロボットを開発するだろう。(200字)
〈解説〉まとまった英文の音声を聞き，その概要を150～200字程度の日本

語で書く問題である。放送は2度ある。英文のトピックはロボットに関するものであるが，IT技術の発展により様々なロボットが作られるようになったこと，ロボットが大きく2種類に分けられること，そしてそれぞれのロボットの特徴をまとめていけばよいだろう。まず，第1パラグラフでIT技術の発展に伴って様々なロボットが作られるようになったことが述べられている。次に，第2パラグラフでロボットが2種類に分けられることと，その特徴が大まかに述べられている。そして，第3パラグラフでは人を直接サポートするようなロボットの事例が述べられている。最後に，第4パラグラフでは人ができないような危険な環境で作業をするロボットの事例が述べられている。

【5】(1)　イ　　(2)　ア　　(3)　ウ　　(4)　エ　　(5)　エ　　(6)　ウ
(7)　ア　　(8)　ウ　　(9)　イ　　(10)　エ

〈解説〉(1)　英文は「コリンズさんは，すぐにでも職を見つけたかった5年前に起業した」の意であり，空欄はMs. Collinsを受ける代名詞が適切である。　(2)　over the next 5 yearsに着目すると，未来を示す表現が適切である。　(3)　空欄の前後にbe動詞と過去分詞のperformedがあることに着目すると，空欄に入るのは副詞が適切である。　(4)　it is 形容詞(for人) to doの形になっていることに着目する。　(5)　空欄の前がnew operators cannot treat informationとなっていることに着目すると，空欄に入るのは副詞が適切である。なお，lessも副詞として使用できるが，treat informationを修飾するという観点では不適切である。

(6)　英文は「(〜に)ふるまうことが日本文化の特徴の1つである」の意であるので，humbly「謙虚に」が適切である。　(7)　英文は「その党の小委員会が36時間連続で開催されているのは，合意できそうな法案の原案をどの委員も(　　)できていないからである」の意であるので，come up with「提案する・思いつく」が適切である。　(8)　英文は「ロイは先祖のほとんどがドイツ人だと思っていたが，実はノルウェーの政治家の直系(　　)であることを知った」の意なので，descendant「子孫」が適切である。　(9)　英文は「ルーシーは自身の作品を外部

の人に客観的に(　　)してもらいたがっているが，それは難しい」の意であるので，appraised「鑑定する(される)」が適切である。

(10)　英文は「彼女はそれ(過激な主張)が信念であると言い続けたが，最終的には発言を(　　)せざるをえなかった」の意であるので，withdraw「撤回する」が適切である。

【6】(1)　ア　　(2)　イ　　(3)　ウ　　(4)　イ　　(5)　エ

〈解説〉(1)　soothは「なだめる・癒す」の意である。　(2)　imposeは「課す・強いる」の意である。a strict dietとseriously overweightに着目するとよい。　(3)　whether the extension is practicableで「延長が可能かどうか」。　(4)　about「～に関する」の意である。　(5)　materialは「原料」の意である。

【7】(記号／語(語句)の順)　(1)　ア／characteristics　　(2)　イ／that
(3)　イ／themselves　　(4)　イ／a　　(5)　イ／is

〈解説〉(1)　「～の1つ」を意味するone of～に続く名詞は複数形になる。
(2)　likeで始まる挿入句を省略せずに表すと，the market price of gold or the market price of silverになる。　(3)　supportが「養う・扶養する」の意味であることに着目すると，themが指すのはimmigrants自身のことであることがわかる。また，代名詞で受けることができる名詞がimmigrantsかthe history of the United Statesしかないこともヒントになるだろう。　(4)　the number of～は「～の数」の意味であり，「たくさんの」を意味するa number of～と混同しないように注意したい。
(5)　widely used in pencilsが挿入された形になっていることに着目すると，元の英文はGraphite is a kind of carbon that is soft enough to draw a line on paperである。

【8】(1)　4番目…キ　　7番目…ア　　(2)　4番目…イ　　7番目…カ
(3)　4番目…エ　　7番目…オ

〈解説〉(1)　exploit an opportunityで「機会を利用する」。完成した英文はI

recommend you exploit that opportunity to practice your Spanish as much as you can.「この機会を利用して，できるだけスペイン語を練習することをお勧めします」となる。youの後にshouldが省略されている。

(2)　完成した英文はI'm certain it won't be a problem because she has an excellent reputation for public speaking.であり，「私は問題ではないと思っています。なぜなら，彼女は人前で話すことに定評があるからです」の意である。　　(3)　完成した英文はApart from job satisfaction, I hope to get a bonus at the end of the year if I do my job well.であり，「仕事のやりがい以外で言えば，仕事をちゃんとやれば，年末にボーナスがもらえたらいいなと思っています」の意である。

【9】(1)　エ　　(2)　ウ　　(3)　ウ

〈解説〉(1)　空欄を含む文の動詞が現在完了形になっていることに着目する。the past few weeksは「ここ数週間で」の意である。　　(2)　空欄の後に主語と動詞が続いていることから，選択肢はifまたはthatに絞られるが，空欄前の動詞がreportであることに着目すると，thatが適切である。　　(3)　空欄を含む英文は「技術的な問題は生じておらず，(　　)は確実にWi-Fi接続を利用できると言っていた」の意である。フリーWi-Fiを導入したバスを試験的に走らせ，乗客の反応を見たことに着目するとよい。

【10】(1)　ア　　(2)　エ　　(3)　ウ　　(4)　ア　　(5)　イ

〈解説〉(1)　第1パラグラフの1～2文目に着目すると，2文目に書かれているものは1文目の例であることがわかる。　　(2)　該当する英文は第1パラグラフの6文目にあり，その文の始まりがAnother exampleとなっていることに着目すると，4～5文目にあるbehavioral processes that occur on a periodic cycleやremarkably timed behaviorの例であることがわかる。(3)　第2パラグラフの4文目に該当する記述がある。一般的には24時間サイクルだと考えられている体内時計であるが，恒暗または恒明の人工的な環境下では，25時間サイクルになったと書かれている。

(4)　第3パラグラフの3〜5文目に該当する記述がある。体内時計とその人がいる現地時間を同期させるためには，その人がいる場所で安定した光と闇のサイクルが必要になると書かれている。　　(5)　第3パラグラフの9文目に該当する記述がある。時差ぼけは1日につき30分〜1時間のペースで治っていくが，人によっては2倍ほど早く治ると書いてある。したがって，早い人では1日につき2時間のペースで治っていくと考えられるため，4時間の時差は最短で2日で治ると考えられる。

【11】(1)　ウ　　(2)　イ　　(3)　イ　　(4)　エ　　(5)　エ

〈解説〉(1)　メール本文の第1パラグラフの1文目に該当する記述がある。
(2)　メール本文の第1パラグラフの2文目と4文目，第2パラグラフの1から3文目に該当する記述がある。どちらも用務員のシフトに関する内容である。　　(3)　設問文でat all timesと聞かれているので，マニュアルの1.①のcの文中のalwaysから，この項目が正答とわかる。
(4)　マニュアルの3.の①に該当する記述がある。follow the instructionsは「説明書の指示に従う」の意なので，エ「操作説明書を読むこと」が適切。　　(5)　メール本文の第3パラグラフの1文目に該当する記述がある。改訂したマニュアルに目を通して考えを聞かせて欲しいと書かれている。

【12】(1)　①　イ　　②　ア　　③　ア　　(2)　あ　compare themselves to the masters　　い　have more opportunity to stretch their limits
(3)　エ　　(4)　Effortful study is struggling with problems just beyond one's level of competence or comfort zone. (15 words)

〈解説〉　(1)　①　第1パラグラフの3〜4文目に該当する記述がある。
②　第2パラグラフの最後の文に該当する記述がある。　　③　第3パラグラフの2文目に該当する記述があるように，Simonは優れたプレイヤーには長期にわたる集中的な学習経験が重要であると主張している。その一方，第4パラグラフの1文目や5文目にあるように，Ericssonが考える優れたプレイヤーの特徴は絶え間のない努力型であり，ある競技

に熟達しても自分と比較して優れた人からずっと新しい情報を得ようとする姿勢があると述べている。　(2)　空欄を含む文は，主に第5パラグラフの情報をまとめた形になっていることに着目する。第5パラグラフでは，チェスのグランドマスターを獲得した最年少プレイヤーが，15歳から12歳に低年齢化したことが述べられており，その背景として，コンピュータによって，昔はできなかったような名人級のソフトウェアプログラムとの対戦ができるようになったと書かれている。(3)　この英文は前半でチェスなどに優れたプレイヤーの特徴を述べ，後半ではその特徴に基づいて，若い優れたプレイヤーが増えてきていることとその背景を述べている。この両方を含意したタイトルが適切である。　(4)　Ericssonが優れたプレイヤーの特徴として述べているのは，自分が熟達してからも気を緩めずに，自分よりも優れた人から学ぶ姿勢のことである。そのため，第4パラグラフで使用されている表現などもヒントにしながら，「自分自身の能力よりも高い人や問題に挑戦しながら学ぶこと」を英語で表現すればよい。

【13】An ALT is a model of an English speaker for students. For example, when conducting a performance test of speaking, it is effective for students to have an ALT provide a specific example of an "A" evaluation. In addition, by incorporating an ALT's perspective when we create rubrics for tests, it is possible to carry out performance tests that are more suitable for actual English use situations. In the performance tests, ALTs can participate in evaluation activities and they can provide more specific feedback to students. (92 words)

〈解説〉英語授業における効果的なALTの活用事例について，英語で答える問題である。生徒への具体的な効果も記述することが求められているため，目安語数が80語であることを踏まえると，事例としては2つ，多くても3つ書ければ十分である。活用方法ばかりを列挙して，その具体的な効果が十分に説明できていないような形にはならないよう注意したい。解答例では主に評価における活用事例が書かれているが，

187

それ以外の活用事例として，ALTに伝えることを目的とした言語活動を設計することが挙げられる。生徒に目的・場面・状況等に応じた言語運用の機会を設けることができ，また，日本人同士のコミュニケーションでのみ通じるような，いわゆる日本人英語だけでは不十分であることを生徒に気づかせる効果が期待できる。

【14】 (1) 「あそこでも，ここでも，ベストセラーになっている」という状態がイメージの基盤として存在するため，all over the worldの方がin the worldよりも適する表現となる。in the worldは「He is the fastest runner in the world.」などのように「範囲」を示す場合に用いるのが適切である。　(2)　全て「いくつかの」という意味で用いられるが，Someは可算名詞・不可算名詞数ともに用いることができ，数についてはseveral, a fewに比べて曖昧さをともなう。several, a fewともに可算名詞のみに用いる。a fewはseveralと同数かそれよりも少ない数を表す。またa fewは「少ないこと」に，severalは「多い」ことに含みを持たせて使用されることが多い。

〈解説〉(1)　in the worldとall over the worldの違いを検討するには，前置詞のinとoverのニュアンスを考えてみるとよいだろう。inは空間的に捉えて「～の中」の意味であるが，overは上方を覆うようなイメージで「～の上に」の意味である。そのため，all over the worldの方が，世界を覆っているようなニュアンスが含意される。したがって，in the worldは単に「世界でベストセラーになった」というニュアンスになるが，all over the worldは「世界の各地で(あちらこちらで)ベストセラーになった」というニュアンスになる。　(2)　解答例を少し補足すると，someはある程度の量や数があることを示すことに重きが置かれるため，あまり具体的な数量までは含意されないことが多い。

【高等学校】

【1】(1) イ ① ウ ① カ ① (2) ④ (3) ③

(4) 会話のトピックを，学習者の習熟度に合わせ，身近な課題や社会問題・環境問題等，何等かの意見対立のあるものにする。その上で，各生徒に割り当てられる役割もその課題に合わせて，何等かの対立関係を持つものにする(例えば，「町の活性化のために大型レジャー施設を誘致したい町職員」と「静かな暮らしを守りたい町民」など)。会話の台本は，そのトピックやどういった意見対立があるのか(役割の設定等)がある程度わかるところまでのものを準備し，続きは，生徒たちにアドリブで進めさせるようにする。…Criteria 1, 3 また，会話を進める上で，事前に条件設定をし，周知しておく(「レジャー施設の建設の可否など，与えられた課題について，何等かの結論にいたること」など)。…Criteria 4 さらに，会話を進める際，それぞれの役割にとって，有利に議論を進められるような使える情報や切り札となるような情報をそれぞれに事前に与えておく(見せ合うことは禁止する)。…Criteria 2 最後に議論の概要や結論についての報告レポートやまとめを英語で書かせ提出させる。…Criteria 3, 4

〔参考〕Criteria 1: Primary focus on meaning Criteria 2: (information) Gap Criteria 3: Own linguistic resources Criteria 4: Communicative outcome

〈解説〉(1) イ rendition「演奏，表現」。下線部を含む英文は「Dialogue活動の場合は，言語使用は機械的なものになることが多く，スクリプトの正確な表現に焦点が当てられている」の意である。

ウ replicate「再現(複製)する」。下線部を含む英文は「Nunan(1989)は現実世界で生じるような状況を再現(複製)したreal-worldタスクと，状況的な真正性ではなく，やりとりの真正性を追求するpedagogicタスクを区別した」の意である。 カ adept「熟練した，巧みな」。下線部を含む英文は「学習者は難しい文法形式の使用を避けることに長けている」の意である。 (2) 下線部①～④の文のうち，文脈に即さないものを選ぶ問題。この英文の第1パラグラフにあるように，この英文

189

のトピックは英語指導におけるタスクと練習について，具体的な活動例と併せて説明をしている。その上で，従来の英語指導の中心であった練習だけでは不十分であることから，タスクを取り入れることの重要性と，その際の留意点が述べられている。このことを踏まえると，練習だけでコミュケーション能力を高めることができると書いてある④が不適切である。また，④を含んだ文の次の文でも，タスクに基づいた活動が必要であると述べられている。　(3)　まず，空欄を含んだ英文と並列的に書かれている，その次に文に着目したい。「Table 11.2に示されているCandidates for a Jobのタスクは，産出中心で，意見にギャップがあり，現在完了形の形式に焦点が当てられている」と書かれている。また，Activity2: Spot the Differenceの項には，「Spot the Differenceのタスクは，ペアになった生徒にそれぞれ絵を与え，お互いの絵の中の5つの違いを見つけるために，絵に描かれていることを伝えあう活動である」と述べられている。このことから，Spot the Differenceも，エ(産出中心の)タスクであることがわかる。その一方，使用される言語形式は様々であることから，言語形式には，オ(焦点が当てられていない)と言える。　(4)　この英文の第1パラグラフに書かれているタスクの4つの条件として，言語活動の焦点が意味に当てられていること，情報のギャップがあること，学習者の言語的または非言語的な知識を活用する必要があること，そして，言語活動の結果が重要であることが挙げられている。一般的なDialogue活動は，与えられた英語をそのまま覚えて言うだけの活動であって，上記の条件を1つも満たしていない。そのため，まずは話す内容を生徒に考えさせるようにする必要がある。その際，1人1人の生徒が持っている知識を利用できそうなトピックにすることや，英語で話し合いを行う必然性がある状況を設定するとよい。

【２】(1)　B　　(2)　②　　(3)　②　　(4)　②，③　　(5)　In English classrooms in Japan, teachers try new teaching methods to give students more active roles in their classroom. Cooperative Language Learning(CLL) is one of those methods. However, traditional approaches are still helpful in specific teaching situations. Here, I am going to look at the advantages and disadvantages of CLL and traditional approaches. One of the advantages in CLL classrooms is that students can practice "real-life" conversations by working in groups, where they are encouraged to actively communicate with each other. The task itself may not be "real," but in order to achieve the goal, they must try to convey what they mean in English just as we do in real-life. However, in traditional language teaching, students have few opportunities to communicate in groups and interact with other students. They work mainly on activities such as pattern practice, role play, and translation to improve their knowledge of English, but not their skills to actually use it. However, CLL has disadvantages, too. In CLL classrooms, teachers organize group work, facilitate communication tasks, or intervene to teach collaborative skills. If the teacher does not have proper skills or knowledge to play those roles, it will be difficult for students to achieve the goal of English learning. In traditional language teaching, teachers are the center of the classroom and can easily control the class. To sum up, CLL is suitable to implement a more active way of learning, but some traditional approaches are still useful depending on the goal of the lesson. (249 words)

〈解説〉(1)　与えられた英文は「これらの問題に対処する際，言語教師はこれまで普通教室で行われてきたアプローチから多くのことを学ぶことができる」の意である。「これらの問題」とあることから，空欄の前に問題などが列挙されていることが推測できる。すると，生徒にとってよい学習環境を整えるために言語教師が行うべきことが，第1パラグラフ3文目以降に述べられていることに着目すればよい。

(2)　空欄前後の文で，伝統的な教育環境では少数派の生徒が脱落してしまう懸念があることや，教育者たちはこれらの伝統的な教育の課題を踏まえて協働学習を提案していることが述べられていることに着目する。よって，空欄を含む英文は「教育者たちは伝統的な教室学習のモデルが教師主導であり，イ(協力)よりもア(競争)を促し，そして多数

派の生徒を優遇するものであることを懸念していた」の意となるのが適切。　(3)　空欄を含む英文の前の文では，第2言語習得における協働学習は教室内におけるコミュニケーション活動を促進するものと述べられており，また，さらにその前に列挙されている協働学習の具体的な方法論を踏まえると，協働学習は学習者主導の教育方法であることがわかる。よって，空欄を含む英文は「それは，エ(教師主導の)授業方法よりも優れたウ(学習者中心の)指導法として捉えられている」の意となるのが適切。　(4)　②　practice through competitive interactionが誤り。協働学習においては競争ではなく協力が重要である。
③　assuming a more active role in their learningが誤り。協働学習において，授業の中心は教師ではなく生徒である。　(5)　協働学習と伝統的な指導法の利点と欠点を150～250語の英語で書く問題である。Table 13.1に言及しつつ具体的な理由まで書くことを考えると，それぞれの利点と欠点をただ書くのではなく，解答例にあるように，協働学習と伝統的指導法の利点と欠点を対比させながら書くのがよいだろう。その際，英文で使用されている表現なども参考にするとよい。

2020年度　実施問題

【中高共通】

Script

[There are three speaking roles for this test: Directions , Man(M), and Woman(W).]

Directions : Please turn the test paper over. The Listening Comprehension Test will now begin. You may take notes while listening.

【1】 Directions : Section A.

Please listen to the following conversations. After each conversation, a question will be asked, and four possible answers will be read. Choose the best answer and circle the corresponding letter on your answer sheet. Each conversation, the question, and the answers will be read only once.

Directions : Conversation 1.

W : You are a real YouTube junkie, aren't you, Alex?

M : I'm not a junkie: I'm fastidious about the contents I watch.

W : You're kidding! It seems your whole afternoon has been wasted in front of the computer monitor.

M : I know what I'm doing, mom. So, don't try to tell me what to do.

Directions : What is Alex's mother worrying about?

A.　The way Alex studies.

B.　The way Alex spends his time.

C.　The manner Alex talks to her in.

D.　The YouTube content Alex has chosen.

Directions : Conversation 2.

W : Do you have any problems, sir?

M : You've just lost my business.

W : If you talk to me what the problem is, maybe I'll try to do something to help solve it.

M : All right. If you want to know it, I'll tell you now. I purchased something by mail-order but I have never received it yet. And this is the third time it's happened!

Directions : How can the woman help the man?

A. She can help him get more business.

B. She can tell him what the problem is.

C. She can help him get what he wants.

D. She can give him a mail-order catalog.

Directions : Conversation 3.

M : Emily, you're so fortunate to get a babysitting job! It seems like easy money.

W : I don't think babysitting is easy, Mike.

M : Oh, yeah? Why is it so difficult?

W : Well, babysitters have serious responsibilities to do. We have to observe the kids and make sure they don't go into dangerous situations.

M : Hmm... I've never thought about that.

W : We even have to check on them when they are sleeping.

M : Wow, I guess your job involves a lot more than I expected!

Directions : What does Mike learn?

A. Actually, babysitters can't earn much money.

B. Kids are not always well-behaved.

C. Babysitting involves a lot of responsibility.

D. It is hard to get a job as a babysitter.

Directions : Conversation 4.

M : Hey, so what are you up to over the long holidays in this weekend?

W : My family and I are driving down to Chicago to visit my grandfather. It's his 90th birthday, so we want to give him a surprise birthday present.

M : He'll be so glad to see everyone. Is he in a nursing home now?

W : No, I don't know whether you can believe it or not, but he lives alone in his house.

M : That's amazing!

W : Yeah, and he still prepares most of his meals and does all of the housework by himself.

Directions : What can we find about the woman's grandfather?

A. He still drives sometimes.

B. He just moved to Chicago.

C. He is still independent.

D. He visits his family often.

(☆☆○○○○)

【2】 Directions : Section B.

Please listen to the following two passages. After each passage, two questions will be asked. Four possible responses to each question are listed on the answer sheet. Choose the best one and circle it. Each passage and question will be read only once.

Directions : Passage 1.

M : Have you ever sent an e-mail and had it "bounce back" ? You may have sent it three or four times to a friend, classmate, or colleague only to have it return to you. This is usually called "barfmail" by IT experts. Barfmail is not entirely as problematic as spam, but it's troublesome. Barfmail appears for several causes. In certain situations, the receiver's e-mail filter confuses a genuine message with spam, so it blocks the e-mail and returns it or files it as junk mail. In other situations, the mailer might have entered an incorrect e-mail address for the receiver by mistake — in such cases the mailer is causing the trouble.

Barfmail complicates our business and social activities because we must spend more and more time to deal with it. In other words, barfmail is confusing our e-mail inboxes. A lot of IT systems managers are recommending users to make sure their receiver addresses are accurate by checking them elaborately before sending, and also to modify their spam filters so that apposite e-mail gets delivered. With a few moments to do them, these small steps could dramatically reduce the amount of barfmail in the world.

| Directions | :　Question 1.　What is barfmail?

A.　A type of spam with e-mail.
B.　An e-mail blocking system.
C.　An e-mail transmission error.
D.　A junk mail manager.

| Directions | :　Question 2.　What is one solution IT systems managers recommend?

A.　Getting more powerful computers.
B.　Deleting unnecessary junk e-mail.
C.　Upgrading communication applications.
D.　Verifying the receiver's address.

Directions : Passage 2.

M : It's predictable to think that the greening of the peninsula might signal the appearance of global warming, which has been debated so much, and it is caused by the accumulation in the atmosphere of carbon dioxide and other gases released by the fossil fuels burning. As you've already known, in 1978 a paper in the journal *Nature* made an assertion for scientists to pay attention to Antarctica for early signs of what we call the greenhouse effect — especially the collapse of ice shelves off the Antarctic Peninsula.

While the prediction is taking on a reality, it is unclear that global warming is the cause. There has been a half-degree rise in average temperatures in the whole world in this past century or so, but that could be part of some sort natural cycle, uninfluenced by human activity.

Directions : Question 1. What were scientists asked to pay attention in Antarctica?

A. Release of carbon dioxide and other gases.

B. Human activities.

C. A signal of global warming.

D. Burning of fossil fuels.

Directions : Question 2. How much do we know about the temperature rise in the whole world?

A. It's not clear whether it's man-made or not.

B. The greenhouse effect has set in.

C. Its totally unrelated to what we do.

D. World temperatures are going down steadily.

(☆☆☆○○○○)

【3】 Directions : Section C.

Please listen to the following two conversations. After each conversation, two questions will be asked. Four possible responses to each question are listed on the answer sheet. Choose the best one and circle it. Each conversation and question will be read only once.

Directions　Conversation 1.

W : Hi, James. Where are you headed?

M : Hi, Christie. I'm on my way to the student union. As it's the beginning of a new term now, our dance club is inviting new members. We've got a desk set up nearby outside the student café.

W : I remember. You did the same work at the opening of the school year, didn't you? What happened to do that?

M : Great. Well, moderate great. We found lots of new members — 17 to be exact — but almost all of them were women. That'd be OK if we were a hip-hop group, but social dancing is much more fun if there is an equal number of men and women.

W : So you don't want to invite any more women? That's too bad. To tell the truth, I was thinking of joining your dance club.

M : Oh, we're not setting a limit to the number of women who want to join. The more members, the merrier. It's just that we hope to find a few more men who are going to learn how to dance with a partner. Do you know anyone?

W : Well, my boyfriend's on the football team. It's off-season for them now, so they should have time. I think I can persuade some of them that social dancing would be the best way for them to keep in shape and meet some nice partner at the same time.

Directions :　Question 1.　Where is the man going?

A.　To football practice.

B.　To a dance performance.

C.　To the student union.

D. To a student café.

Directions : Question 2. What kind of problem is the man's club holding?

A. A shortage of new members.

B. A shortage of financial support.

C. An imbalance between sexes.

D. A lack of practice space.

Directions : Conversation 2.

M : Professor Westbrook, I'd really like to receive your advice about something I've been thinking about. Could I talk to you?

W : Sure, John. Have a seat. Anyway, it's my office hours right now, and I'm always glad to talk to an advisee.

M : I'm graduating next year and, well now, I'm not certain about what to do afterward.

W : I see, and considered your performance here as an economics major — I think you had straight A's in your economics courses — you'll have a lot of options to choose.

M : That's the problem. It is still difficult for me to make up my mind about what I want to do. I think it's one idea to go right on to graduate school, either in economics or business. But maybe it would be good for me to work for a while and have some experience before continuing my studies.

W : This is the same agony many of our excellent students undergo. I'm afraid I can't present a single answer. It depends on you.

M : That's what I thought you'd say.

W : I do have one good suggestion. Maybe you are thinking too much seriously about this as an either/or choice. Maybe you could both work and continue your studies?

M : What does that mean?

W : Why not take an exciting job with your favorite company and at the same time enroll part-time in an evening program, just like an MBA program? Take some night classes.

M : I never thought of that before. That sounds really promising. Maybe I'll visit the Career Planning Office soon and research about the part-time graduate programs around here.

Directions : Question 1.　What can be inferred about the man?

A.　He rarely meets with his advisor.

B.　He is probably a very good student.

C.　He may decide to change his major again.

D.　He will not be able to graduate next year.

Directions : Question 2.　What does the woman suggest the man do?

A.　Consult with an academic counsellor.

B.　Contact as many company employers as possible.

C.　Concentrate more on his current courses.

D.　Consider working and studying at the same time.

(☆☆☆○○○○)

【4】 Directions :　Section D.

The following article will be read twice. Please write a summary of the contents in Japanese. The summary should be between 150 and 200 characters. There will be six minutes to write the summary after the second reading. You may take notes and begin summarizing while listening. Now, please listen to the article.

M : More than 70 percent of the world's business companies are owned and managed by only one person, mainly because of the ease of foundation this type of company affords. However, while the "personal business" remains by far the most usual type of business organization today, we have no doubt that the major form of business around world is the corporation, stock company. Although not all corporations are huge multi-national enterprises, it can commonly be said that the power of corporations to influence the economy, politics, and culture of a country greatly exceeds that of any other form of business.

The incorporation of human beings in search for a common purpose is as old as history. Nevertheless, the general idea of a corporation as an existence separate and distinct from the individuals who compose it arose at the early period of the colonial era, just about the early 17th century. Legally, the corporation is an artificial "person," which is able to conduct business transactions in the same way as the owner of a personal business would. Unlike the business owned by a single individual, though, the life of a corporation potentially exists permanently. It does not end when the owner dies or when its members take turns.

The principal cause why the corporation has become the most influential form of business in the world is that it is the most practical type of organization for supplying funds. To obtain the manufacturing plants, the equipment, and the marketing outlets necessary to compete with other large companies, we have to procure capital that may run into hundreds of millions of dollars. Because of any individual or even some members of shareholding, multiple owners can hold the corporation. In conjunction with the development of a capital market for the impersonal purchase and sale of stock, this structure has significantly assisted corporations to obtain the funds they need to operate on a wide scale.

Another advantage the corporation has over other forms of business companies is that it provides the management independently. In other words, business executives who, separate from the owners or shareholders, are paid to supervise and manage the company. This typically results in more professionl and expert management and has evolved to be a more important feature in corporate profitability.

(379)

Directions : Now, listen again.

M : *repeat*

Directions : Stop writing, please. This is the end of the listening test.
Thank you.

参考文献(すべて全面的に加筆修正)
・『DAILY　30日間　英検準1級集中ゼミ』(旺文社・2009年)
・『TOEFL　ITP　TEST　実戦問題集』(語研・2011年)
・『英検1級完全模試(全5回)』(アルク・1997年)

(☆☆☆☆☆○○○○)

【5】次の(1)～(10)の英文の_____に入る最も適当な語(句)を，ア～エ
の中からそれぞれ1つ選び記号で答えなさい。

(1)　The auditory canal, a pipe going to the external ear canal, is seen only in
animals having eardrums inside _____ heads.
　　ア　itself　　イ　theirs　　ウ　its　　エ　their

(2)　_____ as overweight, a man or woman who is an adult should have a
body weight 10 to 20 percent more than other adults of the same size and
sex.
　　ア　Defined　　イ　Define　　ウ　To define　　エ　To be defined

(3)　According to botanists, a plant species _____ depending upon
atmospheric temperature, sunlight exposure, and richness of the soil.
　　ア　flourished　　イ　flourishes　　ウ　flourishing　　エ　flourish

(4)　The Federal Reserve Board _____ seven members who are assigned
by the president of the United States and who have to have responsibilities

during their fourteen-year terms.

ア is composed of   イ   which composes   ウ   is composing

エ   composed of

(5)   Evolutionary psychology _____ all emotions of human beings arise because they heighten the possibility of survival in some way.

ア   assuming that   イ   is assumed of   ウ   assumes that

エ   assumed that

(6)   In the opening address, the president said that people elected him to lead _____ country.

ア   one's   イ   those   ウ   his   エ   these

(7)   Applicants should _____ the completed application form for admission to the registrar's office personally or by post.

ア   submit   イ   be submitted   ウ   submitting   エ   submitted

(8)   A native extract from the plant has been used in Africa to treat respiratory diseases for more than 20 years with _____ success.

ア   to be surprised   イ   surprising   ウ   surprised

エ   to surprise

(9)   The maker ensured that if it is appropriately operated, the machine will work well _____ any problem for at least ten years.

ア   beyond   イ   that   ウ   without   エ   over

(10)   More than 200 years ago, a settlement was constructed on the other side of the river from _____ is now the center of industry in this area.

ア   what   イ   he   ウ   that   エ   it

(☆☆○○○○)

【6】次の(1)～(5)の英文において下線部に最も近い意味の語(句)をア～エの中からそれぞれ1つ選び記号で答えなさい。

(1)   The company decided to do away with its only indicated smoking area to protect the health of all employees.

ア   designated   イ   embraced   ウ   abolished   エ   restricted

(2)　The room was so noisy that we could catch only <u>snatches</u> of the famous actor's speech.

　　ア　frictions　　　イ　proportions　　　ウ　fragments　　　エ　flakes

(3)　Some viruses may lie <u>hidden</u> in the human body for a long time before they become active and start to do harm.

　　ア　compatible　　　イ　lenient　　　ウ　dormant　　　エ　exploited

(4)　At the shelter for the homeless, many local citizens <u>cooperated</u> by donating either their time or money to help the less fortunate.

　　ア　gave out　　　イ　pitched in　　　ウ　got through

　　エ　dreamed up

(5)　Ricky <u>compensates</u> his lack of an extensive background in mathematics by studying hard every night to master the subject.

　　ア　gives out　　　イ　brings up　　　ウ　makes up for

　　エ　gets out of

(☆☆☆○○○○)

【7】次の(1)～(5)の英文において不適切な箇所を，下線部ア～エからそれぞれ1つ選び記号で答え，正しい形，または，適切な語(句)にしなさい。

(1)　ア<u>In</u> the middle of 19th century, イ<u>the</u> industrial revolution made the ウ<u>beginning</u> of mass production, technological innovation, and エ<u>transportation of public</u>.

(2)　ア<u>It</u> is difficult for writers to find detailed mistakes in イ<u>his</u> own work, so a copy editor ウ<u>is usually</u> asked to do エ<u>that</u> task.

(3)　Great attention must be paid when ア<u>producing</u> silicon chips, both to イ<u>prevent</u> contamination by dust ウ<u>or</u> to avoid エ<u>defects</u> of manufacturing.

(4)　Environmental ア<u>demolition</u> caused by イ<u>pollution air</u> and water contamination costs major urban ウ<u>areas</u> a large amount of money in エ<u>annual</u> clean-up costs.

(5)　Although ア<u>some</u> of Wisconsin's corn crop is consumed イ<u>by</u> humans, much of ₍ゥ₎<u>itself</u> is used as animal ₍エ₎<u>feed</u>.

(☆☆☆◎◎◎◎)

【8】次の(1)～(3)の英文において〔　　〕内の語(句)を正しく並べかえて文章を完成するとき,〔　　〕内の語(句)の4番目と7番目にくる語(句)を, それぞれ1つ選び記号で答えなさい。

(1) Stephanie, an exceptional student, was〔ア　was　　イ　master　ウ　mathematics　エ　able to　　オ　advanced　　カ　since　キ　she〕very young.

(2) She is〔ア　father's side　　イ　on　　ウ　the Maori people　エ　of　　オ　descended　　カ　from　　キ　her〕the family.

(3) His occasional〔ア　was　　イ　his insistence　　ウ　a real　エ　inconsistent　　オ　impoliteness　　カ　with　　キ　he was　ク　that〕gentlemen.

(☆☆◎◎◎◎)

【9】次の英文において空欄(1)～(3)に入る最も適当な語を, ア～エの中からそれぞれ1つ選び記号で答えなさい。

The changing manner of top business school graduates are specifically (1). These are people who have choices, who often boast several years of steady experience and get a number of job offers in all but the very worst of economic climates. At one time, many (2) to firm power, to be the managers at some giant company. But now more and more of them, especially those at or near the top of their grade, want to (3) out a niche of their own rather than slip into one offered by a corporation.

(1) ア　remaining　　イ　revealing　　ウ　concealing　　エ　receding
(2) ア　respired　　イ　ascended　　ウ　aspired　　エ　discouraged
(3) ア　cover　　イ　corner　　ウ　curve　　エ　carve

(☆☆☆◎◎◎◎)

【10】次の英文を読み，あとの(1)～(5)を文意に合うようにするため，最もふさわしいものをア～エの中からそれぞれ1つ選び記号で答えなさい。

The forest is one of the most important properties for us in Japan. But we are allowing our beautiful public forests, which account for almost 20 percent of Japan's gross area, to deteriorate.

We should preserve the public forests by maintenance of roads and rivers leading into them, by cutting down trees selectively and selling them, and by planting young plants. Unfortunately the present conditions aren't true. The government agency which supervises these activities, the Forest Agency, has a special program which is sure to be self-sufficient. That is, the income which is earned from vending lumber cut down from public forests is supposed to be allocated to paying for the various forest maintenance activities. The program has been going into the red for several years and this budget shortage ensures that not all the maintenance activities can be executed.

The reasons for the budget shortage are mostly caused by the increase in the use of imported lumber. Domestic lumber cannot contend with the cheaper imported lumber. Also, pressure from environmentalists has caused that more attention is required towards ameliorating the scenery of forests, rather than increasing revenue. While many people may agree with limiting felling operations in public forests, it is important to retain that these operations are an indispensable source of revenue and, decently carried out, can truly be beneficial to forests. When revenue is decreased, there may not be enough money to plant young plants and maintain hiking courses.

Public forests aren't the only areas on the verge of a crisis. Private forests, which account for 70 percent of all the forest area, are also being allowed to retrogress. These private forests are just as indispensable as public ones when it is connected with protecting the natural environment and water resources in Japan. Since they are privately owned, if the owners don't try to maintain them properly, there is no one else to preserve them. Contributing to the plight of many of these private forests is the depopulation of many isolated communities in mountainous areas. The residents there actively participated in their maintenance and kept them from decisively falling into disrepair.

Now is the time to face this problem, before it becomes worse than now.

Public support for the forests is widespread in Japan. According to a certain survey, more than 60 percent of people said they would like to preserve the forests in some way. We should make more people to have more interests in the fate of our country's forests and we should also search solutions to the problem of funding programs to maintain this indispensable national resource.

(1)　The maintenance of Japan's public forests

ア　is overseen by the Forest Agency under a special program.

イ　relies on the helping of self-supporting volunteers.

ウ　goes well as far as the trees of public forests are cut down selectively and sold.

エ　is very hard as they cover as much as a fifth of the gross area.

(2)　The revenue for forest keeping activities has fallen short

ア　because the program has been going into the red.

イ　mainly because lumber from forests in Japan is more expensive than imported one.

ウ　partly because of more lumber of better quality imported from abroad.

エ　because consumption of wood has decreased as other materials are used to build houses.

(3)　The writer of this article explains that

ア　environmentalists should be more interested in improving the scenery of the forests.

イ　the cutting down of trees within measure is good for the forest.

ウ　a lot of money should be used to build more wooden houses.

エ　old trees should be cut down to plant new kinds of trees which will earn more profit.

(4)　Forests owned privately are as indispensable as public ones in that

　　ア　they account for 70 percent of all Japan's forest area.

　　イ　they defend Japan's environment against natural disaster.

　　ウ　they protect sources of water supply for Japanese people.

　　エ　they contribute to the predicament of isolated communities.

(5)　With regard to the problem of Japan's forests,

　　ア　more than 50 percent of the people surveyed showed no interest.

　　イ　we should not prematurely give up hope worrying about it.

　　ウ　people's interest is divided between economic development and preservation of forests.

　　エ　there are pressing financial problems to be solved.

(☆☆〇〇〇〇)

【11】次の英文を読み，あとの各問いに対する答えとして最も適当なものをそれぞれ1つ選び記号で答えなさい。

　　The world's volcanoes are categorized into types based chiefly on how they have formed. This classification is a result of the kinds of materials that have erupted from them, the speed at which the materials have been spouted, and the length of period over which the eruptions have happened.

　　The most general type of volcano, the shield volcano, is a gradually sloping dome gently built up for a long period by thin layers of volcanic dust and a series of lava flows. These flows are comparatively thin, rarely surpassing seven meters in thickness, and made from lava that flowed out slowly. Any fragmental materials such as volcanic rock and volcanic boulders thrown out by eruptions are insignificant and have practically no influence on the shape of the mountain. With the growing of the shield volcano, eruptions of lava gradually cease to originate from the volcano's central crater and instead lava flows out of secondary cracks on the slopes of the volcano. Finally, the main column of lava is no longer capable of reaching the top of the volcano, and all the eruptions come from the secondary vents. From then on the volcano increases in diameter but not in height.

The second type of volcano is created when several smaller lava domes unite as they grow in size, forming a compound volcano. For instance, the island of Hawaii has been formed by the combination of five such lava domes. In a compound volcano, lava domes are formed by thick lava that runs out from the vent at the top of each dome; with time a compound volcano can grow to an incredible size as its various vents form its base. Some of compound volcanoes have risen from thousands of meters under the sea's surface to form islands or chains of islands.

Compared with this, the third type, a composite volcano, which is also sometimes called a "stratovolcano", develops a form dominated by rock fragments erupted from the highest crater of a single volcano that are interspersed with the lava that flows from its central vent. Compared to the size of the whole mountain, which may rise more than 3,000 meters above its base, the crater that forms the central vent is entirely small, rarely ever more than a few hundred meters in diameter. A volcano of this type usually exhibits a steep slope and appears symmetrical when viewed from far away. Mt. Kilimanjaro in Tanzania, Mt. Nevado del Ruiz in Colombia, and Mt. Fuji in Japan are probably the most famous examples of composite volcanoes.

(1)　The passage is mostly concerned with

　　ア　the distribution of volcanoes all over the world

　　イ　the physical forms of volcanoes

　　ウ　the dangers caused by volcanoes

　　エ　the formation of new volcanoes

(2)　Which factor is NOT referred to in paragraph 1 as playing a role in the creation of a volcano?

　　ア　How long a volcano has been in activity

　　イ　What kinds of materials a volcano has discharged

　　ウ　The place a volcano has occurred

　　エ　How fast lava and rock have erupted

(3)　The word "rarely" in line 6 is the most similar in meaning to

　　ア　hardly

　　イ　unfortunately

　　ウ　ordinarily

　　エ　seldom

(4)　Deduce than the passage. Which kind of volcano may be most generally seen in the Pacific Ocean?

　　ア　Shield volcanoes

　　イ　Stratovolcanoes

　　ウ　Compound volcanoes

　　エ　Composite volcanoes

(5)　Which of the following best distinguishes the structure of the passage?

　　ア　Cause and result

　　イ　Chronological development

　　ウ　An extended story

　　エ　A classification of types

（☆☆○○○）

【12】Read two passages and answer the questions below.

Summer Intern Wanted

Communications Position Open at Ayers Associates

Ayers is a consultant for online marketers all over the world. We were established in 1990, and we are (　あ　) for the traditions of our outstanding customer service and business methods. We are currently looking for a summer intern who can support one communications department.

Responsibilities contain:

・Support with writing and editing ad copy, e-mail messages, memos and other kinds of documents

・Plan meetings

・Monitor trends of he industry

・Implement market research

・Make reports

Requirements:

・Previous experience in communications setting desirable

・Excellent written and verbal communications abilities recommended

・Computer literacy

This is a magnificent career chance for college students who are planning to （ い ） the communications field. We are looking for superior professionals who can keep severe deadlines. For prompt consideration, please send your resume as an e-mail attachment with a cover letter.

To: info@ayers.net

From: caitlyn@nls.com

Subject: Summer Intern Position

Dear Sir or Madam,

I'm writing （ う ） to your ad for a summer intern. So far, I'm working on a journalism degree in college. Until now, I worked in the school office treating the school's communications every summer. My duties ［ ア ］, so I think I'm very eligible for the job you're giving publicity. I'm also able to handle the computer remarkably and am familiar with many kinds of software applications.

I'm a very industrious student and am hoping to someday find employment in communications or journalism. Please run your eyes over my resume and let me know if you think ［ イ ］. I'm excited to get your reply.

Sincerely yours,

Caitlyn Smith

(1) Choose the best word or phrase from among the four choices for each blank, (あ)～(う). Write the number of the answer.

あ ① well known ② invested many times

　③ supported quickly ④ hardly reported

い ① getting used to ② get into

　③ looking forward to ④ known about

う ① as an announcement ② in my opinion

　③ down my field ④ in response

(2) Complete the sentence in ［ ア ］ and ［ イ ］ so that the passage will make sense. Fill in each blank within 10 words.

(3) What is one of the responsibilities of the position? Choose the most suitable answer below.

ア To report the news by e-mail and memos

イ To operate meetings

ウ To make an investment in the market

エ To check what's popular in various industries

(4) What is required for the position? Choose the most suitable answer below.

ア The candidate must be over 20.

イ The candidate must have excellent speaking and writing skills.

ウ The candidate must have a computer science magazine.

エ The candidate must have some experiences about management.

(5) What did Caitlyn annex with her e-mail? Choose the most suitable answer below.

ア A recommendation

イ A picture of her

ウ A resume

エ　An enclosure

(☆☆○○○○)

【13】As for the developments of English teaching plans, we can make good use of Kyoto as a teaching material. Write a composition about one of them concretely including the points to keep in mind in English. The composition should be 80 words or more.

(☆☆☆○○○○)

【14】授業中に生徒が次の(1)と(2)の質問をしました。あなたは英語の先生としてどのように説明しますか。それぞれについて日本語で答えなさい。(説明の一部に英語を交えても差し支えない)

(1)　「私の兄は，私の頭をたたいた。」という意味になるよう，"My brother hit my head." という英文をつくったところ，ALTの先生から "My brother hit me on the head." が正しいと言われました。なぜこんな変な形の文になるのですか？

(2)　理由を表す接続詞としてbecauseを習いましたが，他にもas / since もあると知りました。この3つの言葉の用法の違いを教えてください。

(☆☆☆☆○○○○)

【高等学校】

【 1 】Read the passage and answer the questions below.

> Sunyoung is a Korean teacher of English, who has a master's degree in teaching English to speakers of other languages (TESOL). In her class, she organizes lots of communicative group tasks that give her students opportunities to improve their spoken English through using it.

EXPERIENCE

(中略)

In the following Experience, the students are practicing the function of "making arrangements to meet." Sunyoung sets the scene by reminding the class of the objectives of the unit they have been working on. (The last class was based on several short conversations in which the people were making arrangements to meet.) She then divides the class into two. One group receives the Student A Worksheet, while the other group receives the Student B worksheet (see Figure 1).

Sunyoung: So, tonight we're going to do an information-gap task. You all know what an information-gap task is — we did one last week, remember? You're going to work in pairs, and you have the same task to do, but you have different... what? Different... ?

Eunha: Informations.

Sunyoung: Right. Good, Eunha, different information. And you have to share your information. You have to share it. OK? So before we do that, I want you to look at your worksheet. I want to make sure you understand the words. Work together in your groups, and look at the activities on the worksheet. This is what people are doing on the weekend, on Friday, Saturday, and Sunday, OK? Now, which activities are related to work and which are not? Discuss among yourselves and decide. Some are work activities, and some are personal activities, If you don't know some words, you can ask me. I'll give you five minutes to make sure you know the words.

Student A Worksheet

	Friday evening	Saturday afternoon	Saturday evening	Sunday afternoon	Sunday evening
Bob	work late	————	meet boss at airport	————	prepare for a meeting
Karen	————	free	————	go shopping	————
Philip	free	————	free	————	free
Joan	————	take car to garage	————	bake cookies	————

Student B Worksheet

	Friday evening	Saturday afternoon	Saturday evening	Sunday afternoon	Sunday evening
Bob	_____	go to meeting	_____	free	_____
Karen	clean apartment	_____	visit aunt in hospital	_____	free
Philip	_____	play tennis	_____	study for exam	_____
Joan	free	_____	go to concert	_____	free

Figure 1. Sample task: Making arrangements to meet.

While the students are checking the words, she shuttles back and forth among the groups. When she is sure that the students understand the words, she claps her hands.

Sunyoung: OK, now, it's time to get into pairs. So I want one person from Group A to pair up with one person from Group B. But don't show each other your worksheet—don't share your worksheets. This is an info-gap task. You have to share your information—not show it.

The students rearrange their chairs so that they are sitting in pairs.

Sunyoung: Right, so—ready? S.K., ready? Good. So this is what you have to do. Take a look at your worksheets. What are the names of your friends on the worksheets? Their names.

S.K.: Bob, Karen, Philip, and, er, Joan.

Sunyoung: Bob, Karen, Philip, and Joan. So, on the worksheets, you can see some of the things they have to do this weekend. Some of the things that they have to do are related to work, and same are not. You and your partner want to go to the movies some time over the weekend with your friends.

Understand? Good—off you go.

As the students complete the task, the teacher circulates among the pairs and ensures that they are completing the task correctly. When all pairs have finished, she claps her hands together and points to one of the pairs.

Sunyoung: So, Eunha and Kelly. Did you manage to find a time slot when everyone is free?

Eunha: No, no slot, free slot.

Sunyoung: No free slot?

Eunha: No free slot.

Sunyoung: So what did you do? Decide not to go to the movies?

Kelly: We decide Sunday evening.

Sunyoung: Sunday evening. Why Sunday evening?

Kelly: Because only one person isn't free.

Sunyoung: Which one?

Kelly: Bob.

Eunha: Yes. Bob.

Sunyoung: So, poor Bob misses out! (laughs)

Eunha: Yes. Bob have to miss out.

Sunyoung: Do the rest of you agree?

Students: Yes, yes.

Sunyoung: OK. So, now I want you to change one thing about each person's schedule, just one thing, all right? Then I want you to change partners—find a new partner and do the task again.

WHAT IS TASK-BASED LANGUAGE TEACHING?

Task-based language teaching(TBLT) has its origin in a number of philosophical positions and ⁊empirical traditions in education, applied linguistics, and psychology. These include experiential learning and humanistic education, learner-centered instruction, and process-oriented and analytical approaches to syllabus design.

In this section, I build on the opening classroom Experience to describe and illustrate some key principles of TBLT, first showing how it fits into a larger historical curriculum framework and, second, offering a definition of the concept. I then look at its philosophical and empirical bases.

The Experience you just read is an extract from a lesson based on principles of TBLT. What do you notice about the extract? First, the learners are engaged in exchanging meanings, not memorizing and repeating utterances presented by the teacher or the textbook. In fact, the language they need to

216

complete the task was practiced in a previous lesson. The learners exchange meanings based on the worksheet they have been given and do not simply repeat someone else's meaning. While the task is a pedagogical one (you would not see two people doing a task like this outside the classroom), there are clear connections between the in-class task and the real-world task of making plans and arrangements. Finally, the success of the task is assessed in terms of a communicative goal (negotiating and coming to an agreement about the best time to meet friends), not in terms of successfully manipulating linguistic forms. (中略)

Task defined

It is now time to look more directly at what we mean when we talk of tasks. TBLT belongs to a family of approaches to language pedagogy that are based on what is known as an analytical approach to language pedagogy (Wilkins, 1976). Here I describe this approach, contrasting it with the synthetic approach in the next section of this chapter. Before I look at the conceptual and empirical bases of TBLT, however, I need to clarify what I mean when I talk about tasks.

Tasks have been defined in various ways. As I mentioned when discussing the Experience that begins this chapter, I draw a basic distinction between pedagogical tasks, which are things that learners do in the classroom to acquire language, and real-world or target tasks, which are the uses to which individuals put language to do things in the world outside the classroom. In an early and rather programmatic definition, Long(1985) characterizes real-world tasks as "the hundred and one things people do in everyday life, at work, at play and in between." He provides a long list of these things, including domestic chores such as painting a fence, dressing a child, and writing a check and workplace tasks such as weighing a patient, typing a letter, and sorting correspondence.

217

```
                    X
```

In Sunyoung's classroom the learners had to exchange and negotiate information to find the most suitable time to go to the movies with their friends. The learners, working in pairs, have access to (イ) but (ウ) pieces of information. This is known as an information-gap task, a basic task type in TBLT. Other task types include (エ), (オ), and values clarification[1]. Notice that, although there is no explicit focus on pronunciation, grammar, or vocabulary, students need to _カmobilize their linguistic resources to achieve the goal of the task. Notice also that there is a concrete outcome that goes beyond the manipulation of linguistic forms. The task has a sense of completeness, and at the end of the task, learners are able to evaluate how well they have done.

In short, while pedagogical tasks should always have some kind of relationship to real-world tasks, the relationship may be somewhat _キtenuous. However tenuous the relationship might be, the link between the classroom and the world beyond the classroom should be clear to the learners.

Despite their(ク), most definitions of *task* in the literature have several characteristics in common. Skehan(1998) synthesizes the views of a number of writers and suggests that pedagogical tasks exhibit five key characteristics. If you refer back to the discussion of the Experience earlier in this chapter, you will find exemplification and elaboration of _ケthese features.

ENDNOTES

1 *Values clarification* is a classroom activity in which students are asked to examine the values that they hold and articulate why these values are important in their lives; often, the activity involves assigning a ranking (e.g., from 1 to 5) to a list of values.

(1) Choose the best statement that describes the meaning of each of the underlined words ア, カ, and キ from among the choices for each word. Write the numbers of the answer.

ア empirical

① based on a situation that is not real, but that might happen

② based on scientific testing or practical experience, not on ideas

③ relating to the study of ideas, especially scientific ideas, rather than to practical uses of the ideas or practical experience

カ mobilize

① to encourage people to support something in an active way

② to help something to move more easily

③ to start to use the things you have available in order to achieve something

キ tenuous

① definite and specific

② not easily broken or damaged

③ uncertain, weak, or likely to change

(2) Put the following sentences in order so that the part ☐ X ☐ will make sense.

① Creating an inventory of real-world tasks, that is, listing the actions that learners will actually or potentially need to perform outside the classroom is a first step in the development of a TBLT curriculum.

② Pedagogical tasks, on the other hand, are what learners do in the classroom to activate and develop their language skills.

③ Such tasks involve learners in comprehending, manipulating, producing, or interacting in the target language to achieve a non-linguistic outcome.

④ The next step is to turn these into pedagogical tasks.

(3) Choose the beat pair of the words from among the choices for (イ)

and (　ウ　). Write the number of the answer.

① イ　obvious　　　ウ　unknown

② イ　related　　　ウ　different

③ イ　unrelated　　ウ　similar

(4) Choose the TWO best task types from among the choices for (　エ　) and (　オ　). Write the numbers of the answer.

① opinion exchange

② prepared speech

③ problem solving

④ skit performance

(5) Choose the best word from among the choices for (　ク　). Write the number of the answer.

① diversity

② simplicity

③ uniqueness

(6) As for $_{\textit{ケ}}$these features, among the following seven choices, choose the TWO sentences that are NOT appropriate for those features. Write the numbers of the answer.

① Learners are not given other people's meanings to simply repeat.

② Meaning is primary.

③ Task completion has least priority.

④ Task completion has some priority.

⑤ The assessment of the task is in terms of outcome.

⑥ There is some sort of relationship to comparable real-world activities.

⑦ What learners do in the task is barely connected to the real world.

(7) Think of another activity using the same worksheets that Sunyoung used (Student A Worksheet and Student B Worksheet) and describe the procedure in English. The activity must be based on TBLT principles. You can start it as the second activity in her lesson in the passage as if you were Sunyoung.

＊Also, set TWO OR MORE goals of the activity and write them down in the answer sheet. Start the sentences to describe the goals with "Students can."

(☆☆☆○○○)

【2】 Read the passage and answer the questions below.

Tests have a way of scaring students. How many times in your school days did you feel yourself tense up when your teacher mentioned a test? The anticipation of the upcoming "moment of truth" may have provoked feelings of anxiety and self-doubt along with a fervent hope that ①you would come out on the other end with at least a sense of worthlessness. The fear of failure is perhaps one of the strongest negative emotions a student can experience, and ②the most common instrument inflicting such fear is the test. ③You are not likely to view a test as positive, pleasant, or affirming, and, ④like most ordinary mortals, you may intensely wish for a miraculous exemption from the ordeal.

And yet, tests seem as unavoidable as tomorrow's sunrise in virtually all educational settings around the world. Courses of study in every discipline are marked by these ア periodic milestones of progress (or sometimes, in the perception of the learner, confirmations of inadequacy) that have become conventional methods of measurement. Using tests as gatekeepers—from classroom achievement tests to large-scale standardized tests—has become an acceptable norm.

Now, just for fun, take the following quiz. These five questions are sample items from the verbal section of the Graduate Record Examination (GRE®). All the words are found in standard English dictionaries, so you should be able to answer all five items easily, right? [A] Okay, go for it.

Directions : In each of the five items below, select the definition that correctly defines the word. You have two minutes to complete this test!

1. onager
   a. large specialized bit used in the final stages of well-drilling
   b. in cultural anthropology, an adolescent approaching puberty
   c. an Asian wild ass with a broad dorsal stripe
   d. a phrase or word that quantifies a noun

2. shroff
   a. (Yiddish) a prayer shawl worn by Hassidic Jews
   b. a fragment of an ancient manuscript
   c. (Archaic) past tense form of the verb to *shrive*
   d. a banker of money changer who evaluates coin

3. hadal
   a. relating to the deepest parts of the ocean below 20,000 feet
   b. one of seven stations in the Islamic *haji* (pilgrimage) to Mecca
   c. a traditional Romanian folk dance performed at Spring festivals
   d. pertaining to Hades

4. chary
   a. discreetly cautious and vigilant about dangers and risks
   b. pertaining to damp, humid weather before a rainstorm
   c. optimistic, positive, looking on the bright side
   d. expensive beyond one's means

5. yabby
   a. overly talkative, obnoxiously loquacious
   b. any of various Australian burrowing crayfishes
   c. a small, two-person horse-drawn carriage used in Victorian England
   d. in clockwork mechanisms, a small latch for calibrating the correct time

Now, how did that make you feel? Probably just the same as many learners feel when they take multiple-choice (or shall we say multiple- (　イ　)?), timed, "tricky" tests. To add to the torment, if this were a commercially administered standardized test, you would probably get a score that, in your mind, demonstrates that you did (　ウ　) than hundreds of people! (中略)

Of course, this little quiz on infrequently used English words is not an appropriate example of classroom-based achievement testing, (　エ　) is it intended to be. It's simply an illustration of how tests make us feel much of the time.

[　B　] Can they instead build a person's confidence and become learning experiences? Can they become an integral part of a stndent's ongoing classroom development? Can they bring out the best in students? The answer is *yes*. That's mostly what this book is about: helping you create more authentic, intrinsically motivating assessment procedures that are appropriate for their context and designed to offer constructive feedback to your students.

To reach this goal, it's important to understand some basic concepts:

· What do we mean by *assessment*?
· What is the difference between assessment and a test?
· How do various categories of assessments and tests fit into the teaching-learning process?

ASSESSMENT AND TESTING

ォAssessment is a popular and sometimes misunderstood term in current educational practice. You might think of assessing and testing as synonymous terms, but they are not. Let's differentiate the two concepts.

Assessment is "appraising or estimating the level or magnitude of some attribute of a person" (Mousavi, 2009, p.35). In educational practice, assessment is an ongoing process that encompasses a wide range of methodological techniques. Whenever a student responds to a question, offers a comment, or tries a new word or structure, the teacher subconsciously appraises the student's performance. Written work — from a jotted-down phrase to a formal essay — is a performance that ultimately is "judged" by self, teacher, and possibly other stedents. Reading and listening activities, usually require some sort of productive performance that the teacher observes and then implicitly appraises, however peripheral that appraisal may be. A good teacher never ceases to assess students, whether those assessments are incidental or intended.

Tests, on the other hand, are a subset of assessment, a genre of assessment techniques. They are prepared administrative procedures that occur at identifiable times in a curriculum when learners muster all their faculties to offer peak performance, knowing that their responses are being measured and evaluated.

In scientific terms, a test is a method of measuring a person's ability, knowledge, or performance in a given domain. Let's look at the components of this definition. [　C　] A test is first a *method*. It's an instrument — a set of techniques, procedures, or items — that requires performance on the part of the test-taker. To qualify as a test, the method must be explicit and structured: multiple-choice questions with prescribed correct answers, (　カ　), an oral interview based on a question script, or a checklist of exspected responses to be completed by the administrator.

Second, a test must *measure*, which may be defined as a process of quantifying a test-taker's performance according to explicit procedures or rules (Bachman, 1990, pp.18-19). Some tests measure general ability, whereas others focus on specific competencies or objectives. ⑤<u>A multiskill profiency test determines a general abillty level</u>; a quiz on recognizing correct use of definite articles measures specific knowledge. ⑥<u>The way the results or measurements are communicated may vary</u>. Some tests, such as (　キ　), may earn the test-taker a letter grade accompanied by marginal comments from the instructor. ⑦<u>Others, particularly large-scale standardized tests, provide a total numerical score, a percentile rank, and perhaps some</u>

224

subscores. ⑧If an instrument specifies a form of reporting measurement — a means to offer the test-taker some kind of result — then that technique cannot appropriately be defined as a test. [　D　]

Next, a test measures an *individual's* ability, knowledge, or performance. Testers need to understand who the test-takers are. What are their previous experiences and backgrounds? Is the test appropriately matched to their abilities? How should test-takers interpret their scores?

A test measures performance, but the results imply the test-taker's ability or, to use a concept common in the field of linguistics, competence. Most language tests measure one's ability to perform language, that is, to speak, write, read, or listen to a subset of language. On the other hand, tests are occasionally designed to tap into a test-taker's knowledge *about* language: defining a vocabulary item, reciting a grammatical rule, or (　ク　). Performance-based tests sample the test-taker's actual use of language, and from those samples the test administrator infers general competence. A test of reading comprehension, for example, may consist of several short reading passages each followed by a limited number of comprehension questions — a small sample of a second language learner's total reading behavior. But the examiner may infer a certain level of general reading ability from the results of that test. [　E　]

Finally, a test measures a given *domain*. For example, in the case of a proficiency test, ⑨even though the actual performance on the test involves only a sampling of skills, the domain is overall proficiency in a language — general competence in all skills of a language. ⑩Other tests may have more specific criteria. ⑪A test of pronunciation might well test only a limited set of phonemic minimal pairs. A vocabulary test may focus on only the set of words covered in a particular lesson or unit. ⑫One of the biggest obstacles to overcome in constructing adequate tests is to measure the desired criterion and inadvertently include other factors. (中略)

A well-constructed test is an instrument that provides an accurate measure of the test-taker's ability within a particular domain. The definition sounds fairly (ケ) but, in fact, constructing a good test is a (コ) task involving both science and art.

(1) Among the choices [A] to [E] throughout the passage, choose the best place where the following statement should be put.

Here's the bottom line: Tests need *not* be degrading or threatening to your students.

(2) Part of one of the underlined sentences ①～④ has been changed so that the sentence won't fit in the context. Choose that sentence and write the number of the answer.

(3) Part of one of the underlined sentences ⑤～⑧ has been changed so that the sentence won't fit in the context. Choose that sentence and write the number of the answer.

(4) Part of one of the underlined sentences ⑨～⑫ has been changed so that the sentence won't fit in the context. Choose that sentence and write the number of the answer.

(5) What does the writer mean by ァ periodic milestones of progress? Answer in one word used in the passage.

(6) Fill in the blanks (イ), (ウ), and (エ). *One word for each blank.

(7) The following are statements about ォ Assessment. Write "T" if the statement is true, or "F" if it is false.

a. Assessing is antonymous to testing though many people think otherwise.

b. What matters is that teachers never stop assessing students, regardless if they do it deliberately on accidentally.

c. When assessing students, teachers should imply the appraisal, which should be peripheral.

(8) Choose the best example from among the choices for blanks, (カ), (キ), and (ク). Write the number of the answer. *You cannot use

one number for two or more blanks.

① a classroom-based, short-answer essay test

② a writing prompt with a scoring rubric

③ identifying a rhetorical feature in written discourse

(9) Choose the best pair of the words from among the choices for (ケ) and (コ). Write the number of the answer.

① ケ abstract コ creative

② ケ simple コ complex

③ ケ technical コ elementary

(10) Which do you think is more effective to improve students' proficiency in English, assessment or tests? Write your opinion about it.

i. Your essay should consist of 150-225 WORDS.

ii. You should refer to TWO OR MORE pieces of the information mentioned in the passage.

iii. You should have specific reasons or details to support your opinion.

(☆☆☆○○○)

解答・解説

【中高共通】

【1】 Conversation 1 B   Conversation 2 C   Conversation 3 C
Conversation 4 C

〈解説〉日常会話を聞いて，読みあげられる選択肢で答える形式。やや難解な単語が含まれているものもあるが，対話の全体的な流れがつかめれば，仮に理解できない単語があっても問題ない。ただし放送は1度のみなので，聞き逃しがないように気をつけなければならない。

【２】Passage 1　Question 1　C　　Question 2　D

　　Passage 2　Question 1　C　　Question 2　A

〈解説〉Passage 1は200語程度，Passage 2は120語程度からなる英文を聞い
　て，印刷されている選択肢で答える形式。放送は1度のみで，パッセ
　ージ1つにつき，質問が2つである。選択肢からトピックを予測する。
　Passage 1はbarfmailについて，Passage 2は温暖化についてである。

【３】Conversation 1　Question 1　C　　Question 2　C　　Conversation 2

　　Question 1　B　　Question 2　D

〈解説〉Conversation 1は学生同士の会話，Conversation 2は教授と学生の
　会話を聞いて，印刷されている選択肢で答える形式。放送は1度のみ
　で，対話文1つにつき，質問が2つである。やや長めの対話文である。
　特定の語句を聞き取る問い(Conversation 1　Question 1のstudent union)も
　あるが，大半は概要をつかんでいるかを問う設問で構成されているの
　で，細かいところよりも話の流れを追うように聞くことを心がける。

【４】世界の主要な事業形態は株式会社であり一国の経済，政治，文化に
　対する影響力はその他の事業形態より大きい。一個人によって所有さ
　れる事業と違い，所有者が死んだり構成員が交代したりしても株式会
　社は存続する。株式所有という仕組みによって複数名による所有が可
　能になり，株式の個人購入以外の売買のための資本市場が発達した。
　株式会社では経営者は事業保有者や株主とは分かれており，企業の監
　督，運営のため雇われている。(199字)

〈解説〉350〜400語程度の英文を聞いて，要旨を150〜200字の日本語で記
　述する形式。放送は2度流れるが，記述に与えられている時間は6分で
　ある。出題形式が独特なので，同様の練習をつんで，コツをつかんで
　おかないと上手く解答することは難しいと思われる。聞きながらメモ
　をとり，それを膨らませるかたちで文章を構成する。

【5】(1) エ　　(2) エ　　(3) イ　　(4) ア　　(5) ウ　　(6) ウ
(7) ア　　(8) イ　　(9) ウ　　(10) ア
〈解説〉(1)「外耳に通じる管，耳道は，頭の中に鼓膜がある動物にだけ
見られる」。animalsの所有格が入る。　　(2)「肥満と定義するには，成
人男性または女性は，同じ身長と性別の成人より体重が10〜20％以上
多くなければならない」。　　(3)「植物学者によると植物種は気温，日
光照射，土壌の豊かさ次第でよく育つ」。speciesは単複同形。ここでは
単数形。　　(4)「連邦準備制度理事会は合衆国大統領に任命され，4年
の任期の間責任を負う7人のメンバーで構成されている」。be composed
of 〜「〜から成る」。　　(5)「何らかの方法で生き延びる可能性を高く
するので，人間のあらゆる感情は生じるのだと進化心理学は仮定して
いる」。assume that 〜「〜と思い込む，仮定する」。　　(6)「国を導くた
めに人々は自分を選んだのだと，大統領は冒頭のあいさつで言った」。
(7)「入学志願者は記入済の願書を教務課に直接，または郵送で提出し
なければならない」。submit 〜「〜を提出する」。　　(8)「天然の植物エ
キスは，20年以上アフリカで呼吸器疾患の治療に使われ，非常に役立
ってきた」。with success「成功して」。　　(9)「メーカーは，正しく操
作すればその機械は最低でも10年は問題なく作動すると保証した」。
(10)「200年以上前に，現在のこの地域の産業の中心地から川向こうに
開拓地がつくられた」。what S is now「現在のS」。

【6】(1) ア　　(2) ウ　　(3) ウ　　(4) イ　　(5) ウ
〈解説〉(1)　indicated, designated「指定された」。　　(2)　snatch「一部，
断片」。fragment「かけら，破片」。　　(3)　hidden「隠れて」。dormant
「潜在して，休止の」。　　(4)　cooperate「協力する」。pitch in「(金を)出
し合う，出して協力する」。　　(5)　compensate, make up for「償う，埋
め合わせる」。

【7】(1)　記号…エ　　語(句)…public transportation　　(2)　記号…イ
語(句)…their　(3)　記号…ウ　　語(句)…and　(4)　記号…イ　　語(句)

229

…air pollution　(5)　記号…ウ　　語(句)…it

〈解説〉(1)　public transportation「公共交通機関」。　(2)　「作家たちの作品の中に」なのでtheirが適切。workはここでは不可算名詞扱い。

(3)　both A and Bで「AとBの両方」。「粉塵汚染を避けるためと製造欠陥を防ぐ両方のために」。　(4)　air pollution「大気汚染」。　(5)　「ウィスコンシンのトウモロコシ収穫のいくらかは人間によって消費されているが，それの多くは動物の飼料として使われている」。Wisconsin's corn cropをitで受ける。

【8】(1)　4番目…ウ　　7番目…ア　　(2)　4番目…イ　　7番目…エ
(3)　4番目…カ　　7番目…キ

〈解説〉(1)　整序すると，able to master advanced mathematics since she was となる。　(2)　整序すると，descended from the Maori people on her father's side of となる。be descended from ～「～の子孫である」。father's side of the family「父方の親族」。　(3)　整序すると，impoliteness was inconsistent with his insistence that he was a real となる。be inconsistent with ～「～に矛盾する」。

【9】(1)　イ　　(2)　ウ　　(3)　エ

〈解説〉(1)　「経営学の学院生の変わりつつあるふるまいが特に明らかである」。　(2)　「かつては多くが安定した権力，大会社の経営者になることを熱望した」。　(3)　「しかし今では彼らのますます多くは，特に成績がトップかそれに近いものたちは，会社に与えられた所に入り込むより自分自身の適所を作りたがっている」。

【10】(1)　ア　　(2)　イ　　(3)　イ　　(4)　ウ　　(5)　エ

〈解説〉(1)　日本の公有林の維持は，ア「特別なプログラムの下，林野庁によって監督されている」。第2段落3文目参照。　(2)　森林維持活動のための収入は，イ「主に日本の森林からの木材は輸入ものより高価であるため」十分ではない。第3段落2文目参照。　(3)　この記事の

筆者は，イ「適度に木を伐採することは森林のためによい」と説明している。第3段落の4文目参照。　(4)　私有林は，ウ「それらが日本人の水の供給源を守るという点で，公有林と同様に不可欠である」。第4段落3文目参照。　(5)　日本の森林問題に関しては，エ「解決すべき差し迫った財政上の課題がある」。第6段落3文目参照。

【11】(1)　イ　　(2)　ウ　　(3)　エ　　(4)　ウ　　(5)　エ
〈解説〉(1)　主として火山の大きさや形について述べられていることから，「このパッセージはほとんど，火山の物理的形状に関してである」となる。　(2)　第1段落では，the kinds of materials, the speed, the length of periodの3要因が挙げられている。　(3)　rarelyは「めったに～ない，おおよそ～ない」と頻度を打ち消す副詞でseldomと同義。hardlyは程度を打ち消す副詞である。　(4)　問いは「どの種類の火山が太平洋で最も一般的に見られるか，推測せよ」。ハワイ諸島の例が挙げられていることから複合火山であると考えられる。　(5)　第2～第4のそれぞれの段落で，shield volcano, compound volcano, composite volcanoの3つの火山について説明をしている。段落構造を区別しているものとして，「火山タイプの分類」が正しい。

【12】(1)　あ　①　　い　②　　う　④　　(2)　ア　were similar to what you described in your ad　　イ　I'd be suitable for your company
(3)　エ　　(4)　イ　　(5)　ウ
〈解説〉(1)　あ　インターン募集広告の会社の紹介部分で，①「弊社は1990年に設立され，際立った顧客サービスとビジネス方法で知られております」。be known for ～「～で有名である」。　い　②「コミュニケーション分野に就職しようと思っている大学生にはとっては，最高のキャリアチャンスです」。get into ～「～に就職する」。　う　学生の申し込みのメールで，④「私は夏のインターンの広告に返信しています」。in response to ～「～に応じて」。　(2)　ア　前文の「学校のオフィスで働いた経験があること」と，空所後の「自分が広告にある仕事

にふさわしい」を踏まえて書く。解答例は「私の務めは広告に記載されているものと似ていました」。　イ　履歴書に目を通し，連絡をしてほしいと述べている部分である。解答例は「私が貴社にふさわしいとお考えであれば」。　(3)　広告中にすべきことが列挙されている。アについては，広告中で「サポート」するとあるので誤り。イについては「計画する」とあるので不適。ウについては記述がない。広告中のMonitor trends of the industryやImplement market researchから，エ「様々な業界で何が人気があるか調べる」が適切。　(4)　このポジションに必要とされているものは，広告中のExcellent written and verbal communications abilities recommendedから，「志願者は優れたスピーキングとライティングのスキルを持っていなければならない」が適切。(5)　Caitlynがメールに添付したのは，resume「履歴書」。

【13】 I assign the interview to the foreigner at the sightseeing spot to students as homework of the summer vacation to raise their ability for English communicative competence. The students write a report about the results and give speeches in the English class. Working on this task, they can get the ability of the presentation in English, too. They can make interview to a lot of foreigners visiting Kyoto at the sightseeing spot around the school area. It is necessary to tell them to be careful about safety during interview, for example, they have to ask their parents to go with them. (101 words)

〈解説〉設問は「ティーチングプランの発展に関連して，教材として京都をうまく利用することができる。そのプランについて具体的に80語以上で書け」というもの。解答例では，夏季休業中に観光地で外国人観光客へインタビューし，結果をレポートに書き，授業で発表する活動を挙げている。学習成果の発表として，学校周辺の隠れた名所を紹介するガイドブックを配布するなどもアイデアとして考えられる。

【14】(1)　感情が入った場面で(たとえば喧嘩の場面などで)頭をたたく場合には，1つ目の文を用いることになります。2つ目の文が成立する場

合があるとすれば，客観的に感情を交えない場合，たとえば兄が自分のことを起こそうとして(善意で)頭をたたいている場合が想起されます。　(2)　3つの接続詞は，用法の違いとしてbecauseとas/sinceの2つに分けられます。becauseは聞き手がまだ知らない情報を表す時に用い，as/sinceは聞き手がすでに知っている情報を表す時に用いるのが基本です。たとえば，"Since it's raining, the baseball game got cancelled."(雨が降っているので，野球の試合は中止になった)では，「雨が降っている」のは聞き手も知っている情報ですが，"I'm training because I'm going to run a marathon."(私はマラソンを走るのでトレーニングしています)では，「マラソンを走る」ことは聞き手にとって初めて聞く情報になります。

〈解説〉(1)　目的語にmy headが来ると，たたいた場所に重点を置く言い方となる。　(2)　as/sinceは理由が前提となっていたり，自明であったりする場合に使われるので，主節の前に置かれる。

【高等学校】

【1】(1)　ア　②　　カ　③　　キ　③　　(2)　②→①→④→③

(3)　②　　(4)　①，③　　(5)　①　　(6)　③，⑦

(7)　Goals of the Activity EXAMPLE… ・Students can negotiate and make an arrangement to go to the movies with all the members of the group.

・Students can listen to and understand the other group members.

・Students can tell the other group members what they want to do or do not want to do.

・Students can persuade their group members when necessary.

Procedure EXAMPLE…(After the first activity in the text,)　1. Have students make groups of four.　2. Have students decide who will be Bob, Karen, Philip and Joan.　3. Before starting the activity, in 5 minutes, have each student decide which of their plans can be rearranged and which plans cannot (＋why).(Students are not allowed to tell others their intention.)

4. Have students start negotiating to make an arrangement to go to the movies

with all the members of the group. In the process of negotiating, students can offer the change of the plans or refuse it but they must tell others why. They have 8 minutes.　　5. Have one of the students in each group tell the result in class and briefly explain how they are able to reach an agreement (or how they are not).

〈解説〉(1)　ア　empirical「経験に基づいた，経験による」。
カ　mobilize「行使する」。　キ　tenuous「内容のない，薄い」。
(2)　②のon the other handに着目。前段のreal world taskに対して，pedagogical taskについて述べられている段落である。→①のfirst stepは「教室外で学習者が実際に，または可能性として行う行動をリストアップする」。→④The next stepに着目。「それらをpedagogical taskに変えること」。→③taskについての説明。　(3)　information gapの活動は「ペアで作業する学習者は，関連しているが異なる情報にアクセスする」ことで成立する。　(4)　空所後の記述より，学習者に達成感があったり，タスク終了後にできたことを評価したりできるタスクタイプを選択する。prepared speechやskit performanceは当てはまらない。　(5)直後に「タスクのほとんどの定義には，文献において，いくつかの共通の特徴がある」が続く。despite their diversity「それらが多様であるにもかかわらず」が適切。　(6)　Experienceにある，pedagogical taskの5つの特徴から解答を導く。③「タスク完了は最下位の優先度である」と⑦「タスクで学習者がしていることは実社会とほとんど関係がない」が誤り。　(7)　解答例では，学習者が表中の4人になり，スケジュールを調整するという場面をつくり出している。交渉したり説得したりするプロセスが設定されたことで一層，実社会とのつながりが深いタスクとなっている。

【2】(1)　B　　(2)　①　　(3)　⑧　　(4)　⑫　　(5)　tests/Tests
(6)　イ　guess　　ウ　worse　　エ　nor　　(7)　a. F　b. T
c. F　　(8)　カ　②　　キ　①　　ク　③　　(9)　②
(10)　I think that assessment is more effective than tests to improve students'

proficiency in English. I have two reasons.

First, assessment is more effective to intrinsically motivate students. What is most important when people want to improve something is "motivation." This is also true when learning a language. As mentioned in the passage, tests often cause students to lose their confidence. When you cannot have confidence, it is almost impossible to have motivation. If teachers choose appropriate words and timing to give assessment, students will receive more positive feedback, which will greatly help them make progress, and may even lead them to become more motivated.

Second, assessment gives students more opportunities to improve their English. According to the passage, compared to tests, assessment can be done throughout the year, the day, or the lesson, which means teachers have many more chances to give students proper feedback. As a result, students have many more opportunities to look back on their performance, fix it, and try again. In contrast, there are only a limited number of tests in a certain period and sometimes students can get the wrong message from the results.

For these reasons, I believe assessment is more effective to improve students' proficiency in English. (205 words)

〈解説〉(1) 挿入文は「肝心なことは, テストが生徒を侮辱したり脅かしたりする必要はないということだ」。まとめとして, テストの在り方について述べている段落に入ると考えられる。Here's the bottom line「要するに, 言いたいことは」。 (2) ①少なくとも無駄ではなかったという気持ちと共に, 反対の結果になるという「切なる希望」a fervent hopeであれば文意が通る。 (3) ⑧「手段が測定をレポートする形式を定めなければ」に対して「そのテクニックはテストとして適切に定義されない」であれば文意が通る。 (4) ⑫「テストは既定の分野を測るものである」という段落の流れがある。よって下線部「適正なテストをつくるときに克服すべき最も大きな障害の1つは, 望ましい規準を測ることと他の要因をうっかり含めてしまうことである」の前者はこの文脈には適さない。 (5) 下線部は「定期的な進歩のマ

イルストーン」。that以下で，「測定の従来の方法」とあることからも，testを指している。　(6)　イ　例示されている選択肢式の問題を揶揄していることから，choice「選択」をguess「当てずっぽう」などに言い換える。　ウ「これが営利的に行われている規格テストであったら」に続く文で「あなたはおそらく何百人以下の悪い出来だと証明するスコアを取ると想像するだろう」。do badly「出来が悪い」。　エ　例示されている選択肢式の問題について言及している部分で，「教室ベースの達成テストのふさわしい例でもなければ，それを意図しているものでもない」。not A nor B「AでもなければBでもない」。is itの語順は倒置。　(7)　a.「多くの人はそう考えていないが，assessingはtestingの反意語である」。多くの人は同意語だと考えている。　b.「大切なことは，よく考えてか，偶然にやっているかに関わらず，教師が生徒を評価することをやめないことである」。本文にA good teacher never ceases to assess students, whether those assessments are incidental or intendedという記述がある。　c.「生徒を評価する時，教師は重要でない評価を伝えるべきである」。これは明らかな誤りである。　(8)　カ　テストとして資格のあるものは，②「採点の注釈がある作文」。　キ「受験者に取るに足らないコメントを添え文字による成績を与える」という内容から，①「教室ベースの短い論文式テスト」。　ク　受験者の言語知識に入り込むよう意図されているテスト内容として，③「書かれている文章の修辞的特徴をつきとめること」が適切。　(9)　補充後の文意は「よく構成されたテストは特定の領域内で受験者の能力を正確に測る手段である。この定義はかなり単純であるが，実際に良いテストをつくることは人文と科学の両方を含む複雑な作業である」。

(10)　問いは「生徒の英語力を向上させるためには，評価とテストのどちらが有効だと考えるか，本文で述べられている情報に言及しながら，意見を支える理由や詳細を交え150～225語で書け」というもの。解答例では，テストとの比較を上手く取り入れながら意見をまとめている。As mentioned in the passageやaccording to the passageなどの語句を使い，本文を適度に引用しながらまとめるとよい。

2019年度　実施問題

【中高共通】

Script

[There are three speaking roles for this test: Directions , Man(M), and Woman(W).]

Directions : Please turn the test paper over. The Listening Comprehension Test will now begin. You may take notes while listening.

【1】

Directions : Section A.

Please listen to the following conversations. After each conversation, a question will be asked, and four possible answers will be read. Choose the best answer and circle the corresponding letter on your answer sheet. Each conversation, the question, and the answers will be read only once.

Directions : Conversation 1.

W : Aren't you dressed rather scantily for such a cold day?

M : Don't worry. I'm going to put on some more clothes before I go out.

W : Why don't you take this scarf with you?

M : No, thank you. I'll put on that overcoat. I think that's enough.

Directions : What is the man probably wearing?

A. The man is wearing a thick sweater.

B. The man is wearing a T-shirt.

C.　The man is wearing a scarf.

D.　The man is wearing a wool jacket.

Directions：　Conversation 2.

W：　Thanks so much for babysitting my son, David.

M：　Don't mention it. We enjoyed playing with him.

W：　Didn't he do anything wrong?

M：　Never. He is such a polite boy. I only wish that some of his politeness would rub off on my two boys. They are too naughty!

Directions：　What does the man want his sons to do?

A.　He wants them to be more polite.

B.　He wants them to play with David.

C.　He wants them to help their father.

D.　He wants them to work as babysitters.

Directions：　Conversation 3.

M：　I hear that the annual scone campaign held by Cornwall Cafe was a huge success this year. The owners were able to raise 1,180 pounds. Did you buy any scones?

W：　Oh, my, I forgot all about it, and I really would have liked to have supported the campaign. When was it?

M：　It was during the last week of May. The scones were sold at half price, and all proceeds were sent to a nonprofit organization that provides aid to the homeless. Don't you think it's a lovely gesture? I'm so glad they made a lot of money.

W：　I think so, too, but I wish I had taken the opportunity to help their cause.

M：　It's not too late. I'm sure you could still send money directly to the organization.

W : That's sounds nice! Please tell me how to do it.

Directions : What is the woman probably going to do?

A. She is going to buy some scones directly from the nonprofit organization.

B. She is going to make some scones at Cornwall Cafe.

C. She is going to think about other ways to help the homeless.

D. She is going to make a donation directly to the nonprofit organization.

Directions : Conversation 4.

M : I hear you've been learning how to dance recently.

W : Yes, I'm actually learning how to dance the samba and I'm having so much fun. The music is so catchy, so full of energy, and I just love those rhythms.

M : I don't know much about the samba. I think it's from Rio de Janeiro in Brazil.

W : Now it's Brazil's national music, but it has an interesting story. Its origins go back much further to Africa.

M : Oh, really? How did it become popular in Brazil?

W : Long time ago, Africans who were forced to go to Brazil as slaves brought it with them. It mixed with European and Latin American dance.

M : Interesting! I want to know more about it.

W : I bet you will like it. Why don't you come with me to a class?

Directions : What is the wrong information about the samba?

A. It's Brazil's national music.

B. Its birthplace is Rio de Janeiro.

C. African people brought it to Brazil.

D. It is a mixture of European and Latin American dance.

(☆☆○○○○)

【２】

Directions : Section B.

Please listen to the following two passages. After each passage, two questions will be asked. Four possible responses to each question are listed on the answer sheet. Choose the best one and circle it. Each passage and question will be read only once.

Directions : Passage 1.

M : Welcome, all attendees, to the Fifth Annual Conference on 'Sustainable Development'. We have a few announcements about cancellations and room changes for today's events. The presentation "Present Situation of Global Warming" scheduled for 2:00 p.m. this afternoon has been canceled. The presentation on the introduction of alternative energy scheduled for 9:00 a.m. today has been rescheduled for tomorrow at 11:00 a.m. in Conference Room 1. Also, the session on teleconferencing scheduled for 10:00 a.m. in Silver Hall has been rescheduled for 2:00 p.m. in the same room. We regret to announce that our keynote speaker today, Dr. Robert McNiell, has been delayed in transit. He will give the keynote address tomorrow instead at 1:00 p.m. in the main hall.

Directions : Question 1. What is the program which all the participants will not be able to attend?

A. "Present Situation of Global Warming".

B. The introduction of alternative energy.

C. The session on teleconferencing.

D.　Dr. McNiell's speech.

Directions ：　Question 2. When and where should the participants go to attend the keynote address?

A.　To the Conference Room 1 at 11:00 a.m. today.

B.　To the Silver Hall at 10:00 a.m. tomorrow.

C.　To the main hall at 2:00 p.m. today.

D.　To the main hall at 1:00 p.m. tomorrow.

Directions ：　Passage 2.

M ：　Hello. I'm Martin Scofield, president of Skylark Education Foundation. At this time, Skylark Education Foundation is asking for donations for the Lakeside City school district. S.E.F.'s goal this year is to provide new tables and chairs for the elementary school cafeteria, brass instruments for the middle school band, and 3-D printers for the high school science labs. Last year, your donations provided 100 new DVDs for the middle school library. We also raised money to pay for new uniforms for the varsity baseball and hockey teams. If you wish to donate, you can send a check to Skylark Education Foundation. Newcomers are welcome to attend S.E.F. meetings at the Lakeside City Community Center at 335 Park Avenue. We meet on the first and third Thursday of every month at 7 p.m. Hope to see you there!

Directions ：　Question 1. What is the announcement mainly about?

A.　Asking for donations to Skylark Education Foundation.

B.　Looking for some staff in the Lakeside City school district.

C.　Asking for participation in the varsity baseball and hockey teams of Lakeside City.

D.　Asking for attendance to the meetings of Skylark Education Foundation.

Directions : Question 2. What facility is going to have more equipment this year?

A. Cafeteria at the middle school.

B. High school science labs.

C. Middle school library.

D. Lakeside City Community Center.

(☆☆☆◎◎◎◎)

【3】

Directions : Section C.

Please listen to the following two conversations. After each conversation, two questions will be asked. Four possible responses to each question are listed on the answer sheet. Choose the best one and circle it. Each conversation and question will be read only once.

Directions : Conversation 1.

W : Hi John. You look so sick. What's wrong?

M : I haven't been feeling well since last week.

W : Have you caught a cold? Or did you drink too much?

M : No. I feel a lot of stress from work.

W : I can't believe it! What happened?

M : Do you remember Tom, my colleague? He's taking a week off to see his daughter in Los Angeles, so I have to take his place while he is away.

W : That's too bad. You said now is the busiest time of the year.

M : Yeah, Tom and I are in charge of the Internet Sales Section.

W : You should enjoy your favorite food and have a good night's sleep. I heard a calcium-rich diet also helps you reduce stress and irritation. Try some fruits and milk. Don't eat too much snacks.

M : All right. Thanks.

Directions : Question 1. What is the man's main problem?
  A. He has to work for his colleague during the week.
  B. He has caught a cold.
  C. He drinks too much.
  D. He is responsible for the decrease of Internet Sales.

Directions : Question 2. What is not true about the woman's advice?
  A. The man should sleep well.
  B. The man should eat something full of calcium.
  C. The man should not eat too much snacks.
  D. The man should take a week off.

Directions : Conversation 2.

M : According to today's news, a cyberattack that began last Friday has affected more than 200,000 victims. How terrible!

W : I heard the virus spread throughout 150 countries! It could affect anyone.

M : Yes. And many people may be involved, too. Digital crime is becoming more common.

W : I've heard some hackers demand ransoms to be paid in digital currency. Since they aren't issued by any government, digital currencies are much harder to trace than regular currencies.

M : In today's interconnected world, these criminals could be anywhere and their tricks have been cleverer and cleverer, but now national and international police agencies are working very closely to stop these kinds of crimes.

W : Let's hope they're caught soon. In the meantime, we have to be careful not to open suspicious attachments, especially from people you don't know.

M ： Exactly. It's also important to make sure we have the latest security patches. We have to stay cyber-safe.

Directions ： Question 1. According to the woman, why do some hackers demand ransoms to be paid in digital currencies?

A. Because digital currencies have been more and more common.

B. Because digital currencies are issued by the government.

C. Because digital currencies are more difficult to trace.

D. Because digital currencies are tolerant to the virus.

Directions ： Question 2. What is true about the woman's suggestion in order to stay cyber-safe?

A. You should not send attachments to people you don't know.

B. You should not open suspicious attachments.

C. You should have the latest security patches.

D. You should follow the directions from international police agency.

(☆☆☆○○○○)

【4】

Directions ： Section D.

The following article will be read twice. Please write a summary of the contents in Japanese. The summary should be between 150 and 200 characters. There will be six minutes to write the summary after the second reading. You may take notes and begin summarizing while listening. Now, please listen to the article.

M ： From my experience as a director of a recruitment company, I'd like to mention some dos and don'ts for people who want to succeed at their new job. When you start a new job, you will be very nervous and wonder whether you will be able to meet the employer's expectations. However, there are some tips to reduce your worries and achieve good results.

When you begin a new job, what you should be most concerned with as an employee is to simply try to please your employer. In my current position, I've listened to a lot of employers. It's very important that employees do things their employer's way —no matter how they've learned to do them. Learn what to do from your present employer. Another point is that employers don't often have time, time to thoroughly train new employees, so they expect them to show initiative. You won't gain anything if you just wait until your employer tells you what to do. These are very important points about standards of a professional.

Of course being able to perform your duties is necessary, but office politics can also play a role in your success. One important thing to remember is that new employees should never take sides in office disputes. It doesn't necessarily mean you should agree with both sides, but try to understand the argument both for and against the subject. And most of all, never discuss a colleague unfavorably with other coworkers.

If you are new to the workforce, creating a professional image is important. Watch how you dress. Always present a businesslike image no matter how informally other people in your office may dress.

You can also project a professional image by watching what you say. For example, don't swear and don't talk about silly things like how much you had to drink the night before. It's true people want to share something personal about themselves, but new employees have to be careful about bringing up their private life in the office. You don't want to become the subject of office gossip. Uh...which reminds me — it is very important to be discreet. If someone tells you something personal, don't repeat it to others. Not only will this show that you're professional, it also proves you can be trusted.

　　If you want to be treated well as an employee, you absolutely have to act like a professional. Show your employer that you are responsible, mature, dedicated, and hardworking, that you are interested in being as productive as possible, and then your employer will take care of you.

Directions : Now, listen again.

M : *repeat*

Directions : Stop writing, please. This is the end of the listening test. Thank you.

(☆☆☆☆☆◎◎◎◎)

【5】次の(1)～(10)の英文の_____に入る最も適当な語(句)を，ア～エの中からそれぞれ1つ選び記号で答えなさい。

(1)　This hat will not _____ with a blue dress, so I won't choose it.
　　ア　go　　イ　do　　ウ　keep　　エ　suit

(2)　The goods we ordered online _____ expected to arrive in a few days.
　　ア　has　　イ　are　　ウ　have　　エ　will have

(3)　We cannot process the order _____ we get a copy of the purchase order.
　　ア　when　　イ　that　　ウ　until　　エ　because

(4)　We enjoyed our vacation in Hawaii _____ the bad weather we experienced.
　　ア　for　　イ　even　　ウ　despite　　エ　although

(5)　There is no non-stop flight _____ from Japan to Miami, but there is a direct flight which stops over at an intermediate point.

ア admirable イ predictable ウ touchable エ available

(6) The hotel which you said was new _____for 10 years by the time this year ends.

ア was open イ has opened ウ has been open

エ I will have been open

(7) Commercial builders downplayed _____ a bust in the superheated housing market.

ア concerning イ concerns about ウ concerned that

エ the concerns of

(8) The audience thanked her with a standing ovation, which was _____ remarkable considering that the concert was nearly canceled.

ア all the more イ many more ウ most of エ too much

(9) I'm going to the landerette because my washing machine has _____ .

ア gone out イ turned down ウ worn out

エ broken down

(10) The state of Maine generally has cooler temperatures than _____ .

ア there ara most other states

イ most other states have

ウ having most other states

エ most other states which have

(☆☆○○○○)

【6】次の(1)～(5)の英文において下線部に最も近い意味の語(句)をア～エの中からそれぞれ1つ選び記号で答えなさい。

(1) Tom procrastinated the matter until it was too late.

ア put off イ shoved off ウ warded off エ turned off

(2) My brother has squandered every penny of the money legacy from our parents.

ア extended イ activated ウ wasted エ increased

(3) Soil on the mountain slopes is susceptible to erosion.

　　ア　massive　　イ　plagued　　ウ　fragile　　エ　subject

(4)　I was <u>blown away</u> by his donation of a million dollars to charity.

　　ア　saddened　　イ　grateful　　ウ　suspicious　　エ　impressed

(5)　The coming decades will likely see more <u>intense</u> clustering of jobs, innovation, and productivity in a smaller number of bigger cities and city-regions.

　　ア　determined　　イ　concentrated　　ウ　emotional　　エ　brilliant

(☆☆☆◎◎◎)

【7】次の(1)～(5)の英文において不適切な箇所を,下線部ア～エからそれぞれ1つ選び記号で答え, 正しい形, または, 適切な語(句)にしなさい。

(1)　<u>ア My friendes tell</u> the <u>イ English exam</u> is <u>ウ quite difficult</u>, but I'm not <u>エ worried</u>.

(2)　The orangutan's hands and feet are designed <u>ア for</u> holding and grasping branches, and its <u>イ powerful immensely</u> arms enable it <u>ウ to</u> climb and swing in trees <u>エ without difficulty</u>.

(3)　The butcher should not <u>ア have been</u> so careless <u>イ as</u> to leave the door of the house unbolted <u>ウ when</u> he <u>エ had gone</u> to bed.

(4)　We are not <u>ア sure if</u> <u>イ what</u> <u>ウ that means</u> to the members <u>エ that voted</u>.

(5)　Long <u>ア thought of as</u> <u>イ a quiet, stuffy place</u> where <u>ウ people</u> just borrowed books, libraries <u>エ have been changing</u> their images dramatically over the last few years.

(☆☆☆◎◎◎)

【8】次の(1)(2)の英文において〔　　〕内の語(句)を正しく並びかえて文章を完成するとき,〔　　〕内の語(句)の4番目と7番目にくる語(句)を, それぞれ1つ選び記号で答えなさい。

(1)　I〔ア song / イ this / ウ without / エ cannot / オ father / カ being / キ my / ク reminded / ケ of / コ sing〕.

(2)　Nobody〔ア than / イ comes / ウ knows / エ to / オ it /

カ　when / キ　brother / ク　fishing / ケ　my / コ　more].

(☆☆〇〇〇)

【9】次の英文において空欄(1)～(3)に入る最も適当な語(句)を，ア～エの中からそれぞれ1つ選び記号で答えなさい。

Suddenly, there bursts forth the wild scream of a (1) _____ woman. I knew that it was my sister's voice, I rushed into the corridor. By the light of the corridor lamp, I saw my sister at the door of her room, her face (2) _____ and her hands groping for help and her whole figure (3) _____ unsteadily.

(1)　ア　exciting　　イ　rejoicing　　ウ　talented　　エ　terrified

(2)　ア　shining with makeup　　イ　glowing happiness

　　　ウ　pale with terror　　エ　worn out

(3)　ア　swaying　　イ　dancing　　ウ　balancing　　エ　loitering

(☆☆☆〇〇〇)

【10】次の英文を読み，あとの各問いに対する答えとして最も適当なものを1つ選び答えなさい。

Traveling can be tricky for newbie. If you want to take a trip to a new place abroad or a place which is far away from where you live, you may need to make a good plan in order to avoid troubles during the trip. So once you know where you want to go, you should decide when and how you are going to go there.

Many people take a trip during holidays because that is the time when they can take a break from work, or studies. Unfortunately, traveling during holiday season may not be a good choice as prices for flight tickets and hotel rooms are usually higher than the off-season period when tourism is not booming. If you have a limited budget, you may consider taking a day off work during the off-season when prices are lower and discounted.

Your budget will also determine which means of transportation you are going to use. Taking a road trip might be cheaper, but you should be in good shape and prepare your car for a long trip. If you choose to fly, you may have to take public transportation to get around in your holiday destination. Whether you take a taxi, a subway or a bus, you should know where you are going based on the itinerary that you have planned before and make sure you know the routes and the fares.

Next, calculate your costs. What kind of accommodation do you want? If you take a road trip, you may prefer to stay in a motel. Hostels are cheaper, but today you can search online and find hotels offering rooms with low rates. If the costs are more than you can afford, make cuts where you can. You may cut expenses for eating out or even cut the trip short and get back before the holiday season ends.

Once you are exactly sure of where and when you want to go, how you will get there and where you are going to stay, make your reservations. You can book your flight and accommodation online. Many attractions even have ticket sales online so you can skip the lines and enjoy the attraction right in. You may also consider taking travel insurance. You will have some protection in case you could not travel during the time your tickets are booked for. If you plan to travel internationally, keep your passport, travel documents, visas and similar items in one place to ease you in accessing them.

Lastly, pack light. Heavy luggage will only restrict your movement and cause discomfort. A few basic shirts and pants or shorts will <u>do</u> and roll them when packing to save room for souvenirs.

(1)　When is the best time to take a cheap trip?
　　ア　During the day off.
　　イ　During the off-season.
　　ウ　During the holiday season.
　　エ　During the peak period.

(2)　What is the advantage of taking a road trip compared to flying?
　　ア　A road trip is longer.
　　イ　A road trip is usually safe.
　　ウ　A road trip is usually cheaper.

エ A road trip requires you to be in good shape.

(3) If your budget for accommodation is very limited, you can do the following, EXCEPT:

ア Cut your trip short.

イ Find a low rate hotel room.

ウ Stay in a hostel.

エ Sleep in the open.

(4) According to the author, what is travel insurance for?

ア To give protection when traveling.

イ To protect your health during the trip.

ウ To give protection if you lose your luggage.

エ To give protection if you should cancel your booking.

(5) Which is the closest meaning to the underlined word "do" in the last paragraph?

ア suffice

イ supply

ウ bring

エ take

(6) Why should you take light luggage?

ア To save your energy.

イ To restrict your movement.

ウ To make moving around easier.

エ To make space for camping equipment.

(☆☆○○○○)

【11】 次の英文を読み，あとの各問いに対する答えとして最も適当なものを1つ選び記号で答えなさい。

Comprehensive lifestyle changes including a better diet and more exercise can lead not only to a better physique, but also to swift and dramatic changes at the genetic level, U.S. researchars said on Monday. In a small study, the researchers tracked 30 men with low-risk prostate cancer who decided against conventional medical treatment such as sugery, radiation or hormone therapy.

The men underwent three months of major lifestyle changes, including eating a diet rich in fruits, vegetables, whole grains, legumes and soy products, moderate exercise such as walking for half an hour a day, and an hour of daily stress management methods such as meditation. As expected, they lost weight, lowered their blood pressure and saw other health improvements. But the researchers found more profound changes when they compared prostate biopsies taken before and after the lifestyle changes. After three months, the men had changes in activity in about 500 genes—including 48 that were turned on and 453 genes that were turned off. The activity of disease-preventing genes increased while a number of disease-promoting genes, including those involved in prostate cancer and breast cancer, shut down, according to the study published in the journal Proceedings of the National Academy of Sciences.

The research was led by Dr. Dean Ornish, head of the Preventive Medicine Research Institute in Sausalito, California, and a well-known auther advocating lifestyle changes to improve health."It's an exciting finding because so often people say, 'Oh, it's all in my genes, what can I do?' Well, it turns out you may be able to do a lot," Ornish, who is also affiliated with the University of California, San Francisco, said in a telephone interview." 'In just three months, I can change hundreds of my genes simply by changing what I eat and how I live?' That's pretty exciting," Ornish said. "The implications of our study are not limited to men with prostate cancer."

(1)　Which of the following does the article basically state about a healthy lifestyle?

ア　It is good for the environment.

イ　It has no effect on your genes.

ウ　It can alter your genes for the better.

エ　It can lead to daily stress management methods.

(2) Which of the following is mentioned about the men in the study apart from eating healthy food and exercising?

ア They had undergone medical surgery for three months.

イ They were taught stress management methods.

ウ They were under a lot of stress.

エ They were given half an hour for meditation.

(3) How many genes, approximately, changed as a result of the healthy lifestyle in total?

ア 500.

イ 453.

ウ 48.

エ 30.

(4) What happened to some of the disease-promoting genes?

ア There was a very little change in their activity.

イ There was very little change in their number.

ウ The number of the genes decreased.

エ Their activify decreased.

(5) Which of the following is NOT mentioned in the article?

ア The men in the study lost weight.

イ The men in the study lowered blood pressure.

ウ The men in the study complained about their genes.

エ Dr. Dean Ornish expressed his optimism about this research in a telephone interview.

(☆☆○○○)

【12】 Read about three students who tried the same task for a month and answer the questions below.

George, 21:After just a few days I understood how difficult the task was. I also began to realize how powerful advertising is. After watching an ad, for a new CD for example, I want to go out and get it! To stop

253

myself buying things I tried not to watch TV — there are just too many ads. However, I bought some magazines and books — so that ［　ア　］！ I love going to the movies, but I saved money by watching DVDs at home.

My friends often asked me out, and I couldn't say no for a whole month. Once we went ten-pin bowling and I spent a bit of cash that evening. 〈　A　〉 I also had to buy a prepaid card for my cell, my alarm clock needed new batteries, and I had a haircut, too. The total I spent was $ 180.

Sandra, 23:When I'm (　あ　) it's not too bad, but it's difficult with friends because they always want to go shopping. The first two weekends were hard;the last two weekends were (　い　)! I used my credit card to buy clothes — tops, a skirt and two pairs of shoes. I also bought myself another pair of jeans. I know I don't need another pair, but they looked so nice. Then I paid for a jacket to go with the jeans, and some more sandals. I needed some shampoo, but I bought loads of make-up at the same time.

My favorite band was also playing in concert and so I went to see them with my friends — I couldn't stop myself. Unfortunately, the price of the tickets was quite high because we wanted good seats but it was worth it. 〈　B　〉 Of course I didn't have to go — but I love films!

Then it was my best friend's birthday, and so of course I had to buy her a present. I also went to the hairdresser before the party. So now at the end of the month, I see I have spent quite a lot of money. 〈　C　〉 I'm a little taken aback, especially as I was trying not to spend anything! My total was $ 900.

Benjamin, 19:There are just many people trying to make you buy things! Advertising is the worst, of course — not just on TV but also while waiting for a bus, in magazines, in shops. It's difficult to (う) it. To help me not buy anything unnecessary I asked myself, "Do I nead this? Do I really want this? ☐ イ ☐ if I buy this?" Of course, the answer was always "no". I didn't have to buy anything really. I could always do without.

I like music, so it was hard not to buy any new CDs, but I decided to listen to all the ones I don't play anymore—and in fact there are quite a lot. So listening to them made me feel I had something new. I didn't waste money buying clothes either—〈 D 〉 I watched my favorite DVDs yet again instead of going lo the movies. My sister cut my hair and I could borrow books and magazines from friends. My total for the month was $20.

(1) Choose the best word or phrase from among the four choices for each blank, (あ)～(う). Write the number of the answewer.

あ ① in a good mood　　② in despair　　③ on my own
　 ④ in a hurry

い ① possible　　② imposible　　③ much better　　④ so-so

う ① afford　　② accept　　③ produce　　④ ignore

(2) Complete the sentence in ☐ ア ☐ and ☐ イ ☐ so that passage will make sense. Fill in each blank below within 10 words.

ア :However, I bought some magazines and books—so that _____ !

イ : _____ if I buy this!

(3) Choose the best place for ①～③ below to put in from 〈 A 〉, 〈 B 〉, 〈 C 〉, and 〈 D 〉. Write the alphabet of the answer.

① I also went to the movies a few times.

② I realize I've got enough at the moment.

③ It's difficult to find activities to do that don't cost anything.

(4) Which of the following sentence is NOT true in the passage? Write the number of the answer.

① All of them did something to take care of their hair during the month.

② Both George and Benjamin found that advertisement was strong enough to make them buy something unnecessary.

③ Benjamin thinks his CDs he doesn't usually listen to helped prevent him from buying new CDs.

④ Sandra spent a lot of money, but she could save more money than she usually does.

(5) What seems to be the task they all tried to achieve during the month? Choose the best phrase which describes their task correctly.

① the task to try not to spend money on anything

② the task to research on what kind of advertisement is the most effective

③ the task to think about how different the interest in clothes between men and women is

④ the task to report how they made on effort to get along well with their friends

(☆☆○○○○)

【13】 If you could learn one thing about your future, what would you like to ask about? Write a composition about what you are most interested in about your future in Englieh. The composition should be 80 words or more.

(☆☆○○○○)

【14】 授業中に生徒が次の(1)と(2)の質問をしました。あなたは英語の先生としてどのように説明しますか。それぞれについて日本語で答えなさい(説明の一部に英語を交えても差し支えない)。

(1) "If I had my own computer, I could get some information on the Internet"と"If I have my own computer, I can get some information on the Internet."の違いを説明してください。

(2) "I saw a little boy crossing the street by himself."と"I saw a little boy

cross the street by himself."において，ing形を用いる場合と原形を用いる場合，「私」が見た内容はどのように異なりますか。

(☆☆○○○○)

【高等学校】

【 1 】 The following is a part of the research on EFL learners' motivational dynamics at N University in Japan. Referring to the following chart and figure, read the passage and answer the following questions.

Research Questions:

(1)　How do learners explain the factors and processes that resulted in their decision to take (or not to take) LC classes semester by semester?

(2)　How do they explain the ebbs and flows in their motivation over the eight semesters?

(3)　略

Method:

Participants (interviewees)	Ten students (five females and five males) who took and completed *LC classes offered by N University
Style of the interviews	30-70 minute conversation
Preparations	Ask each participant to draw a line on a graph indicating his or her motivational trajectory over the eight semesters
Analysis	① Analyzed the participants' comments into 5 categories: (1)　affective reactions (2)　desire and will (3)　appraisal of LC as a learning situation and appraisal of learner's needs (4)　metacognition of learning (5)　social and contextual factors. ② Used Valsiner's (2007) model to situate each coded experience in three domains: (1)　the microgenetic domain: learners' experiences are mostly superficial and contingent (2)　the mesogenetic domain: learners start to find that their experiences in LC classes are meaningful to their lives. (3)　the ontogenetic domain: learners' value, thought patterns and habits as users of English are deeply internalized in them

*LC classes: a semester-long non-credit English program (mostly oral-aural) offered by N University in Japan in an on-campus language institute open to all students wishing to take extra lessons.

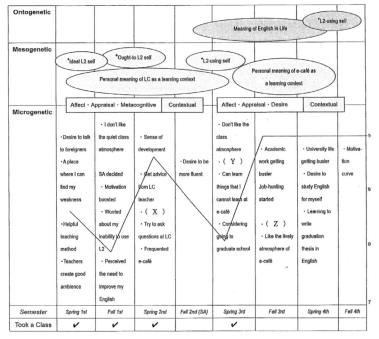

Figure 18.3

*L2: the second language

*Ideal L2 self: Learners are imagining their highest goal as users of the second language.

*Ought-to L2 self: Learners are thinking that they ought to reach to a certain level in using their second language.

*L2-using self: Learners are actually using their second language for their own purpose.

Aya's comments, coded and categorized, are summarized in Table 18.3.

Figure 18.3 shows her attendance at the LC and her motivational curve, with open-coded comments placed along the timeline.

Aya's comments include a large amount of metacognitive talk, which shows that she (ア) her learning and the progress she has made. In the spring semester of her first year in college, she regarded the LC as a place where she could practice speaking and (イ) (Appraisal, Metacognitive). She also appreciated the teaching method as well as the way the teacher made it easier for the participants to speak up by sometimes switching to Japanese (Appraisal, Affect). She decided to apply for a study abroad (SA) program in October of her first year, and later that year she was selected to be a member of such a group (Contextual). This decision boosted her motivation but also made her worry about her English level, as can be seen in her comments, ' [_____A_____] '(Metacognitive). This realization motivated her to study hard, her attendance at the LC triggered by her ought-to L2 self. This ought-to L2 self was categorized in the mesogenetic domain together with the personal meaning of LC as a learning place.

With the ought-to self emergent at the mesogenetic level, her seriousness about learning is reflected in her metacognitive comments, which increased in frequency in the spring semester of her second year. Also, effort seemed to begin to pay, as seen in her comments: 'I was able to say a sentence in response to questions', and 'I was able to understand what the teacher was asking'. As regards the different functions of LC and *e-café, she said, 'I learn what I can do and what I cannot do at LC. [_____B_____] . I then put the advice into practice at e-café'. She gradually frequented e-café more often and became a familiar face there.

Aya is one of the most highly motivated learners among the interviewees. She is also the one who seemed to have at least some vague vision of her ideal L2 self even at an early stage. She related an episode in her high school days about meeting an *NS instructor working in the school where her mother was an English teacher. [_____< I >_____] We therefore entered the ideal L2 self, formed at an early stage in her learning, in the mesogenetic domain.

Figure 18.3 shows that Aya's self-perceived motivation rose in the fall of her third year in the maximum possible level and (　ウ　), indicating that the motivational system might be in an attractor state. Nevertheless she stopped attending LC classes. In her third year, following the period of SA, her appraisal of the LC became rather negative, as her comments reveal: '[　　　C　　　]' (Affect), 'In the class, we just watched movies and we were asked questions about the phrases used in the movie, which I thought I could do by myself'(Appraisal and Affect (dissatisfaction)), and 'I would rather have discussions'(Desire). After returning from SA, the LC (　エ　) for Aya. Instead, the e-café emerged as an alternative that filled the gap between her needs and what the LC could offer, even though she perceived that in some LC classes there were discussion sessions on given topics, something e-café did not offer. Thus, we entered the personal meaning of e-café in the mesogenetic domain in Figure 18.3. Comparing the two learning contexts, there was constant appraisal of what was being taught and how useful it was to her. Here, we see her agency in maintaining an optimum learning environment, a learner able to (　オ　) and adapt her learning in ways she believes to be appropriate.

Aya's SA experience seems to have (　カ　) her attitude toward English, resulting in greater motivation to further improve her English writing and speaking through a realization that '[　　　D　　　]'and a feeling of a 'desire to learn English coming from within myself'. In her third year, she chose to enrol in a seminar in the law faculty that required her to write a thesis in English. This gave her renewed interest in learning academic English and made her realize that there was a great deal to learn, wishing to 'learn English for my own self, not because I had to'. Thanks to advice from good English teachers, she felt a sense of improvement as an L2 writer. Attending this seminar and interacting with teachers in this learning situation changed her outlook on learning English as she learned in greater depth about the language and its structure. Thus, we feel that the meaning of English, or her L2-using self, solidified in her life. We therefore placed it in the ontogenetic domain in part because we sense that this L2 self will remain with her as a meaning structure that will guide her to $<$ Ⅱ $>$ <u>study and use English for some time to come, possibly throughout her life.</u>

> *e-café: a coffee lounge in N University where several native speakers of English can always be found as conversational partners

> *NS instructor: instructor whose mother tongue is English

(1) Choose the best phrase from among the choices for (ア)～(カ). Write the number of the answer.

  ① constantly checks

  ② cultivate learning contexts

  ③ identify her weak points in her English

  ④ lost significance

  ⑤ qualitatively changed

  ⑥ was maintained at that level

(2) Choose the beat statement from among the choices for ☐ A ～ ☐ D . Write the number of the answer.

  ① I can ask teachers questions and the teachers give me advice for improving further

  ② I didn't feel comfortable with the atmosphere in the LC class because many students were just waiting to be called upon

  ③ I was not good enough

  ④ I was shocked to find myself unable to speak or listen to English

(3) Put the following sentences in order so that the part ☐ $<$ Ⅰ $>$ ☐ will make sense.

  ① Although she was not able to say much, she remembers the encounter as the frustrating but joyful experience of trying to communicate in English.

  ② Her dream in high school was to work for an international

organization, such as the World Health Organization.

③　This early image of her future self, combined with her mother's influence (among other factors), helped her self-organize her learning behavior toward taking LC classes and applying for study abroad.

④　This episode sowed a seed of desire to communicate in English fluently, and this has remained with her ever since.

(4)　Among the four choices, choose the sentence that is most accurately mentioned in the passage.

①　An LC class Aya participated in in the spring semester of her first year prohibited students from speaking in Japanese.

②　None of the LC classes in N University offered any opportunity of discussion, which students could experience at e-café.

③　In Aya's third year, she was too busy working in the law faculty to continue to study English.

④　Through learning how to write a thesis in English, Aya stopped thinking that she had to study English and instead started to have a new purpose and interest of studying English.

(5)　Among the three choices, choose the best statement that should be put into (　X　), (　Y　), and (　Z　) in figure 18.3.

①　Choose e-café for its flexibility

②　Learn what I can do and cannot

③　Unsatisfied with the class content

(6)　Referring to the underlined part ＜ Ⅱ ＞, what do you think JTEs can do to help their students to imagine their future when they use English and study English throughout their lives? Write your idea within 50 words.

(☆☆☆◎◎◎)

【２】Read the passage and answer the questions below.

The first words I heard in English were from my grandmother Ilse Gamez, who I remember as 7a magical presence in my childhood. Everything about her seemed legendary to me. Among the stories she used to tell, my favorites were about her life in New Orleans, where she and her family arrived from Europe and where she spent her childhood until she was 14, when they set sail again, bound for Nicaragua, fulfilling her parents' wish to return definitively to their country of origin. Her stories of New Orleans were filled with references and names in English (frequently also in French), and those mysterious words, so different from the ones I heard in everyday speech, produced in me an irresistible fascination. They sounded like strange music, an exotic melody coming from faraway fantastic places where life had an agitation, a rhythm, an acceleration unknown and unheard-of in the peaceful world I shared with my parents, sisters, and brothers. We were all part of an enormous family that included grandparents, great-aunts, great-uncles, uncles, aunts, and first cousins, as well as a second and third level of blood relatives, followed immediately by all the other people in the category of relatives included in the family universe and its state of perpetual expansion.

The English I heard from my grandmother Ilse had nothing to do with ₍the English I was taught in kindergarten₎ through songs teaching us to count from one to ten, or the language that appeared in the English textbooks we studied in the second and third grade of primary school:"See Dick. See Jane. See Spot. See Puff. See Spot run. See Puff jump."For me, that English lacked charm, instead sounding like the noise of my shoes crunching in the gravel of the schoolyard during recess. But that other English, the one my grandmother and her sister spoke, possessed multiple and varied registers that always amazed me. Sometimes it sounded like the trill of a bird, light and crystalline, and at other times flowed in dense, thick amber like honey. It would rise in high notes with the lonely, nostalgic sound of a flute, or swirl in a whirlpool like the frenzied crowds I imagined rushing around the streets of a big metropolis…

Before long, my ears began to discern another way of speaking the language. It was not the cryptic and fantastic English full of attractions and mystery that I loved to listen to, nor the tiresome, repetitious one that sounded like a cart struggling over cobbled streets. No, this other English expressed things in a different way that was not enigmatic and seductive, nor dumb and monotonous, but dramatic and direct: whatever the characters said, happened simultaneously. For example, a character that was evidently crying, would say:"I'm crying."Another one, obviously hiding something, would declare:"I'll hide this!"

It was the English I started to learn from cartoons on television, where the characters expressed thoughts, emotions, and feelings in a straightforward way:"Out! Help! Stop it! Don't go away! I'll be back! Let's go!"I learned phrases and words that communicated necessity in a fast, precise manner. The language of cartoons also introduced me to metaphors. The first time I heard characters in a downpour shouting their heads off with the phrase"The sky is falling, the sky is falling!" I believed it was the proper way to say in English,"It's a downpour,"or " ウ ."

I had no choice but to learn yet another kind of English from cowboy movies, because my cousins constantly used it in their games. Also, in a mechanical ways, I learned by heart the English names for all the plays in baseball, the most popular sport in Nicaragua.

Gradually, the English that was so dull to me in the first grade of school expanded and deepened, with readings transforming it into a beautiful language that kept growing inside, becoming more and more a part of my consciousness, invading my thoughts and appearing in my dreams. Understanding the language and speaking it in a natural way became integral to my being, my way of appreciating literature, especially poetry, and enjoying the lyrics of my favorite songs, which I was able to repeat perfectly.

Literature classes were my favorite. To act as a character in any of Shakespeare's plays, or to read an O. Henry short story out loud to my classmates, or a chapter of Robert Luis Stevenson's *Treasure Island*, or a sonnet by Elizabeth Barrett Browning, brightened my day. At the school library, I discovered, among other authors, Walt Whitman, Emily Dickenson, and Edna St. Vincent Millay, then Carl Sandburg and William Carlos Williams. Further along, I encountered William Blake, the sisters Brontë, Jane Austen, and Ernest Hemingway. Years later, while at university, I read the Americans William Faulkner, Ezra Pound, and Gertrude Stein, and the Irish authors William Butler Yeats and James Joyce.

(中略)

But my true encounter with living English (that is, the one spoken in everyday life) happened in the United States, where I went to spend my school vacations in Middletown, Connecticut. (中略) However, what is most deeply imprinted in my memory of that first visit to the U.S. is the shock I received from the language I had believed I understood and spoke correctly.

Almost immediately, I realized that my English, that is, the English through which I expressed myself, sounded strange to everybody. My cousins, not to mention their friends, listened to me with surprise or mocking looks. In turn, their English was almost unintelligible to me because they spoke, of course, in teenage slang. When one of my cousins couldn't stand it anymore, she told me that I was a weirdo, that _(ア)I spoke like a philosopher, some sort of Socrates or something, and asked me to make an effort to try to talk like normal people so I could make some friends. She didn't have a clue about the extreme anguish I was going through trying to understand what was being said around me, trying to decipher everything I misunderstood, assuming one thing for another. Desolate, I thought about the abundant literature I had read up to then, and the songs I had worked so hard to memorize. It was all worthless for learning to speak practical English that would help me establish bonds with boys and girls my own age. On the contrary, the vocabulary I learned from books, especially from the poetry that taught me to love the language, had no place in the everyday speech of my contemporaries.

To be accepted by everybody, I started paying extreme attention to how I expressed myself and to the words I chose. I anxiously searched for ways to adapt my way of speaking, imitating what I heard from others, so I wouldn't be excluded from their conversations or activities. I understood that if I didn't do that, I would _オ<u>be left on the fringes of the main current, the mainstream</u> where all U.S. teenagers lived, with space only for themselves. The barrier was not easy to cross, and when I couldn't do it, my consolation was to take refuge in the library of the house, where I read, during that first vacation, an English translation of Fyodor Dostoevsky's *Crime and Punishment*.

I was 14 years old when I went to the States for the first time—the same age as my grandmother Ilse when she watched New Orleans fade into the distance from the deck of a steamship—and ever since then I've understood what it means to live in direct contact with a language through the people who speak it, through their culture, and through their vision of the world.

(1)　Among the four choices, choose the best phrase which correctly describes the writer's feelings towards her grandmother in the underlined part ア. Write the number of the answer.

① 　fear and suspicion

② 　anger and despise

③ 　strangeness and curiosity

④ 　warmth and respect

(2)　Among the four choices, choose the best sentence which describes the underlined part イ. Write the number of the answer.

① 　It didn't attract the writer's attention.

② 　It sounded like a bird's singing.

③ 　It included various styles of speech.

④ 　It was neither monotonous nor dramatic.

(3)　Fill in the blank ウ within five words so that the sentence makes sense.

(4)　Among the four choices, choose the best sentence which describes the reason for the underlined part エ. Write the number of the answer.

① 　The writer imitated her grandmother's way of speaking English.

② 　The writer's ability to speak English was just to be able to communicate necessity fast and precisely.

③ The writer's way of speaking English was mainly based on literature.

④ Kindergarten and primary school didn't teach the writer practical English.

(5) Among the four choices, choose the best sentence which describes the underlined part オ. Write the number of the answer.

① The writer would completely belong to the writer's big family including a lot of relatives.

② The writer would not be accepted by the group of teenagers around her.

③ The writer would be indifferent about what's going on in the world and fall behind the times.

④ The writer would try hard to look better and cleverer than she really needed to.

(6) Among the four choices, choose the sentence that is most accurately mentioned in the passage. Write the number of the answer.

① The writer's grandmother left Nicaragua for the United States with her parents when she was 14 years old.

② Nothing about English which the writer learned in primary school let her realize the importance of the language at all.

③ The writer was suffering from poor communication between her and the people around her, and one of her cousins didn't know the pain the writer was feeling.

④ The writer didn't make any effort to get along well with her relatives and their friends and just spent her time reading her favorite books to escape from reality.

(7) Find the place where the following sentences should be put in the passage. Write the two words right before the place they should be put in.

That is to say, a word was an act; words and action occurred at the same time. An activity was named at the very moment it took place.

(8)　Write your opinion about teaching English through literature written in English.

It should　1)　include advantages and disadvantages with specific reasons or details to support your opinion.

2)　include the arguments which are found in the passage.

3)　have 150-200 words.

(☆☆☆◎◎◎◎)

解答・解説

【中高共通】

【１】Conversation 1　B　　Conversation 2　A　　Conversation 3　D
Conversation 4　B

〈解説〉男女間の2～4回のやり取りを聞いて，読みあげられる選択肢で答える形式。質問も「男性は息子にどうして欲しいと思っているか」，「女性は次に何をするだろうか」など，対話の流れを理解することで容易に解答することができる。ただし放送は1度のみなので，聞き逃しがないように気をつけなければならない。

【２】Passage 1　Question 1　A　　Question 2　D
Passage 2　Question 1　A　　Question 2　B

〈解説〉120語程度のアナウンスを聞いて，印刷されている選択肢で答える形式。放送は1度のみで，パッセージ1つにつき，質問が2つである。イベントのキャンセルや変更点を正確に聞き取ることが求められている。

【３】Conversation 1　Question 1　A　　Question 2　D
Conversation 2　Question 1　C　　Question 2　B

〈解説〉男女間の4～5回のやり取りを聞いて，印刷されている選択肢で答える形式。放送は1度のみで，対話文1つにつき，質問が2つである。問題【1】に比べて，対話が長くなり，語彙や話題が難しくなっているので，やや難度が上がっている。「男性が抱える主な問題は何か」や「それに対する女性のアドバイスは何か」など概要に関する質問が主である。

【4】新しい仕事で成功するためには，まず雇用者のやり方で主体的に仕事をして雇用者を喜ばせると良い。社内での駆け引きでは，議論のどちらか一方の味方をすべきではない。服装は常にビジネスに適したものにし，口が堅く，信用に足る人物であることを示すべきだ。自分がプロであること，つまり責任感があり，成熟し，献身的で働き者であり，生産的であろうと努めていることを雇用者にわかってもらえれば，目をかけてもらえるだろう。(199字)

〈解説〉428語からなる記事を聞いて，要旨を150～200字の日本語で記述する形式。放送は2度流れるが，記述に与えられている時間は6分である。指定語数でまとめるには，基本的には，メインアイディア，展開部，まとめの文の構成とし，展開部の長さを調整しながら書き始めることになるであろう。英文を聞き取る力もさることながら，短時間で，書き留めた情報を取捨選択し，文章を構成する力も求められており，かなり難度の高い出題である。150～200字を6分でまとめる文字量や制限時間の感覚をつかむために，相当練習をしておく必要がある。

【5】(1) ア (2) イ (3) ウ (4) ウ (5) エ (6) エ (7) イ (8) ア (9) エ (10) イ

〈解説〉(1)「この帽子は青いドレスに合わない」。go with ～「～と調和する」。suit ～「～に似合う」。 (2)「ネットで注文した品物は数日で届くはずだ」。be expected to ～「～すると予想される」。 (3)「注文書のコピーをもらうまで注文を処理することができない」。 (4)「私たちが経験した悪天候にもかかわらず，ハワイでの休暇を楽しんだ」。

despite 〜は前置詞で,「〜にもかかわらず」。althoughは接続詞。

(5)「日本からマイアミへの利用可能な直行便はない」。available「利用できる」は後置修飾する場合も多い。　(6)「あなたが新しいと言ったそのホテルは, 今年の末までに開業10年になる」。未来完了形。主語にあたる部分では, 関係代名詞の直後にyou saidが挿入されている。

(7)「コマーシャル製作者は過熱した住宅市場の懸念を軽視した」。concern about 〜「〜に関わる心配, 不安」。　(8)「観客は総立ちで彼女に感謝した。コンサートがもう少しでキャンセルされるところだったということを考えると一層それは注目に値した」。all the more「いよいよ, さらに」。　(9)「洗濯機が故障したのでコインランドリーに行くつもりだ」。break down「故障する」。　(10)「メイン州は他の多くの州よりひんやりした気温である」。than以下は, most other states have (cool temperature)である。

【6】(1)　ア　　(2)　ウ　　(3)　エ　　(4)　エ　　(5)　イ
〈解説〉(1)　procrastinate 〜「〜を引きのばす」。　(2)　squander 〜「〜を浪費する」。　(3)　susceptible「影響を受けやすい」。　(4)　be blown away「感動する, 驚く」。　(5)　intense「集中した, 激しい」。

【7】(記号, 語(句)の順)(1)　ア, My friends say　　(2)　イ, immensely powerful　　(3)　エ, went　　(4)　ア, sure　　(5)　イ, quiet, stuffy places
〈解説〉(1)　tellがthat節を伴う場合, 通例tell＋O＋that 〜となる。

(2)「非常に力強い腕は, オランウータンを難なく木に登らせぶら下がらせる」。immenselyは副詞でpowerfulを修飾する。　(3)「その肉屋の主人は寝る時に家のドアのかんぬきをはずしたままにするような不注意であるべきでなかった」。when節内は過去時制が適切。　(4)「私たちは投票したメンバーにとってそれが何を意味するのか分からない」。

(5)「(図書館は)人々がただ本を借りる静かで風通しの息苦しい場所と長く考えられていたが」。librariesが主語なのでplaceを複数形とする。

【8】(1)　4番目…ア　　7番目…ク　　(2)　4番目…ケ　　7番目…オ

〈解説〉(1)　整序すると，cannot sing this song without being reminded of my
fatherとなる。「私はこの歌を歌うと必ず父を思い出す」。　(2)　整序
すると，knows more than my brother when it comes to fishingとなる。「釣
りのことになると，私の兄ほど詳しい者はいない」。

【9】(1)　エ　　(2)　ウ　　(3)　ア

〈解説〉(1)　「突然おびえた女性の激しい叫び声が聞こえた」。　(2)　「彼
女の顔は恐怖で青ざめ」。　(3)　「彼女の全身はゆらゆらと揺れて」。

【10】(1)　イ　　(2)　ウ　　(3)　エ　　(4)　エ　　(5)　ア　　(6)　ウ

〈解説〉(1)　「安価で旅行をするのに一番良い時はいつか」。第2段落の最
後の文より，イ「オフシーズンの間」が正解。　(2)　「飛行機旅行に比
べ，車での旅行の利点は何か」。第3段落の1文目より，ウ「たいてい
車での旅行の方が安い」が正しい。　(3)　宿泊予算が限られているな
ら，ア「旅行を縮める」，イ「安価のホテルの部屋を探す」，ウ「ホス
テルに泊まる」ことができる。エ「野外で寝る」は記述がない。
(4)　「筆者によると旅行保険は何のためか」。第5段落の5文目より，エ
「万が一予約をキャンセルすることになれば，補償されるから」。
(5)　下線部を含む文意は「数枚の基本的なシャツと長ズボンまたは短
パンがあれば間に合う」。do「役に立つ，間に合う」。suffice「十分で
ある」。　(6)「なぜ軽い鞄を持って行くべきか」。第6段落の2文目より，
ウ「動き回ることを容易にするため」。

【11】(1)　ウ　　(2)　イ　　(3)　ア　　(4)　エ　　(5)　ウ

〈解説〉(1)　「健康的なライフスタイルについてこの記事は基本的に次の
どれを述べているか」。第1段落の1文目より，ウ「遺伝子をよりよい
方向に変える」。　(2)　「研究中の男性について，健康的な食事をした
り運動したりすることを除いて，次のどれが述べられているか」。第2
段落の1文目より，イ「ストレス管理の方法を教えられた」。

(3)　「すべての健康的なライフスタイルの結果として，およそいくつの遺伝子が変化したか」。第2段落の4文目より，ア「500」。　(4)　「病気を促進する遺伝子に何が起きたか」。第2段落の5文目より，エ「活動が衰えた」。　(5)　「記事に述べられていないことはどれか」。第2段落の2文目に，ア「研究中の男性は体重が減った」とイ「研究中の男性は血圧が下がった」は述べられている。最終段落の最後の2文に，エ「ディーン・オーニッシュ博士は電話インタビューの中で，この研究について楽観論を述べた」も述べられている。

【12】(1)　あ　③　　い　②　　う　④　　(2)　ア　I could read instead of watching TV (7words) / I could do without watching TV(6words)　から1つ　　イ　Will my life be better(5words) / Do I really use it(5words)　から1つ　　(3)　①　B　　②　D　　③　A　　(4)　④　　(5)　①

〈解説〉(1)　あ　「私が一人の時は，そんなに悪くないが，友達が一緒だと難しい。なぜならいつも買い物に行きたくなるからだ」。with friendsと対比されている。　い　「最初の2週間は大変だった。後半の2週間は不可能だった」。最終的にサンドラはかなりのお金を使ったことから，②「impossible」が正解。　う　「それ(広告)を無視することは難しい」。
(2)　ア　雑誌や本を買ったのは「広告がたくさんあるTVを見ないため」という種の内容にする。　イ　物を買う時に"Do I need this?"などと自問している場面にふさわしいせりふを入れる。
(3)　①　「私は数回映画に行った」。映画に行ってしまったというサンドラの空欄Bが適切。　②　「今のところ十分(服を)持っていると気づいた」。「服を買ってお金を無駄にすることもなかった」に続く文として，空欄Dが適切。　③　「全くお金がかからない活動を見つけることは難しい」。「一度ボウリングに行って，その晩少しお金を使った」に続く文として，空欄Aが適切。　(4)　サンドラが「特にお金を使わないようにしていたので，(たくさん使って)私は少し驚いている」と言っていることから，④「サンドラはたくさんのお金を使ったが，いつもよりはお金を節約できた」は誤り。　(5)　①「何にでもお金を使わ

ないようにするタスク」が正解。

【13】 If I could ask about my future, the question would be something about my
health. I want to know what kind of disease or injury I would get, and I would
give my full attention to something I should be doing now. I would consider
what kind of food I should be having or avoiding, how much exercise I should
be doing, what I should be careful of not to get the injury and so on. I think
health is the most important thing, so I would ask about my health and want to
learn what I should be doing now.(101 words)

〈解説〉設問は「自分の将来について1つ知ることができるとしたら，ど
んなことについて尋ねたいか，80語以上で書け」というもの。解答例
では，最初の文で1つ話題を挙げ，2，3文目に詳細を，4文目で締めく
くっている。80語であれば4～5文程度を目安にまとめられる。

【14】(1) 前者は，私は「コンピュータを持っていない」ことを示して
いるが，後者は「現在手元にない」ことだけを示しており，実際には
コンピュータを持っているのかどうかは伝わらない。 (2) ing形
は「行動の一部を偶然見た」という意味で用い，原形では「一部始終
(行動の完了まで)見た」という意味になる。

〈解説〉(1) 前者は仮定法なので，裏にI don't have my own computerとい
う現在の事実が隠れていることになる。 (2) 他の知覚動詞でも，知
覚動詞＋O＋現在分詞と知覚動詞＋O＋動詞の原形では同様の違いが
ある。

【高等学校】

【1】(1) ア ① イ ③ ウ ⑥ エ ④ オ ②
カ ⑤ (2) A ④ B ① C ② D ③ (3) ①→④
→②→③ (4) ④ (5) X ② Y ③ Z ①
(6) (例1) In class we can set the situation where students actually use
English in their future such as writing a résumé in English. Such activity is

very useful for them to think that they need English when they want to get a certain job. (43 words)　　　(例2)　We can introduce people who are working all over the world to your students. Such people often appear in the textbooks. By learning about them, students can easily understand that the people are successful partly because they have good command of English. (42 words)

〈解説〉(1)　ア　アヤのコメントが何を示しているかを問うている部分。①「それは彼女が自身の学習や成しえた進歩を絶えずチェックしていることを示している」。　イ　大学1年の春学期に彼女はLCの授業をどのように見ていたかが問われている。③「スピーキングの練習ができて，自身の英語の弱点を確認できるところだと見ていた」。　ウ　3年の秋学期にアヤ自身が感じるモチベーションがどうだったが問いにあたる。⑥「最大可能レベルにまで上昇し，そのレベルで持続した」。　エ　SA後，アヤの学習環境に対する変化として，④「アヤにとってLCは意味を失った」。　オ　最適な学習環境について述べている件。②「学習者が学習環境を作り，適切だと信じる方法で学習を適応させる」。　カ　SA後，英語に対する態度について，⑤「SAの経験は英語に対する態度を質的に変化させた」。　(2)　Aは，1年生の秋学期のコメントを参照。「この決定は彼女のモチベーションを高めたが，A『自分が英語を話したり聞いたりできないことに気づきショックを受けた』というコメントにも見られるように，自身の英語レベルを心配させることにもなった」。　Bは，2年生の秋学期のコメントを参照。前後の文意は「LCとe-caféの異なる機能に関して，彼女は『LCで自分ができることとできないことを知る。先生に質問をすることができ，先生はさらに進歩するために自分に助言をくれる。そして私はその助言をe-caféで実行に移す』と言った」。　Cは3年生の春学期のコメントを参照。「SA後の3年次にLCへの評価は彼女のコメントC『多くの学生が指名されるのを待っているだけなので，LCの授業の雰囲気が快適に感じられなかった』が示すようにむしろ否定的になった」。　DはSA以降のコメントを参照すると「アヤのSA経験は英語に対する彼女の態度を質的に変化させ，自分の力が十分ではないという自覚や自分自身か

ら湧き上がる英語を学びたいという気持ちから，ライティングやスピーキングを更に伸ばしたいというモチベーションを高める結果となった」。　(3)　アヤの高校時代のエピソードに関わる文章を整序する。③の「この早期のイメージ」や④「このエピソード」という指示語に注目すると，①→④，②→③の組み合わせができる。　(4)　第2段落の3文目より，時々日本語に切り替えて授業が行われていたので，①は誤り。第5段落の4文目より，ディスカッションの機会を提供していたのはLCの授業であったので，②は誤り。第6段落の3文目より，アヤは3年次に法学部のセミナーに参加したので③は誤り。第6段落の3文目より，④「英語で論文をいかに書くかを学ぶことで，アヤは英語を勉強しなければならないと考えることを止め，英語を学ぶ新しい目的と興味を持ち始めた」が正しい。　(5)　第3段落の内容より，Xは②「できることとできないことを知る」。　第5段落の内容より，Yは③「授業内容に不満足」，Zは①「融通性からe-caféを選択」。

(6)「生涯英語を使ったり勉強したりする自分の将来を学生がイメージするのを助けるため，JTEができることは何か」という問い。解答例では，実際に英語を使用する場面を授業で設定することや英語が将来の成功につながる一因になりうると理解させることなどを挙げている。

【2】(1)　④　　(2)　①　　(3)　It's raining ［very hard / heavily］

(4)　③　　(5)　②　　(6)　③　　(7)　happened, simultaneously

(8)　There are two advantages in teaching English through literature written in English. First, students can learn people's way of thinking and their historical background in English-speaking countries. Through literature, they will understand cultural differences that need to be recognized when learning English more easily than through other materials. Second, students can learn various ways of expressions in English as the writer mentions. We will acquire more vocabulary, idioms, and grammatical structures to express ourselves while enjoying literature in our mother tongue, and as a result, we will get better at communicating and our lives will become much richer. However, there are some disadvantages. Like the writer mentions, English in literature is not always the same as the one actually spoken in English-speaking countries today. The older the books are, the greater differences there will be from spoken English. The younger they are, the greater gap there will be between English they speak and the one they read in literature. EFL teachers have to make efforts to get rid of the gap. Students need to learn both English in literature and English used in the real world. Teachers should be careful about the balance of them when they teach English. (199 words)

〈解説〉(1)　文意は「私は祖母を神秘的な存在として思い出す」。筆者の祖母への感情として④「温かく尊敬の念」が適切。　(2)　幼稚園で教えられた英語については，次文でthat English lacked charmと述べている。よって①「それは筆者の注意を引かなかった」が正解。　(3)　It's a downpour.「豪雨だ」を他の表現に言い換える。　(4)　第8段落の1文目「生きた英語に最初に出会ったのは合衆国であった」より，そこで筆者の英語が，生きていない英語，即ち文学の中の英語で，人とは違うと気づいたことがわかる。それが，下線部エ「私はソクラテスか何かの哲学者のように話す」と指摘された理由となる。　(5)　第10段落の1文目に，筆者は合衆国で誰にも受け入れられるように，話し方や使う単語に注意を払ったとある，もしそれをしなければ，オ「本流のはずれに取り残されただろう」という文意から，②「筆者は周囲の十代の若者のグループに受け入れられなかっただろう」が正解。

(6)　第9段落の5文目から，いとこが筆者の苦悩を知らなかったことが分かる。よって③「筆者は自分と自分の周りの人々との上手くいかないコミュニケーションに苦しんでいたが，いとこの1人は筆者の感じている痛みを知らなかった」。have a clue「分かっている」。　(7)　挿入文は「言い換えると，言葉は演技だった。言葉と演技が共起した。行動をするとすぐに，それは名がつけられた(言葉となった)」。第3段落のドラマチックで直接的な英語の記述部分が適切。挿入文の次に「例えば，明らかに泣いている人物は『私は泣いている』と言うだろ

うし，明らかに何かを隠しているまた別の人物は『これを隠そう』と宣言するだろう」と具体的例が来る。　(8)　設問は「英語で書かれた文学を通して英語を教えることについて意見を書け」。解答例では，利点として「人々の物の考え方や歴史的背景を容易に理解することができる」，「様々な英語の表現方法を学ぶことができる」，不利な点として「現代の英語と差異があること」などを挙げ，バランスよく両方を学ばせることが大切だとまとめている。

2018年度　実施問題

【中高共通】

Script

[There are three speaking roles for this test: Directions , Man , and Woman .]

Directions : "Please turn the test paper over. The Listening Comprehension Test will now begin. You may take notes while listening."
＜3 seconds＞

【1】

Directions : "Section A.

Please listen to the following conversations. After each conversation, a question will be asked, and four possible answers will be read. Choose the best answer and circle the corresponding letter on your answer sheet. Each conversation, the question, and the answers will be read only once."
＜2 Seconds＞

Directions : "Conversation 1."
Man : Guess what! I'm on cloud nine.
Woman : Did you win the lottery or something?
Man : I passed the bar exam.
Woman : Congratulations!
＜2 Seconds＞

Directions : "How is the man feeling?"

＜2 Seconds＞

    A.   He is so bummed.

    B.   He is a little tipsy.

    C.   He is in distress.

    D.   He is filled with joy.

＜5 Seconds＞

Directions	:	"Conversation 2."
Woman	:	Oh no! The train is going to be late!
Man	:	What time will it get here?
Woman	:	At a half past three. What's the time now?
Man	:	It's five to three. We'll have to wait another thirty five minutes.

＜2 Seconds＞

| Directions | : | What time will the train arrive? |

＜2 Seconds＞

    A.   At two fifty-five.

    B.   At three fifteen.

    C.   At three thirty.

    D.   At three thirty-five.

＜5 Seconds＞

Directions	:	"Conversation 3."
Woman	:	Excuse me, do you mind if I sit down?
Man	:	No. Let me move my bag.
Woman	:	Thanks. By the way, do you live in the dorm? I think I've seen you there.
Man	:	Yes, I just moved in last week.
Woman	:	I live in the dorm, too.

Man : Oh, really? Do you like it?

Woman : Yeah, it's okay. It takes me about 5 minutes to get to my first class in the morning.

Man : I'm not so lucky. My first class is on the other side of the university. But I've got a bicycle, so it doesn't take too long.

Woman : I've got a bike, too. But I haven't needed it this semester.

Man : Well, this is my stop coming up. By the way, my name's Bob.

Woman : Hi, Bob. I'm Sylvia.

Man : Nice meeting you, Sylvia. I'll probably see you around.

Woman : Okay. Bye, Bob.

＜2 Seconds＞

Directions : What is the last thing the man says to the woman?

＜2 Seconds＞

A.　He says he has to stop seeing her.

B.　He says he will likely see her again.

C.　He says he has to get off the bus.

D.　He says he is going to come by her room.

＜5 Seconds＞

Directions : "Conversation 4."

Woman : Hi Steve. So that was your car I saw. I thought you always ate at the dorm.

Man : Hi Julia. Most of the time I do. But on Fridays and weekends, I like to go out.

Woman : Listen, you want to help me finish my fries? I shouldn't have ordered the large.

Man : Thanks, they look good. Uh, by the way, Julia, can I ask where you're from?

Woman : I'm from Isabela, a town in Puerto Rico. Why?

| Man | : | Well, you speak English fluently, and your Spanish is perfect. |

| Woman | : | I've used both languages ever since I can remember. My parents made sure I attended schools where they spoke English. |

| Man | : | I'd love to be billingual. I've studied Chinese for five years, but I know I'll never speak like a native. |

| Woman | : | Let me ask you something, Steve. Do you ever dream in Chinese? |

| Man | : | Um, yes, I do sometimes. Is that a good sign? |

| Woman | : | It shows that you're making progress. I bet you know more Chinese than you think you do. |

<2 Seconds>

| Directions | : | What does the woman say about the man's Chinese? |

<2 Seconds>

A. He doesn't speak it very well.

B. He already speaks it like a native.

C. He probably speaks it better than he thinks.

D. He will speak it fluently if he practices more.

(☆☆☆○○○)

【2】

| Directions | : | "Section B.

Please listen to the following two passages. After each passage, two questions will be asked. Four possible responses to each question are listed on the answer sheet. Choose the best one and circle it. Each passage and question will be read only once."

<2 Seconds>

Directions : "Passage 1."

Man : Hello. Passengers of flight 17 bound for Caracas, with stops in Atlanta and Miami. The departure gate has been changed to 30B. Also, there will be a slight departure delay due to inclement weather outside. The ground crew is in the process of deicing the wings in preparation for departure. It also looks like the flight is slightly overbooked, so we are offering complimentary round-trip tickets to a few passengers willing to take a later flight. We should be bording about a quarter to the hour. Thank yon for your patience.

＜2 Seconds＞

Directions : Question 1

What change has been announced?

A. The flight number issues

B. The arrival time

C. The destination

D. The gate number

＜10 Seconds＞

Directions : Question 2

Who is probably making the announcement?

A. A pilot

B. A ticket agent

C. A flight attendant

D. A ground crew member

＜10 Seconds＞

Directions : "Passage 2."

Man : "The banjo is a musical instrument which originated in

Africa. Because African music is very much based on rhythm, the banjo looks very much like a drum and probably developed from a drum. It also has a neck and from four to six strings. The banjo was probably brought from Africa to America by slaves in the 16th and 17th centuries. In the United States, white county musicians began using the banjo to play their dance music. Eventually, the four-string banjo became an integral part of early jazz, called Dixieland and the five-string banjo became the foundation of a kind of fast country music called bluegrass.

＜2 Seconds＞

Directions ： Question 1

What would be the most likely source of this passage?

A.　A music appreciation lecture

B.　A radio advertisement

C.　A political speech

D.　A TV situation comedy

＜10 Seconds＞

Directions ： Question 2

If this passage continued, what would the next topic probably be?

A.　Types of drums in Africa

B.　The problem of slavery in America

C.　Some famous banjo players

D.　Classical music today

(☆☆☆○○○)

【3】

Directions : "Section C.

Please listen to the following two conversations. After each conversation, two questions will be asked. Four possible responses to each question are listed on the answer sheet. Choose the best one and circle it. Each conversation and question will be read only once."

＜2 Seconds＞

Directions : "Conversation 1."

Woman : Wow, what a snow storm. And they say it's not going to stop for another five hours. Have you heard anything about classes?

Man : Not yet. I guess the administration hasn't decided. I can't imagine that the faculty could make it to campus with today's weather the way it is.

Woman : Year... Well, I for one could use a break. But you know what that means. We'll have double the work for the next class.

Man : Why don't we take advantage of the lull and get some work done at the library computer center? I just called and it's open, at least for now.

Woman : That's a great idea... Then after that, let's get a cup of coffee at the library café. My treat!

＜2 Seconds＞

Directions : Question 1

What will the students probably do next?

A. They will probably head to the library computer center.

B. They will probably get a cup of coffee at the library café.

C. They will probably do an extra assignment for their class.

284

    D.   They will probably call the administration about the schedule.

＜10 Seconds＞

Directions ： Question 2

What do the students think will happen to the day's classes?
A.   They think the classes will be called out.
B.   They think the classes will be held off campus.
C.   They think the classes will be canceled.
D.   They think the classes will be twice as long.

＜10 Seconds＞

Directions ： "Conversation 2."

Man ： Phew, the line was long. I've got popcorn for both of us.

Woman ： Thank you so much. Ah, it's so delicious. I can't get enough of it! Crunchy and light as air!

Man ： You know, it's a certain type of corn, where the kernel is hard on the outside and soft and starchy on the inside, and the inside contains a little bit of moisture so it expands when it's heated—just the inside, not the hard exterior.

Woman ： Oh, that's why when you heat it up, it ends up exploding. I wonder when and where the way to cook popcorn was found.

Man ： People have heen popping corn for food for centuries. Ancient Peruvians were doing it as early as 4700 BC. The oldest known popcorn cooker comes from around the third century AD, and it was a small pot with a handle and a hole on top. Then, in the 19th century, the first popcorn machine was invented. With its steam-powered engine, the popcorn was heated with salt, lard, and butter, and then it was stirred and kept warm.

Woman : Now we can also cook it with a microwave oven.

Man : Yes. A man named Percy Spencer discovered how to microwave popcorn in the 1940s. Today, Americans are the biggest consumers of popcorn in the world, and there are all sorts of flavors to choose from. Plain is the healthiest, but there's caramel flavoring, and all sorts of cheese flavoring.

Woman : When you add too much butter and salt, it may not be great for your body.

Man : I know, but that won't stop me from eating it every now and then because it's delicious!

＜2 Seconds＞

Directions : Question 1

According to the dialog, why do the corn kernels explode when they are heated?

A. Because the inside of them is dry and the outside is soft.

B. Because the inside of them is moist and the outside is soft.

C. Because the inside of them is hard and the outside is moist.

D. Because the inside of them is moist and the outside is hard.

＜10 Seconds＞

Directions : Question 2

How did people in the 19th century cook popcorn?

A. They used a small pot with a handle and a hole on it.

B. They used a microwave oven.

C. They used a popcorn machine with a steam-powered engine.

D. They flavored with caramel or cheese.

<10 Seconds>

(☆☆☆☆○○○○)

【4】

Directions : "Section D.

The following article will be read twice. Please write a summary of the contents in Japanese. The summary should be between 150 and 200 characters. There will be six minutes to write the summary after the second reading. You may take notes and begin summarizing while listening. Now, please listen to the article."

<3 Seconds>

Man : Everyone, please think of your biggest personal goal. For real -- you can take a second. You've got to feel this to learn it. Take a few seconds and think of your personal biggest goal, okay? Imagine deciding right now that you're going to do it. Imagine telling someone that you meet today what you're going to do. Imagine their congratulations, and their high image of you. Doesn't it feel good to say it out loud? Don't you feel one step closer already, like it's already becoming part of your identity?

Well, bad news: you should have kept your mouth shut, because that good feeling now will make you less likely to do it. The repeated psychology tests have proven that telling someone your goal makes it less likely to happen. Any time you have a goal, there are some steps that need to be done, some work that needs to be done in order to achieve it. Ideally you would not be satisfied until you'd actually done the work. But when you tell someone your goal and they acknowledge

287

it, psychologists have found that it's called a "social reality." The mind is kind of tricked into feeling that it's already done. And then because you've felt that satisfaction, you're less motivated to do the actual hard work necessary.

So this goes against conventional wisdom that we should tell our friends our goals, right? So they hold us to it.

So, let's look at the proof. 1926: Kurt Lewin, founder of social psychology, called this "substitution." 1933: Wera Mahler found when it was acknowledged by others, it felt real in the mind. 1982, Peter Gollwitzer wrote a whole book about this, and in 2009, he did some new tests that were published.

It goes like this: 163 people across four separate tests. Everyone wrote down their personal goal. Then half of them announced their commitment to this goal to the room, and half didn't. Then everyone was given 45 minutes of work that would directly lead them towards their goal, but they were told that they could stop at any time. Now, those who kept their mouths shut worked the entire 45 minutes on average, and when asked afterward, said that they felt that they had a long way to go still to achieve their goal. But those who had announced it quit only after 33 minutes, on average, and when asked afterward, said that they felt much closer to achieving their goal.

So if this is true, what can we do? Well, you could resist the temptation to announce your goal. You can delay the gratification that the social acknowledgment brings, and you can understand that your mind mistakes the talking for the doing. But if you do need to talk about something, you can state it in a way that gives you no satisfaction, such as, "I really want to run this marathon, so I need to train five times a week and kick my ass if I don't, okay?"

<8 Seconds>

Directions : "Now, Listen again."

<3 Seconds>

Man : *repeat*

<6 Minutes>

(Directions) : "Stop writing, please. This is the end of the listening test. Thank you."

(☆☆☆☆◎◎◎)

【5】 次の(1)～(5)の英文の_____に入る最も適切な語を，ア～エの中か らそれぞれ1つ選び記号で答えなさい。

(1) If you're not sure what to do, just watch the fellow working beside you and try to do _____.

　ア equivalent 　イ after 　ウ same 　エ likewise

(2) As a cop, he has seen much of the _____ side of life.

　ア sear 　イ seamy 　ウ wry 　エ hectic

(3) You should have attended that lecture on durability testing of fibers; it really was most _____.

　ア stimulating 　イ reluctant 　ウ feasible 　エ irrelevant

(4) Hardly had my wife left home _____ my son started to play a video game.

　ア any 　イ as 　ウ when 　エ so

(5) He has been _____ of murder in the death of his business partner.

　ア aborted 　イ accused 　ウ lodged 　エ processed

(☆☆☆◎◎◎)

【6】次の(1)～(5)の英文の_____に入る最も適切な語句を，ア～エの中からそれぞれ1つ選び記号で答えなさい。

(1) I left my country so that _____ a better life.

　　ア　to have　　イ　I have　　ウ　I can have　　エ　I could have

(2) Not only _____ more brittle than hard maples, but they are also less able to withstand high winds.

　　ア　soft maples　　イ　soft maples are　　ウ　are soft maples

　　エ　they are soft maples

(3) Alabama was occupied by the French and Spanish before _____ to England in 1763.

　　ア　it was ceded　　イ　was ceded　　ウ　ceded it

　　エ　ceded to it

(4) Economics is a social science that _____ the factors that determine the production, distribution, and consumption of goods and services.

　　ア　concerns about　　イ　concerns with　　ウ　is concerning

　　エ　is concerned with

(5) Despite its wide range of styles and instrumentation, country music has certain common features _____ its own special character.

　　ア　given it　　イ　give it that　　ウ　that give it　　エ　that gives it

　　　　　　　　　　　　　　　　　　　　　　　　　　(☆☆☆○○○)

【7】次の(1)～(5)の英文において下線部に最も近い意味の語句をア～エの中からそれぞれ1つ選び記号で答えなさい。

(1) High-ranking officials are not <u>exempted</u> from paying taxes.

　　ア　included　　　　　　イ　containing similar qualities

　　ウ　free from a task　　エ　to stop the action

(2) Despite the <u>meager</u> income, Harrison's boyhood was enjoyable, with much of it spent outdoors fishing or hunting.

　　ア　scarce　　イ　commendable　　ウ　genuine　　エ　close

(3) Through constant practice, a <u>tyro</u> will be changed into an expert.

ア youth イ beginner ウ professional エ veteran

(4) I'm going to <u>see</u> my old friends tomorrow.

ア come across イ hook with ウ hook up to

エ hang out with

(5) I'm considering whether to apply or not. Let me <u>sleep on it</u>.

ア feel laid back イ think it over ウ come up with it

エ deal with it

(☆☆☆☆○○○○)

【8】次の(1)～(5)の英文において不適切な箇所を，下線部ア～エからそれぞれ1つ選び記号で答え，正しい形，または，適切な語句にしなさい。

(1) Acrylic _ア<u>paints</u> are _イ<u>either</u> aplied _ウ<u>using</u> a knife or diluted and _エ<u>supreading</u> with a paintbrush.

(2) _ア<u>Many of the satellites</u> _イ<u>of space</u> carry telescopes and other instruments _ウ<u>used in astronomy</u> to _エ<u>look at the stars</u>.

(3) It is amazing what _ア<u>discovered Faraday</u> in the field _イ<u>of science</u> _ウ<u>without the use</u> _エ<u>of mathematics</u>.

(4) In the meeting Mr. Sands _ア<u>put forward a</u> _イ<u>feasible</u> plan for _ウ<u>raising</u> more _エ<u>fund</u>.

(5) Full-time jobs for men are declining, _ア<u>while</u> more women are finding part-time and full-time work. The result _イ<u>is</u> declining social status for men _ウ<u>so</u> they lose their role _エ<u>as</u> the sole financial provider.

(☆☆☆○○○○)

【9】次の(1)～(5)の英文において〔　〕内の語句を正しく並べかえて文章を完成するとき，〔　〕内の語／語句の4番目と7番目にくる語句を，それぞれ1つ選び記号で答えなさい。ただし，文頭にくるものも小文字で表記してあります。

(1) 〔ア he／イ it／ウ play／エ promoted／オ this／カ was／キ who／

291

ク yesterday〕.

(2)　Neither〔ア boss／イ do／ウ has／エ it／オ nor／カ nothing／キ to／ク with／ケ you／コ your〕.

(3)　This movement was a reaction〔ア the／イ place／ウ the world／エ industrialization／オ many／カ in／キ to／ク around／ケ taking／コ economies〕.

(4)　In American universities, every〔ア study／イ be／ウ achieved／エ must／オ requirements／カ of／キ has／ク field／ケ certain／コ that〕.

(5)　〔ア being／イ cheap／ウ ends／エ merchandise／オ money／カ on／キ spent／ク the／ケ up／コ wasted〕.

(☆☆☆☆☆○○○○○)

【10】次の英文を読み，あとの(1)～(6)を文意に合うようにするために，最もふさわしいものをそれぞれ1つ選び記号で答えなさい。

　　Before the grass has thickened on the roadside verges and leaves have started growing on the trees is a perfect time to look around and see just how dirty Britain, that is my country, has become. The pavements are stained with chewing gum that has been spat out and the gutters are full of discarded fast food cartons. Years ago I remember travelling abroad and being saddened by the plastic bags, discarded battles and soiled nappies at the edge of every road. Nowadays, Britain seems to look at least as bad. What has gone wrong?

　　The problem is that the rubbish created by our increasingly mobile lives lasts a lot longer than before. If it is not cleared up and properly thrown away, it stays in the undergrowth for years; a semi-permanent reminder of what a tatty little country we have now.

　　Firstly, it is estimated that 10 billion plastic bags have been given to shoppers. These will take anything from 100 to 1,000 years to rot. However, it is not as if there is no solution to this. A few years ago, the Irish government introduced a tax on non-recyclable carrier bags and in three months reduced their use by 90％. When he was a minister, Michael Meacher attempted to introduce a similar arrangement in Britain. The plastics industry protested, of course. However, they need not have bothered; the idea was killed before it could draw breath, leaving supermarkets free to give away plastic bags.

What is clearly necessary right now is some sort of combined initiative, both individual and collective, before it is too late. The alternative is to continue sliding downhill until we have a country that looks like a vast municipal rubbish tip. We may well be at the tipping point. Yet we know that people respond to their environment. If things around them are clean and tidy, people behave cleanly and tidily. If they are surrounded by squalor, they behave squalidly. Now, much of Britain looks pretty squalid. What will it look like in five years?

(1) It's a good time to see Britain before the trees have leaves because

   ア   you can see the beauty of nature in Britain.

   イ   you can see Britain at its best.

   ウ   you can see the grass thickened on the verges.

   エ   you can see how dirty Britain is now.

(2) Years ago things used to be

   ア   the same abroad.

   イ   better abroad.

   ウ   worse abroad.

   エ   worse, but now things are better abroad.

(3) The problem is that

   ア   rubbish is not cleared up.

   イ   rubbish lasts longer than it used to.

   ウ   our society is increasingly mobile.

   エ   Britain is a tatty country.

(4) Michael Meacher, a former minister,

   ア   followed the Irish example with a tax on plastic bags.

   イ   tried to follow the Irish example with a tax on plastic bags.

   ウ   made no attempt to follow the Irish example with a tax on plastic bags.

エ　had problems with the plastics industry who weren't bothered about the tax.

(5)　It's clear that

ア　it is too late to do anything.

イ　we are at the tipping point.

ウ　there is no alternative.

エ　we need to work together to solve the problem.

(6)　It's considered that

ア　people are surrounded by squalor.

イ　people are like a vast municipal rubbish tip.

ウ　people behave according to what they see around them.

エ　people clean and tidy things around them voluntarily.

(☆☆☆◎◎◎◎)

【11】次の英文を読み，あとの問いに対する答えとして最も適切なものをそれぞれ1つ選び，記号で答えなさい。

Most earthquakes are caused by large-scale movements of the Earth's lithospheric plates and occur at the boundaries between the plates. Experts recognize seven to twelve major plates and a number of smaller ones. The plates take their names from continents (the North American plate): from oceans (the Pacific plate): and from geographic areas (the Arabian plate).

The plates are in very slow but constant motion, so that seen from above, the Earth's surface might look like a slowly moving spherical jigsaw puzzle. The plates move at rates of 2 to 15 cm or several inches in a year, about as fast as our fingernails grow. On a human scale, this is a rate of movement that only the most sophisticated instruments can detect. But on the scale of geological time, it's a dizzying speed. At this rate, those almost-four-billion-year old rocks could have traveled all the way around the Earth eleven times.

The movement of the plates is generally one of three kinds: spreading, colliding or sliding. When plates are spreading, or separating from each other, we call their movement divergent. When they are colliding, or pushing each other, we call the movement convergent. Movement in which plates slide past each other is called lateral (or transform) plate movement. Earthquakes can accompany each of the three types of movement.

The revolutionary theory of plate tectonics originated early in the 20th century, although it did not gain general acceptance until the late 1960s. The German meteorologist, geophysicist, and explorer Alfred L Wegener is now given credit for the first step in understanding the movement of the lithosphere. In the period 1910-1912 he formulated the theory called continental drift and collected evidence from the rocks, fossils, and climate of various continents to show that they had once been joined together. Wegener had little data on the oceanic crust, so he thought that the continents merely moved through that crust.

(1) What parts of the tectonic plates collide when earthquakes occur?

   ア   The bottoms.

   イ   The edges.

   ウ   The centers.

   エ   The peaks.

(2) Why is the phrase "jigsaw puzzle" used in the second paragraph?

   ア   Because of the way the plates fit together.

   イ   Because of the number of plates.

   ウ   To show how complex everything is.

   エ   To show how fast it grows.

(3) Why have the plates travelled so far?

   ア   Because they are moving quite fast.

   イ   Because the Earth is not very big.

   ウ   Because the age of the Earth is advancing.

   エ   Because they have kept moving for almost four billion years.

(4) Why did Wegener's theory take so long to be accepted?

ア　Because he had no understanding of the ocean floor.

イ　Because he made several errors in his theory.

ウ　Because it was very different from previous ideas in this area.

エ　Because he was unknown in the field of earthquake seismology.

(5)　What evidence did Wegener NOT use to support his theory of Continental Drift when looking at two now-distant locations?

ア　The existence of similar rocks.

イ　The existence of similar extinct plants and animals.

ウ　The existence of similar races of people.

エ　The conditions of weather.

(☆☆☆○○○○)

【12】Read the following passage and answers the questions below.

Tomohiro Watanabe, an 18-year-old from Fukushima, was one of those who used their newly acquired right to vote in last summer's Upper House election, the first national poll since the voting age was lowered to 18. He composed a tanka short poem about his experience.

"My right to vote/ I used it/ For the first time/ Apparently, however/ [　A　]."

No, no, it is not too early for you. Please vote in the next election and the one after that.

Again last year, Japan was hit hard by the force of nature. Earthquakes, torrential rains and other natural disasters battered various parts of the nation. Yuka Sasaki, a first-year high school student from Nagano, described a sense of shame she felt after typhoon in her own short poem.

"As a typhoon came/ I expected the cancellation of trains/ Then damage caused by the typhoon/ Made me realize my (　あ　)."

For three decades, Toyo University has been holding an annual student tanka contest called "One Hundred Poems of Modern Students." With this year marking the 30th anniversary of the contest, more than 1.3 million poems composed by students have been entered in the competition.

Here are some of the winners:

"In my mail to a funny friend/ I type in (the kanji character for)'laugh'/ In doing so, however, I'm not smiling."

This poem, composed by Mizuki Takao; depicts [　B　] about her efforts to maintain a good relationship with a friend. Older adults are also often seized by such a sensibility. A poem by Emika Ikeuchi describes girl's bittersweet emotion as [　C　].

"I check my phone/ To see if I have received you message/ Every 10 minutes/ My phone gets/ A new fingerprint."

Shu Ando has composed a poem about working hard in the predawn hours.

"Getting up at 3 a.m./ My hands get cold from milking/ The cow's warmth/ Serves as a pocket warmer."

Misaki Kawanami's piece describes how she, apparently tired from being busy, fights off sleep at her desk.

"My eyes are blank/ I'm so sleepy that it is as if/ My desk is the south pole of a magnet/ While my (　い　) the north pole."

Rin Nagashima has a (　う　) grandfather.

"Classes on Saturdays/ My grandpa always comes to watch/ Now, he is/ Totally a member of the class."

Yuta Akahane finds his relationship with his parents changed after an argument.

"In an argument with my parents/ I talked them down/ Now, whom should I (　え　)?"

[　D　] can make a young person stronger. Seito Ryu has created a poem about the pangs of solitude.

"Studying alone in an empty classroom/ I know my pencil/ is watching my painful struggle."

Yuzuki Seki's poem seems to be about her effort to find[　E　].

"In a rotating coffee cup (in a carousel at an amusement park)/ I'm looking for my starting point/ In the summer of my first high school year."

After rotating and rolling, she will eventually find the way.

(1) Choose the best word or phrase from among the four choices for each blank, (　あ　)〜(　え　). Write the number of the answer.

あ　① courage　　② possibility　③ responsibility
　　④ smallness

い　① forehead　② notebook　③ legs
　　④ teacher

う　① strict　　② annoying　③ lovable
　　④ sensible

え　① persuade into　② live with　③ rebel against
　　④ rely on

(2) Complete the sentence in [　A　] and [　C　] so that the passage will make sense. Fill in each blank bellow within 10 words.

A　It was _____.

C　she eagerly _____ from her boyfriend.

(3) Choose the best phrase for [　B　], [　D　], and [　E　] from among the four. All the choices begin with a small letter. Write the number of the answer.

① a solitary, uncertain struggle for one's future

② inner conflict which an adolescent boy or girl usually suffer from

③ the author's somewhat uncomfortable feeling

④ a safe footing amid rapid and constant change

(4) Which of the following sentence is true in the passage? Write the number of the answer.

① Tomohiro Watanabe did not participate in the last summer's Upper House election although he had the right to vote.

② Yuka Sasaki experienced an earthquake in Nagano when she was in the first year at high school.

③ More than 40 thousand poems have been applied for One Hundred

Poems of Modern Students every year on average.

④　Shu Ando tried to warm the cows with his hands and pocket warmer while working very early in the morning.

(☆☆☆◎◎◎)

【13】If you could live (start) your life over again, what would you do differently? Write a composition to explain. The composition should be 80 words or more.

(☆☆☆☆◎◎)

【14】授業中に生徒が次の(1)と(2)の質問をしました。あなたは英語の先生としてどのように説明しますか。それぞれについて日本語で答えなさい。(説明の一部に英語を使用しても差し支えない)

(1)　単語の最後のeは基本的に読まないと習いましたが，cuteの最後のeを読まないのならcutと同じ発音になるのではないですか?

(2)　I regret to inform you I cannot comply with your request. はどのような状況の時に使われる表現ですか。

(☆☆☆☆◎◎)

【高等学校】

【 1 】Read the passage and answer the questions below.

Parents can be a bit sensitive when it comes to their kids. As a high school science teacher, I probably know this better than most people do. Just last week, I had a two-hour meeting with a parent who, upset about her son's failing grades, decided that 〒I was the problem. "If you gave him passing grades," she insisted, "his self-esteem would improve, and then he might actually start doing better."

Give him good grades that he doesn't deserve, and then true success will follow. She honestly believed this. "I've read 〒studies," she said. "I know what I'm talking about."

299

I can't exactly blame her. She's done some research and read parenting books. Sadly, that "research" was probably the same touchy-feely nonsense that I, too, read as an undergraduate in the 1990s, much of which has been thoroughly proven incorrect by now. So what will I do? For one, I won't give in to her demands. Her son will fail my course if he doesn't change his habits; and as cruel as this might sound, he could be a better student for it.

Unfortunately for today's children, many parents won't agree. Overprotective parents are afraid their children will suffer from low self-esteem if they fail, insisting that their children will fare better in sports and school if they start the learning process with inflated confidence. They hover around teachers and coaches, making sure that their children (ウ) as possible. But in my opinion overprotecting children does more harm than good. When kids aren't allowed to fail or make mistakes, they don't build the skills they need to succeed.

Once upon a time, awards were earned. But if you attend any children's awards ceremony today, you'd be hard-pressed to figure out who actually achieved anything. The worst performing students receive the same praise as the winning teams and the most hardworking scholars. Trophies are no longer reserved for the best, but are handed out like Halloween candy—to anyone who shows up. But does this really help anyone? Could trophies gained through no particular effort actually lower the performance of winners and losers alike?

Perhaps. Rewards motivate when they have value. And a basic law of economics states that the value of anything is inversely proportional to its supply. _エRewards are no different. So by passing them out to, well, everyone, their supply increases to such an extent that they are made worthless. There's no longer a connection between a difficult accomplishment and a reward. Indeed, such rewards lose the very effect that they were designed to produce —they no longer motivate anyone. The result? Marginal players, as well as wining teams and top students, simply stop working so hard. Why bother?

300

After all, they'll each get their prize regardless.

Sadly, it gets worse. A pervasive sense of entitlement makes failure more difficult to accept in the real world—specifically, in the workplace. Here, bosses don't pass out prizes so freely, choosing instead to reward performance. _オCoddled kids—now young adults—have a very difficult time adjusting when they haven't experienced the benefits of meaningful failure in the past. As a teacher, I can tell you that it's triumph over adversity that builds true self-esteem. Jean M. Twenge of San Diego University sums up the problem nicely. In her book *The Narcissism Epidemic: Living in the Age of Entitlement*, she asserts: "The 'everybody-gets-a-trophy' mentality basically says that you're going to get rewarded just for showing up. That won't build true self-esteem; instead, it builds this empty sense of 'I'm just fantastic (カ).'" The effect of limited self-esteem plays itself out every day on the job, where fragile young workers shatter like fine china at the first hint of difficulty.

Ms. Twenge found that "millennials" —children born between 1982 and 1999—are having a particularly tough time of it. After graduation, they aimed for prestigious careers with big paychecks without considering the real effort required to achieve them. When these goals weren't easily attained, they finally experienced the taste of real failure for the first time—and quit. To prevent this from happening, parents must teach their children how to earn rewards from an early age so that they can take that skill with them into the real world.

Failure hurts, but it must be practiced before it can be overcome. When parents are overprotective of their children's self-esteem, they actually hinder their kids' potential for success. Accomplishment feeds self-esteem, not the other way around. Children can only achieve success if they're allowed to make mistakes—and learn in the process.

I don't enjoy failing students; but as in the age-old philosophy, it really is for their own good. The students I fail learn a hard lesson, but it's better than

[　キ　].

(1) Choose the best sentence from among the four choices which explains the underlined part ア, イ, and エ correctly. Write the number of the answer.

ア　I was the problem

① her son's grades had become bad because she overprotected him

② her son's grades had become bad because the writer didn't teach well

③ her son's performance would be worse if the writer failed him

④ her son's performance would be worse if the writer passed him

イ　studies

① They show that you need to give your students better grades than they could actually get in order to improve children's self-esteem and they are no longer believed.

② They show that you need to evaluate your students' good points even if they have bad studying habits and they are still supported by the experts.

③ They show that you need to evaluate your students properly in order to raise their motivation and they are now denied by some educators.

④ They show that you need to fail your students when they don't try to work hard and the writer has read all of them when he was in university.

エ　Rewards are no different.

① Rewards are thought as valuable when they are given to all the people present.

② Rewards are thought as valuable when they are given only to people who have accomplished something difficult.

③ Rewards to top students should be different from those to ordinary students.

④ Rewards are thought as worthless when they motivate both marginal players and top players.

(2)　Choose the best phrase or sentence from among the four choices for
（　ウ　）and（　カ　）. Write the number of the answer.

ウ

①　make as many mistakes in class

②　receive as few prizes in their awards ceremony

③　get over as many difficulties in their school life

④　encounter as few hurdles along the way

カ

①　not only I'm talented but also I made a great effort

②　because I've got a trophy for my great effort

③　not because I did anything but just because I'm here

④　not because I have shown up but because I did something great

(3)　Choose the best sentence from among the four choices which describes
the reason for the underlined part オ.

①　because they were rewarded for everything they did in school but are
only for their good performance in the workplace.

②　because they were praised for their good performance in school but
are no longer in the workplace.

③　because each individuals was respected in school but the organization
is regarded as more important in the workplace.

④　because more and more young people who are mentally weak are
produced in the workplace, not in school.

(4)　Fill in the blank [　キ　] within ten words so that the sentence makes
sense.

(5)　Choose the best sentence among the four choices which the writer would
most likely agree with.

①　Strong children are usually not affected by the pain of failure.

②　Overcoming difficulties is necessary for building real self-esteem.

③　Most overprotective parents never experienced failure themselves.

④　Giving prizes to all participants is only recommended for very young kids.

(6)　Write a short paragraph in order to express an opposite idea to the writer's.

It should　1)　include the statement that you disagree with the writer's idea.

2)　include one reason why you think so and some sentences to support your reason.

3)　be within 50 words.

(☆☆☆☆◎◎◎◎)

【2】Read the following passage and fill in the blanks [　A　]～[　F　] with appropriate sentence from among the six choices. Write the number of the answer.

Does globalization make people around the world more alike or more different? This is the question most frequently raised in discussions on the subject of cultural globalization. A group of commentators we might call 'pessimistic' hyperglobalizers argue in favour of the former. They suggest that we are not moving towards a cultural rainbow that reflects the diversity of the world's existing cultures. [　A　]. As evidence for their interpretation, these commentators point to Amazonian Indians wearing Nike training shoes: denizens of the Southern Sahara purchasing Yankees baseball caps; and Palestinian youths proudly displaying their Chicago Bulls sweatshirts in downtown Ramallah. Referring to the diffusion of Anglo-American values and consumer goods as the 'Americanization of the world', the proponents of this cultural homogenization thesis argue that Western norms and lifestyles are overwhelming more vulnerable cultures. Although there have been serious attempts by some countries to resist these forces of 'cultural imperialism' — for example, a ban on satellite dishes in Iran, and the French imposition of tariffs and quotas on imported film and television—the spread of American popular culture seems to be unstoppable.

But these manifestations of sameness are also evident inside the dominant countries of the global North. American sociologist George Ritzer coined the term 'McDonaldization' to describe the wide-ranging sociocultural processes by which the principles of the fast-food restaurant are coming to dominate more and more sectors of American society as well as the rest of the world. On the surface, these principles appear to be rational in their attempts to offer efficient and predictable ways of serving people's needs. [B]. For one, the generally low nutritional value of fast-food meals—and particularly their high fat content—has been implicated in the rise of serious health problems such as heart disease, diabetes, cancer, and juvenile obesity. Moreover, the impersonal, routine operations of 'rational' fast-service establishments actually undermine expressions of forms of cultural diversity. In the long run, the McDonaldization of the world amounts to the imposition of uniform standards that eclipse human creativity and dehumanize social relations.

One particular thoughtful analyst in this group of pessimistic hyperglobalizers is American political theorist Benjamin Barber. In his popular book *Consumed* (2007), he warns his readers against an 'ethos of infantilization' that sustains global capitalism, turning adults into children through dumbed down advertising and consumer goods while also targeting children as consumers. This ethos is premised on the recognition that there is not an endless market for consumerist goods as was once thought. Global inequality contributes to stifling the growth of markets and of capitalism. In order to expand markets and make a profit, global capitalists are developing homogenous global products targeting the young and wealthy throughout the world, as well as turning children into consumers. [C].

Optimistic hyperglobalizers agree with their pessimistic colleagues that cultural globalization generates more sameness, but they consider this outcome to be a good thing. For example, American social theorist Francis Fukuyama explicitly welcomes the global spread of Anglo-American values and lifestyles, equating the Americanization of the world with the expansion of democracy and free markets. [D]. Some representatives of this camp consider themselves staunch cosmopolitans who celebrate the Internet as the harbinger of a homogenized 'techno-culture'. Others are free-market enthusiasts who embrace the values of global consumer capitalism.

[E]. In fact, several influential commentators offer a contrary assessment that links globalization to new forms of cultural expression. Sociologist Roland Robertson, for example, contends that global cultural flows often reinvigorate local cultural niches. Hence, rather than being totally obliterated by the Western consumerist forces of sameness, local difference and particularity still play an important role in creating unique cultural constellations. Arguing that cultural globalization always takes place in local contexts, Robertson rejects the cultural homogenization thesis and speaks instead of glocalization－a complex interaction of the global and local characterized by cultural borrowing. The resulting expressions of cultural 'hybridity' cannot be reduced to clear-cut manifestations of 'sameness' or 'difference'. (中略) Such processes of hybridization have become most visible in fashion, music, dance, film, food, and language.

[F]. The contemporary experience of living and acting across cultural borders means both the loss of traditional meanings and the creation of new symbolic expressions. Reconstructed feelings of belonging coexist in uneasy tension with a sense of placelessness. Indeed, some commentators have argued that modernity is slowly giving way to a new 'postmodern' framework characterized by a less stable sense of identity and knowledge.

① But the respective arguments of hyperglobalizers and sceptics are not necessarily incompatible

② But optimistic hyperglobalizers do not just come in the form of American chauvinists who apply the old theme of manifest destiny to the global arena

③ It is one thing to acknowledge the existence of powerful homogenizing tendencies in the world, but it is quite another to assert that the cultural diversity existing on our planet is destined to vanish

④　However, looking behind the façade of repetitive TV commercials that claim to 'love to see you smile', we can identify a number of serious problems

⑤　Rather, we are witnessing the rise of an increasingly homogenized popular culture underwritten by a Western 'culture industry' based in New York, Hollywood, London, and Milan

⑥　Thus, global consumerism becomes increasingly soulless and unethical in its pursuit of profit

(☆☆☆☆○○○○)

【3】The passage below is a statement about using L1 (母語) while learning L2 (第二言語). Read the passage and answer the questions below.

In Sociocultural Theory, the use of the L1 is seen as one of the primary means by which learners can mediate L2 learning. It does so in two ways: through private/inner speech and by serving as a cognitive tool for scaffolding production in the L2.

Learners frequently use their L1 in private speech. Because private speech is intended for (　ア　), it is not constrained by the same norms that affect social speech. As a result, L2 learners can feel free to resort to the use of their L1 in their self-directed speech. In fact, as Ushakova (1994) pointed out, even those learners who are successful in learning a second language continue to use their L1 as inner speech. Lantolf (2006) cited studies that indicated that advanced-level learners continue to experience considerable difficulty in using the L2 for inner speech to regulate their own thinking. He considered it unlikely that classroom learners would ever succeed in this and suggested that it might only occur when learners possess an intent and a commitment to live their lives as members of a target language community. He drew on Kramsch's (1993) idea of ₁ a 'third space' (i.e. a world consisting of hybrid cultural models derived from both the L1 and L2) to suggest that only those learners who inhabit such a space succeed in conducting inner speech in the L2. This being so, it is clearly necessary to accept that the L1 will play a major role in most learners' inner world. This need not be seen as a problem however, as there is ample evidence to show that when the L1 is used for private speech, it can facilitate both communication and learning (see, in particular, Ohta, 2001).

There is also plenty of evidence to show that the L1 plays a facilitative role in social interaction involving L2 learners. Antón and DiCamilla (1999), for example, examined the collaborative interaction of adult learners of Spanish. These learners used the L1 not just for metatalk but also to assist each other's production in the L2, as in the following extract, where the students are composing a text about the eating habits of Americans:

G: I don't know the word for snack

D: Um ...

G: Ohm so you just say 'in the afternoon'

D: We we could ... in the afternoon

G: So what time in the afternoon

D: Um

Or do we want to just say in the afternoon?

D: Let's say...

G: *Por la tarde?

D: Por la tarde ... *comen ... what did they eat?

The learners use their L1 to 'overtly address the problem of (　ウ　) needed to express their idea'. Antón and DiCamilla noted that this use of the L1 often arose when the students were faced with a cognitive challenge. When there was no problem, the learners created text directly in the L2.

Nation (2003) claimed 'using the L2 can be a source of (　エ　) particularly for shy learners and those who feel they are not very proficient in the L2'. In other words, the use of the L1 in the classroom can serve as a means of reducing learner anxiety and creating rapport. Allowing learners to use their L1 can also allay the threat to learners' own cultural identity posed by having to use the L2 (Auerbach, 1993). Schweers (1999), building on Auerbach's (1993) sociopolitical rationale for the use of the L1 in *ESL classrooms, argued that when the teacher speaks the students' L1, she is able to show that she respects and values their own culture.

(中略)

However, we know of no studies that have actually demonstrated that the use of the L1 leads to lower anxiety. Also the relationship between anxiety and L2 learning is a matter of some controversy. Krashen (1981) argued that 'acquisition' is facilitated when the 'affective filter' is low. Other researchers (e. g. Scovel, 2001) have suggested that anxiety can have a (　オ　) effect on learning and there is some research that supports this view. Djigunovic (2006), for example, reported that high-anxiety learners produced longer texts in the L2 than low-anxiety learners although they were also less fluent. There is also disagreement as to whether anxiety is to be seen as the cause or the result of poor achievement. Sparks et al. (2000) promulgated the Linguistic Coding Difference Hypothesis, which claims that success in foreign language learning is primarily dependent on language aptitude and that students' anxiety about learning an L2 is a consequence of their learning difficulties. MacIntyre and Gardner (1991) argued that the relationship between anxiety and learning is moderated by the learners' stage of development and by situation-specific learning experiences. Their model hypothesizes that learners initially experience little anxiety so there is no effect on learning. This then has a debilitative effect on learning. This model suggests that the use of the L1 with beginner learners might help to avoid negative learning experiences and attendant anxiety and thus foster subsequent development. There is, however, clearly a need for studies that investigate what impact use of the L1 has on learners' situational anxiety at different stages of their development.

　　*por la tarde: in the afternoon　　*comen: (they) eat

　　*ESL: English as a second language

(1)　Choose the best word or phrase from among the four choices for (　ア　), (　ウ　), (　エ　), and (　オ　). Write the number of the answer.

ア

① both the speaker and the listener

② neither the speaker nor the listener

③ the speaker, not the listener

④ the listener, not the speaker

ウ

① understanding others' statement

② developing their academic awareness

③ getting to know others

④ accessing the linguistic items

エ

① embarrassment　　② confidence　　③ enhancement

④ overprotection

オ

① debilitative　　② facilitative　　③ negative　　④ harmful

(2)　Choose the phrase from among the four choices which is NOT appropriate for an example of the underlined part イ.

①　a New York office of a Japanese company where more than a half of the workers are Japanese

②　an English class in Japanese high school which is conducted mainly in Japanese language

③　a family living in Japan where the learner's father or mother is a

310

native speaker of English

④　a Japanese college where Japanese students can discuss with a lot of students from English speaking countries in everyday class

(3)　Find the part which the following sentence is to be put in the last paragraph. Write two words just before the part.

Subsequently, language anxiety develops if learners have bad learning experiences.

(4)　Write your opinion about "Teachers' using Japanese in English class in Japanese high schools."

It should　1)　include advantages and disadvantages with specific reasons or details to support your opinion.

　　　　　　2)　include the arguments which are <u>NOT</u> in this passage.

　　　　　　3)　have 100-150 words.

(☆☆☆☆☆○○○○○)

解答・解説

【中高共通】

【 1 】 Conversation 1　D　　Conversation 2　C　　Conversation 3　B　Conversation 4　C

〈解説〉短い会話の後に，会話の内容に関する質問と解答の選択肢が放送される。会話，質問，選択肢ともに放送は1回のみである。聞き逃さないように注意しよう。　Conversation 1　Manの最初の発言のon cloud nineは「至福の状態で」。また，2回目の発言でbar exam「弁護士試験」に合格したと言っているので，喜びを表す選択肢Dが適切とわかる。　Conversation 2　Womanは2回目の発言でAt a half past threeと言っているので，3時30分の別の言い方を選ぶ。　Conversation 3　Manは6回目の発言で「多分また君に会えるよ」と言っ

311

ている。　Conversation 4　Womanは6回目の発言で「あなたは絶対に，自分で思っているよりも中国語を知っています」と言っているので，Cの「彼はおそらくもっと上手に話せる」が適切である。

【2】Passage 1　Question 1　D　　Question 2　B

Passage 2　Question 1　A　　Question 2　C

〈解説〉短い英文とその内容に関する質問が2問放送される。放送は1回のみである。解答の選択肢はそれぞれ4つ解答用紙に記載されている。Passage 1　Question 1　スクリプト第3文で「出発ゲートが30Bに変更された」と言っている。　Question 2　スクリプト第6文で「オーバーブッキングなので，後の便に変わってくれる方に，周遊チケットを差し上げます」と言っている。　Passage 2　Question 1　楽器のバンジョーについての内容なので，A「音楽鑑賞の講義」が適切である。Question 2　バンジョーの起源やその歴史についての説明がなされたので，次の話題は演奏者と考えるのが自然である。

【3】Conversation 1　Question 1　A　　Question 2　C

Conversation 2　Question 1　D　　Question 2　C

〈解説〉会話とその内容に関する質問が2問放送される。放送は1回のみである。解答の選択肢はそれぞれ4つ解答用紙に記載されている。できれば先に選択肢に目を通し，聞き取るべき箇所の予測をつけておきたい。　Conversation 1　Question 1　Manは2回目の発言で「図書館のコンピュータセンターに行こう」と提案している。　Question 2　Manの1回目の発言に注目。「今日の天候(大雪)では教授たちは大学での講義ができないだろう」の意味である。faculty「教授陣」。

Conversation 2　Question 1　Manの2回目の発言the kernelからit's heatedまでに「トウモロコシの粒は，外側は硬いが，内側は柔らかくて粘り気と水分があるので，加熱すると破裂する」と言っている。

Question 2　Manの3回目の発言の第5文で，19世紀におけるポップコーンの，動力や作り方が説明されている。

【4】自分の大きな目標を人に話すのはやめよう。それだけでもうゴールに近づいた気になるから。目標を人に話すことが実現の可能性を下げることは心理学の実験で示されている。本来なら実現するまで満足は得られないはずなのに，目標を人に話し認めてもらうと，それが実現したかのように錯覚してしまう。言うことと実行することを取り違える心理を理解し，もし人に言いたくなったら，言ったことで満足をしないような言い方をしよう。(197文字)

〈解説〉長文の英語のスクリプトを聞き，150～200字の日本語に要約する問題である。放送は2回流れる。スクリプトは全部で6つのパラグラフ(段落)から構成されている。第1段落が導入で，第2段落で結論を述べ，第3，4，5段落で理由と検証を行い，最後でまとめる構成である。構文自体は特に難解なものはないので，以上の論理構成を踏まえて，1回目の放送で概要をつかみ，2回目の放送でまとめるようにすればよい。

【5】(1) エ (2) イ (3) ア (4) ウ (5) イ

〈解説〉(1) 「同じように」の意味。 (2) 「不快な」の意味。 (3) 「刺激的な」の意味。 (4) 「～するや否や」の意味。As soon as my wife left home, ～.と書き換えられる。 (5) 「非難する，告発する」の意味で，「accuse＋人＋of…」の受け身である。

【6】(1) エ (2) ウ (3) ア (4) エ (5) ウ

〈解説〉(1) 「もっとよい暮らしができるように」の意味で，目的を表す「so that～can」の構文である。なお，soが省略されることもある。 (2) 強調による倒置構文である。 (3) 節なので主語と動詞が必要である。 (4) 「…と関係する」の意味である。 (5) 直後のitsはcountry musicを指すので先行詞はfeaturesで複数である。したがってこれを受ける動詞に三単現のsをつけるのは誤り。

【7】(1)　ウ　　(2)　ア　　(3)　イ　　(4)　エ　　(5)　イ

〈解説〉(1)　「免除する」の意味。　　(2)　「乏しい，不十分な」の意味。
(3)　「初心者」の意味。　　(4)　「一緒に過ごす」の意味。ここでは，
seeは「会う，会って一緒に過ごす」と考えればよい。なお，come
acrossは「偶然出会う，起きる」の意味なので不適切である。
(5)　「よく考える」の意味。

【8】(1)　記号…エ　　語句…spread　　(2)　記号…イ　　語句…in
space　　(3)　記号…ア　　語句…Faraday discovered　　(4)　記号…エ
語句…funds　　(5)　記号…ウ　　語句…as

〈解説〉(1)　diluted and spread「薄めて塗る」。主語はAcrylic paints「アク
リル塗料」なので，過去分詞にするのが正しい。　　(2)　「宇宙にある
人工衛星」の意味である。位置関係を表すのでinが正しい。
(3)　「ファラデーが発見した物」の意味で，whatは先行詞を含む関係
代名詞である。　　(4)　「財源」の意味なので，複数形が正しい。
(5)　「～につれて」の意味なのでasが正しい。なお，エのasは「…とし
て」の意味である。

【9】(1)　4番目…キ　　7番目…ウ　　(2)　4番目…ア　　7番目…キ
(3)　4番目…ケ　　7番目…オ　　(4)　4番目…キ　　7番目…コ
(5)　4番目…カ　　7番目…ウ

〈解説〉(1)　全体の語順は，イ→カ→ア→キ→エ→オ→ウ→クである。It
was he whoと続くので強調構文であることに注意。　　(2)　全体の語順
は，ケ→オ→コ→ア→ウ→カ→キ→イ→ク→エである。この文では，
neither A nor Bの構文に注意。動詞はBに一致する。　　(3)　全体の語順
は，キ→ア→エ→ケ→イ→カ→オ→コ→ク→ウである。この文では，
take placeが「起こる」という熟語であること，また，takingが現在分
詞の後置修飾であることがポイントである。　　(4)　全体の語順は，ク
→カ→ア→キ→ケ→オ→コ→エ→イ→ウである。カッコの直前にある
everyに何が続くかをまず考えると，field of studyとなる。次の動詞の

部分は，has certain requirementsとmust be achievedが考えられるが，後者を選ぶと後が続かない。後者はthat must be achievedとすればよい。

(5)　全体の語順は，ク→オ→キ→カ→イ→エ→ウ→ケ→ア→コである。まずは，ends upとspent on及びbeing wastedの可能性を考える。次に主語をThe moneyと考えれば，The money spent on cheap merchandiseがわかる。後は，ends up以下を続ければよい。

【10】(1)　エ　　(2)　ウ　　(3)　イ　　(4)　イ　　(5)　エ　　(6)　ウ
〈解説〉(1)　第1段落第1文に注目する。ここでは皮肉を込めて「緑が生い茂っていないと，イギリスがどんなに汚くなったかよくわかる」と述べているのである。　　(2)　第1段落第4文で「現在では海外と同じぐらいに汚い」と言っているので，何年も前には外国の方が汚かったとわかる。　　(3)　第2段落第1文のthe rubbish以下「ゴミが昔より長く残るようになった」に注目する。　　(4)　第3段落第5文のMichael以下「(アイルランドの例と)似た取り決めを導入しようと試みた」。
(5)　第4段落第1文「今，明らかに必要なことは～」に注目する。
(6)　第4段落第4文のpeople以下「人は周囲の環境に反応する(＝環境に染まる)」と述べている。

【11】(1)　イ　　(2)　ア　　(3)　エ　　(4)　ウ　　(5)　ウ
〈解説〉(1)　第1段落第1文のoccur at以下「プレートとプレートの間」と述べているので，edges「両方の端」が適切である。　　(2)　第2段落第1文の最初からmotionまでに注目する。常に流動しているので，境目がそのように(ジグソーパズルのように)見えるのである。　　(3)　第2段落第5文に注目する。プレートは，ほぼ40億年も動き続けてきたのである。　　(4)　第4段落第1文に「1960年代後半になって初めて認められた」とある。この文の後半although以下の「not～until…」の構文に注意。
(5)　第4段落第3文のhe formulated以下でrocks, fossils, climateからデータを収集したとわかる。fossils「化石」には動植物が含まれていると考えればよい。

【12】(1)　あ　④　　い　①　　う　③　　え　④　　(2)　A　too early
for me　　C　waits for a (smartphone) message　　(3)　B　③　　D　①
E　④　　(4)　③

〈解説〉(1)　あ　第5段落の短歌のIからtrainsまでに注目する。台風で電
車が止まることを期待していた自分が小さく見えたのである。　い　第
14段落の短歌のMy deskからmagnetまでに注目する。磁極の南北が引き
合うように自分の額と机が引き合う様子を述べている。　　う　第16段
落の短歌のMy以下に注目する。祖父が孫の様子を見に足繁く通ってく
る様子が述べられている。　　え　第17段落の第1文finds以下と，第18
段落の短歌のwhom以下に注目する。それまでの両親との関係が壊れ
てしまって「誰に頼ればよいのか(そのような人はいない)」という感
情が述べられている。　　(2)　A　第3段落第1文で空欄の文を否定して
いるので，これを肯定文にすればよい。　　C　第10段落の短歌のEvery
以下，「10分ごとにメールをチェックするので，その度に新しい指紋
が付く」と述べている。　　(3)　B　第8段落の短歌のhowever以下，作
者は楽しいと思っていないことがわかる。　　D　第20段落の短歌の
aloneとmy painful struggleから，選択肢①が適切。　　E　第22段落の短
歌の最初からpointまでは「遊園地のコーヒーカップで回転しながら，
自分の出発点を探している」。急速な変化の中，自分の安全な足場を
模索しているのである。　　(4)　①はdid not以下が誤り。第2段落第1文
のI used itは「投票した」ことを指す。②はan earthquakeが誤り。第4段
落第3文sheからtyphoonで「台風に遭った」ことが分かる。③は正しい。
第6段落1文のFor three decadesと同第2文に注目。30年間で130万首なの
で，年平均では4万首以上である。④はtriedからwarmerまでが誤り。第
12段落の短歌のMy handsからwarmerは，「搾乳のため冷えた手を，牛
の体温で温める」と言っているのである。

【13】If I could live my life again, I would stay closer to my parents throughout
my life. I left my parents after graduation from high school and lived far away
from them. I regret not taking care of them at all. Both of them are already

gone, so I don't have a chance to do it. I would stay closer and would talk to them a lot. I would stay closer and would take many foreign countries as they never went abroad. I would stay closer and would spend time together. I would stay closer and would say I love them, and I would express my gratitude for everything if I could live my life again. (116 words)

〈解説〉問題の指示文は，「もしもう一度人生を送ることができるならば」なので，解答文では仮定法過去の帰結部分を使うことが必要である。解答例の文でもI would …が用いられている。解答例では，亡くなってしまった両親のことが述べられているが，例えば，高校や大学時代のことに関して記述することも考えられる。

【14】(1)　最後のeは基本的には読まないが，例外はあるものの，その直前の子音の前にある母音をアルファベットの読み方で発音させる働きをすることが多い。　(2)　手紙などにおいて残念なお知らせをする際に使われるフォーマルな表現。やってしまったことに対する後悔の念を表す言葉ではなく，これからお伝えすることについて「残念なことです」といった意味である。

〈解説〉(1)　生徒への説明なので，特に難しい理論的なことよりも具体的な例などを示すとよい。解答例に加えて，例えば，notとnote，winとwineなどを例示して，発音がアルファベットの読み方に変化(前者ではnoteのo，後者ではwineのi)することを記述するとよい。

(2)　英文の意味は「あなたの要望にはお応えできないことをお知らせするのは心苦しい限りです。」である。簡単に言えば「要望にはお応えできません。」の意味である。構文としては，「inform＋人that節」に注意。

【高等学校】

【1】(1)　ア　③　　イ　①　　エ　②　　(2)　ウ　④　　カ　③

(3)　①　　(4)　learning nothing at all (4 words) / failing in the future (4 words) / not being able to overcome difficulties (6 words) などから1つ

(5)　②　　　(6)　(例1)　I disagree with the writer because failing students is too strict. It may change their lives and have a bad effect on their future. It will be better for teachers to encourage their students to work harder by passing them. (40 words)　　　(例2)　I don't think failing students is a good idea because it is the stupidest way for teachers to punish the students who behave badly. They need instruction, not punishment. Teachers should think of other ways to make their students change their bad habits. (43 words)

〈解説〉(1)　ア　第1段落第4文に「もし合格点をくれたら，自信がついて成績がよくなっていく」と述べている。正答の③は，この文意の表現を変えたものである。②と間違えやすいので注意すること。

イ　第2段落第1文及び第3段落第3文のmuch以下が示しているのは，「実際よりもよい点数を与えれば子どもを改善できるという考えは，全く正しくないと証明されている」ことである。　　エ　まず，下線部は「報酬もまったく同じことである。」の意味である。第6段落第2文及び第3文に注目する。ここでは，経済学の基本的な法則である「ものの価値はその供給に反比例する。」を引き合いに出している。

(2)　ウ　第4段落第4文では，親の過保護を批判している。したがって，④の「子どもがほとんど困難に遭遇しないようにする」が適切である。

カ　第7段落第7文のeverybody-gets-a-trophyとyou're goingからupまでは，「皆が勝者だという考え方によれば，自分が姿を見せるだけで報酬をもらえるということになる」。したがって，③の「自分は何もしなくてもすばらしい存在である」が適切である。　　(3)　第7段落第3文に，職場は成果主義なので現実は厳しいことが述べられている。したがって，①「学校時代はどんな成績でもほめてもらえたが，職場で評価されるのは業績を上げたときだけである」が適切。　　(4)　共通していることは，現在の厳しい状況は将来の失敗よりもよいということである。したがって，文中の表現をとって，making mistakes in the real world, especially in the workplace (10words)などと記述してもよい。

(5)　①は誤り。論旨にはない。②は正しい。第9段落第3及び第4文に同じ意味の記述がある。③は誤り。論旨にはない。④は誤り。第7段

落第8文のThat won't以下に「本物の自信ではなく，内容の伴わない空の自信を生み出してしまう」とある。　(6)　指示文の内容に注意して，条件を間違えないようにすること。なお，否定する際の構文に注意。解答例のいずれもそうだが，主語の後の動詞を否定形にすることがポイントである。例えば，解答例の2で，I think failing students is not a good idea…とすると不自然な文になるので注意すること。

【2】A　⑤　　B　④　　C　⑥　　D　②　　E　③　　F　①
〈解説〉A　第1段落第6文のAsからinterpretationまでと，Amazonianから文末までに注目。世界中の異なる地域で画一化が進んでいると述べている。　B　第2段落第5文のhas been以下では，心臓疾患や糖尿病などの具体的な病名が記述されているので，④「重大な問題を挙げることができる」が適切である。　C　第3段落第2文のan 'ethos of infantilization'以下と同第5文のas well以下に注目する。「市場拡大と利益追求のために，若年層をターゲットにして，世界中で画一化した商品を開発している」の意味である。　D　第4段落第4文と同第5文に注目する。ここでは，選択肢②に対抗する具体的な内容がSomeとOthersという形式で例示されている。　E　第5段落第2文に注目すると，「実際，評論家の間では，グローバリゼーションを新しい形式の文化的表現にリンクさせる様々な考えがある」と述べている。文脈から，この文の前に入るのは，③の「強力な画一化の傾向がある一方，地球上にある文化の多様性は失われる運命にある」が適切である。　F　第6段落第2文に注目する。ここでは，異文化の相互乗り入れは，伝統的なものの消失と，その一方で新たな表現の両方の意味があることを述べている。

【3】(1)　ア　③　　ウ　④　　エ　①　　オ　②　　(2)　②
(3)　on learning　　(4)　There are some advantages in teachers' using Japanese in English class. I have two points.
　　Firstly, especially when you teach beginners, you can speak Japanese to make your instruction clear. They can understand you more easily and enjoy

your class.

Secondly, you can also use Japanese when you explain abstract ideas to intermediate and advanced learners. They often feel frustrated when they can't understand the text completely, so you can help them become familiar with it better by adding some information in Japanese.

However, there are also disadvantages.

Students tend to depend too much on their mother tongue unless you stop using it. They somehow need to be exposed to the situation where they have to use only English. Otherwise, they would never be fluent speakers of English.

If you use L1 in your class, you should think carefully about when and for what to use it. (147 words)

〈解説〉(1)　ア　第2段落第3文に注目する。speakerについての記述である。　ウ　第3段落のGとDの会話では，L1を使えば自分の考えが明確に表現できることを述べている。　エ　空欄直後のparticularly for以下「恥ずかしがりの学習者やあまりよく話せない学習者は」，①のembarrassment「きまり悪く感じる」が適切である。　オ　第6段落第5文のhigh-anxiety以下「(第二言語の学習に対して)強い不安を感じている学習者は，あまり不安を感じていない学習者より長い文章を作る」とある。不安がどのような効果をもたらすか考えれば，②のfacilitative「促進するような」が適切である。　(2)　①，③及び④は適切である。第2段落7行目のhybrid culturalに該当するからである。②には異文化的な要素(hybrid)がないので誤り。　(3)　挿入すべき文のキーワードを探すことが第一である。この第6段落では，9カ所にanxietyという語がある。ところで，挿入すべき文の意味は「その後，言語に対する不安は悪い経験があると大きくなる。」である。したがって，「その後」と関係する内容で，この文の直前に位置する英文を探すと，第6段落第9文(Their Model〜on learning.)が適切だとわかる。よって，この文の最後の2語を記入すればよい。　(4)　指示文の意味は「日本の高校の英語の授業で，教員が日本語を使うことについてあなたの意見を記せ。」

である。1)～3)の条件があるが，注意すべきは2)の「この英文の論旨に含まれない内容を記述すること。」である。つまり，自分の独自の見解を記述することが求められているのである。解答例では，初心者と中級者以上に分けて2点を記述しているが，例えば「文法の説明では，英語のみだとかえって混乱を生じさせる可能性がある」などの主旨の記述をしてもよい。

2017年度　実施問題

【中高共通】

<u>Script</u>

[There are three speaking roles for this test: | Directions |, | Man |, and
| Woman |.]

| Directions | : "Please turn the test paper over. The Listening
Comprehension Test will now begin. You may take notes
while listening."

＜3 seconds＞

【1】

| Directions | : "Section A.

Please listen to the following conversations. After each
conversation, a question will be asked, and four possible
answers will be read. Choose the best answer and circle the
corresponding letter on your answer sheet. Each
conversation, the question, and the answers will be read only
once."

＜2 Seconds＞

| Directions | : "Conversation 1."

| Woman | : "Dr. Lovecraft, you are said to have accurately predicted a
number of events which have recently taken place, like a
modern-day Nostradamus. How do you do it, if you don't
mind my asking?"

322

| Man | : | "I am able to know predetermined events according to the relative positions of heavenly bodies." |

| Woman | : | "I'm sure our viewers would be very interested in learning about future events. Where can they start?" |

| Man | : | "I recommend that everyone buy my new book, called *The Future is Now*. It's available at retailers everywhere for the low price of nineteen dollars." |

＜2 Seconds＞

| Directions | : | "What is Dr. Lovecraft's method for seeing the future?

＜2 Seconds＞

    A.   He reads the newspaper every day.

    B.   He observes the placement of planets and stars.

    C.   He communicates with the spirit of Nostradamus.

    D.   He uses a new book.

＜5 Seconds＞

| Directions | : | "Conversation 2."

| Woman | : | "George, I do wish you wouldn't smoke so much. You know it's bad for your health." |

| Man | : | "But I like smoking. It helps me relax, especially after a hard day's work." |

| Woman | : | "It may help you relax, but if you don't quit, we're both going to get cancer." |

| Man | : | "I think *you* should relax. I can quit any time I want, and besides, scientists still have a lot of research to do in that area." |

＜2 Seconds＞

| Directions | : | "Why does George say he enjoys smoking?

＜2 Seconds＞

    A.   He enjoys smoking all day.

B. His wife enjoys smoking with him.

C. He can quit any time he wants.

D. Smoking helps him relax after work."

＜5 Seconds＞

| Directions | : "Conversation 3."
| Man | : "Ms. Jones, throughout the world, large firms spend colossal amounts of money on advertising. Why do you think this is?"
| Woman | : "Well, it's natural that these corporations should want to introduce new products to potential customers."
| Man | : "Many people say that the true purpose of advertising is to convince people to buy things that they don't really need. How do you respond?"
| Woman | : "I'd like to think that we advertisers help people to discover their latent needs."

＜2 Seconds＞

| Directions |:"Which of the following does Ms. Jones say about the purpose of advertising?"

＜2 Seconds＞

A. Advertising is a natural part of our environment.

B. Advertisers want to convince people to buy things that they do not really need.

C. Advertising is a way for people to recognize needs which they were unaware of.

D. Large firms should reduce their advertising budgets in order to be competitive in the global economy."

＜5 Seconds＞

324

Directions	: "Conversation 4."
Woman	: "Is it true that we are facing an environmental crisis, Doctor Savini?"
Man	: "Yes, indeed. One-tenth of all known species of plants are on the verge of becoming extinct, and without oxygen, food, and water, humans will be next."
Woman	: "Can anything be done to avert this disaster?"
Man	: "It may be possible, but a solution will require strict controls on carbon emissions, pollution, and deforestation. Even so, complete ecological recovery may be beyond our grasp."

＜2 Seconds＞

| Directions | : "What does Doctor Savini not claim about the environmental crisis? |

＜2 Seconds＞

A. Protecting trees is part of the solution for the crisis.

B. Nothing can be done to address the crisis.

C. Humans are in danger of extinction.

D. The environment may not ever fully recover from the crisis."

＜5 Seconds＞

(☆☆☆○○○○)

【2】

Directions	: "Section B.
	Please listen to the following two passages. After each passage, two questions will be asked. Four possible responses to each question are listed on the answer sheet. Choose the best one and circle it. Each passage and question will be read only once."

＜2 seconds＞

325

Directions : "Passage 1."

Woman : "People are looking for alternative sources of electricity that have little impact on the environment. One solution is to make electricity using wind power. Wind turbines are built in areas that receive consistent wind. The blades of the turbines spin and generate energy which can be converted into electricity. Wind generated power seems like a promising way to supplement our current supplies of electricity, but there are some people who oppose the idea. The negative environmental impact of wind energy is less than that of coal or other traditional sources, but noise pollution is a concern. Some nearby residents of wind farms have claimed that the noise causes vertigo, irritability, and other health problems. As technology develops to address this issue, wind power will become an increasingly viable option.

<2 Seconds>

Directions : "Which of the following does the passage cite as a problem with wind power?"

<10 Seconds>

Directions : "What is necessary for wind power to become a more popular source of electricity?

<10 Seconds>

〔Paseage 1〕

Question 1

　A.　Nearby residents oppose the aesthetic impact on their communities.

　B.　Converting the energy to electricity is inefficient.

　C.　Some people feel that turbines are harmful to humans.

　D. The cost of building and maintaining the turbines is too expensive.

Question 2

   A.   Technological advances are necessary to solve the current issues.

   B.   Stronger winds are necessary to increase the energy output.

   C   The government must introduce laws to protect nearby residents.

   D   New medicines are needed in order to address the health issues.

| Directions | : "Passage 2."

| Man | : "Graffiti has existed since ancient times, and could be defined as 'drawings, letters, or symbols made on public property.' Modern graffiti is now most commonly made with spray paint or markers in metropolitan areas. It is often seen in a negative light, but is all graffiti vandalism? Graffiti is certainly used by some gangs to mark their territory, and may be related to drugs, violence, or other criminal activities. On the other hand, graffiti may also contain profound social or political messages and require considerable thought and technical proficiency to create. Some municipalities have designated places specifically for people to create pieces of graffiti art. Graffiti reflects society, and may be an indication of deep social problems, rather than a problem by itself.

＜2 Seconds＞

| Directions | : "Based on the passage, which of the four statements is true?"

＜10 Seconds＞

| Directions | : "What evidence does the passage provide that some cities regard graffiti as valuable?"

＜10 Seconds＞

〔Passage 2〕

Queatien 1

   A.   Artists reject graffiti as a way of conveying important messages.

B. Graffit is universally recognized as an important form of art.

C. Graffiti is a relatively recent occurrence in human society.

D. Graffiti may contain important messages about society.

Question 2

A. Graffiti is most common in urban areas.

B. There are officially appointed areas for the purpose of creating graffit.

C. Some cities officially sponsor prizes for graffiti art.

B. Gangs often use graffiti to mark their territories.

(☆☆☆☆◎◎◎)

【3】

Directions : "Section C.

Please listen to the following two conversations. After each conversation, two questions will be asked. Please write appropriate answers in the spaces provided on your answer sheet. Each conversation and the questions will be read from start to finish twice."

＜2 Seconds＞

Directions : "Conversation 1."

Woman : "Hello?"

Man : "Hello Ms. Banks, this is Carl Miller. I was wondering if the buyer has made up his mind."

Woman : "Good afternoon Mr. Miller. I just got off the phone with him. He has another counteroffer for you to consider."

Man : "Is it close to the asking price?　You know how much I need the money."

Woman : "I understand, sir. He is offering ten thousand less than your asking price."

Man : "I am not really ready to go that low. My legal fees are just too expensive."

| Woman | : "I wouldn't accept it either. Considering the price of real estate in your neighborhood, your home should command a higher price. I assure you that it's nothing to be concerned about, but it may take some time." |

Man : "I don't have time. I would really like to get this taken care of as soon as possible. Since the accident last year, I've just been too busy to think about anything else. Where do we go from here?"

Woman : "We should notify him that you are rejecting his current offer. He might choose to offer a higher price."

Man : "Okay. Please let the buyer know that I am turning down the offer."

Woman : "I will contact him right away and let you know what he says."

＜2 Seconds＞

Directions : (Question No.1) "Why does the real estate agent think that Mr. Miller should reject the buyer's offer?"

＜10 Seconds＞

Directions : (Question No.2) "Why does Mr. Miller need money?"

＜10 Seconds＞

Directions : "Conversation 2."

Man : "Good morning, Helen. The news this morning was really surprising, wasn't it?"

Woman : "I've been here since five AM working on these new contracts, so I haven't had any time to watch the news. What happened?"

Man : "Well, you know about last night's blackout, right?"

Woman : "Of course. The lights were out all night."

Man : "It seems like some people really took advantage of the situation."

| Woman | : "What do you mean by that?" |

Man : "A group of looters hit about four stores downtown while the power was out. They tried to rob the bank too, but luckily its security system has a backup generator."

| Woman | : "Have the criminals been apprehended yet?" |

Man : "They're still on the loose, but our police force is the best in the nation. They can't run for long."

| Woman | : "True, but I live near the bank. I hope we don't have any more blackouts!" |

＜2 Seconds＞

Directions : (Question No.1) "Why were the looters unable to rob the bank?"

＜10 Seconds＞

Directions : (Question No.2) "What is Helen's reason for not watching the news?"

＜10 Seconds＞

(☆☆☆☆☆◎◎◎)

【4】

Directions : "Section D.

The following article will be read twice. Please write a summary of the contents in Japanese. The summary should be between 150 and 200 characters. There will be six minutes to write the summary after the second reading. You may take notes and begin summarizing while listening. Now, please listen to the article."

＜3 Seconds＞

Man : "Sleep is increasingly recognized as being important to

330

public health, with sleep insufficiency linked to motor vehicle crashes, industrial disasters, and medical and other occupational errors. Modern humans sleep around three hours less than other primates, such as chimpanzees, who sleep for about ten hours per day, but has it always been this way?

John Goodson, a professor at the University of Florida, has been conducting extensive research to answer this question. He studied the sleep habits of several different hunter-gatherer communities who have limited contact with modern societies. These communities do not have artificial light, telephones, computers, electricity, or any of the electronic devices that we rely on today.

Perhaps his most surprising finding was that their length of sleep was not significantly different from ours. The average sleep period was between 6.9 and 8.5 hours. When compared to current populations in the United States or Europe, they are actually at the lower end of the range. They clearly do not sleep more than modern westerners. Professor Goodson also found that people in these communities do not go to bed until several hours after sundown, just like humans in industrialized cultures.

One noticeable difference, however, is that very few of them suffered from insomnia. This is probably because hunter-gatherers get a lot of physical exercise during the day, compared to people living in industrialized societies. Exercise is an important factor in restful sleep, and insufficient exercise can result in the mind remaining so active that it becomes very difficult to fall asleep at night."

(255 words)

＜8 Seconds＞

Directions ： "Now, listen again."

＜3 Seconds＞

Man ： *repeat*

＜6 Minutes＞

(Directions): "Stop writing, please. This is the end of the listening test. Thank you."

(☆☆☆☆☆◎◎◎)

【5】次の(1)～(5)の英文の＿＿に入る最も適切な語を，ア～エの中から それぞれ1つ選び記号で答えなさい。

(1) Many junior high schools in Kyoto city were closed temporarily because of a flu ＿＿ last winter.
　ア　doom　　イ　diagnosis　　ウ　epidemic　　エ　remedy

(2) Last week Mr. Brown was advised by his doctor to ＿＿ from smoking for his health.
　ア　abstain　　イ　decline　　ウ　refuse　　エ　reject

(3) "Be careful. These fish are＿＿,　but not those colorful ones."
　"You mean those are poisonous?"
　ア　affable　　イ　edible　　ウ　arable　　エ　gullible

(4) There is a saying that the cold can cause a variety of diseases. If yon do not get proper medical treatment,　it will become＿＿.
　ア　precipitous　　イ　chronological　　ウ　habitual　　エ　chronic

(5) Mike and his wife again argued about her easily ＿＿ their little daughter's demands to watch TV for another 30 minutes before going to bed.
　ア　fitting in with　　イ　coming down with　　ウ　giving in to
　エ　filling in for

(☆☆☆☆◎◎◎◎◎)

【6】 次の(1)～(5)の英文において下線部に最も近い意味の語句をア～エの中からそれぞれ1つ選び記号で答えなさい。

(1) Tomoko speaks French, <u>not to mention</u> Chinese.

　ア　as much as to say　　イ　needless to say　　ウ　so to speak

　エ　not to speak of

(2) Ben <u>has gone through</u> all sort of hardship.

　ア　has avoided　　イ　has required　　ウ　has been destined

　エ　has experienced

(3) Julie <u>hit upon</u> the idea while she and her husband were discussing the problem.

　ア　discovered　　イ　opposed　　ウ　suggested　　エ　supported

(4) James couldn't wait to <u>show off</u> his new watch to his friends

　ア　silently show　　イ　proudly show　　ウ　kindly show

　エ　suddenly show

(5) <u>When it comes to</u> competitions, she is second to none.

　ア　With all　　イ　For all　　ウ　With regard to　　エ　As in

(☆☆☆○○○○○)

【7】 次の(1)～(5)の英文において不適切な箇所を，下線部ア～エからそれぞれ1つ選び記号で答え，正しい形，または，適切な語／語句にしなさい。

(1) ア<u>The</u> corporation イ<u>adopted</u> ウ<u>his</u> エ<u>present name</u> in 1981.

(2) ア<u>Almost</u> students were able イ<u>to find</u> ウ<u>good</u> jobs two to four months エ<u>after graduation</u>.

(3) ア<u>Informations</u> イ<u>about</u> the meetings ウ<u>can be obtained</u> エ<u>by calling</u> the Kiev Chamber of commerce.

(4) ア<u>All household</u> chemicals イ<u>they should</u> be stored ウ<u>well</u> out of the reach エ<u>of children</u>.

(5) ア<u>Perhaps</u> Mr. Hayashi is not イ<u>quite</u> as well qualified for the position ウ<u>as</u> Mr. Wakamatsu エ<u>does</u>.

(☆☆☆○○○○○)

【8】次の(1)～(5)の英文において〔　　〕内の語／語句を正しく並べか
えて文章を完成するとき，〔　　〕内の語／語句の4番目と7番目にく
る語／語句を，それぞれ1つ選び記号で答えなさい。ただし，文頭に
くるものも小文字で表記してあります。

(1) 〔ア his／イ Tom／ウ of／エ an／オ teacher／カ dream／キ becoming／
ク English／ケ realized／コ finally〕, but at the expense of many other
things.

(2) There should be a pile of handouts in the meeting room, but I'll〔ア out／
イ you／ウ print／エ none／オ for／カ there／キ if／ク are／ケ left／
コ one〕.

(3) It〔ア was／イ inform／ウ wrong／エ them／オ of／カ their／
キ teacher／ク of the delay／ケ to／コ not〕.

(4) I will〔ア to／イ along／ウ proposals／エ as／オ be／カ long／
キ happy／ク with／ケ your／コ go〕as my parents are too.

(5) 〔ア but／イ were able to／ウ stretchers／エ most／オ victims／
カ carried／キ seveal／ク were／ケ of／コ on〕walk.

(☆☆☆◎◎◎◎)

【9】次の英文を読んで，あとの問いに答えなさい。

Adults tend to think that children who get hooked on Internet surfing have
trouble developing normal relationships with others. But ①that is not
necessarily the case.

Most children use the Internet to communicate with friends and
acquaintances, such as classmates and other members of their school clubs,
after the school day is over. The Internet ②(to / touch / children / opportunity /
offers / stay / in / with / the) their pals all the time, no matter where they are.
Many children are unable to stop their online commumcations with friends
because they fear doing so will damage their friendships. The problem, then,
is that these children are stuck in a "Catch-22" situation.

There have also been cases in which exchanges on Line and other messaging applications led to serious incidents like suicide caused by bullying, of even murder.

For many children, the greatest risk posed by their online communications is not the possibility of encountering strangers with nefarious intent, but rather pressure from their usual friends to conform.

The Internet is like the automobile. Most adults drive. While driving entails the risk of an accident, and cars are often used in carrying out crimes, the automobile is basically a tool that (③) people's life. The Web has made it easier for junior and high school students to interact with people of different schools, ages and areas.

This being the case, perhaps parents should make greater efforts to help their children learn how to avoid potential dangers while using the Internet. We suggest that each family should establish certain rules, such as making children use their smartphone in the living room while everybody else is present.

Some experts advise parents to use the same messaging applications and social networking sites as those used by their children. Doing so will help parents understand the risks involved and allow them to set an example to their children on where the line should be drawn in revealing private information or expressing personal thoughts and feelings.

Children feel they are under ④enomous pressure to gain acceptance from those they view as their peers. Despites this desperation to be accepted, peer pressure often comes into play and some children end up being ignored and excluded by the group. Sadly, this kind of narrow-mindedness is not uncommon in our society. Adults also display this same tendency.

Children need to develop relation with others outside their schools and clubs to avoid being confined to their usual circle of friends and trying to live up to the expectations of others. We urge children to value their private lives and focus more on their own interests.

Children need to understand that it is a healthy part of a relationship to disagree with others. It doesn't mean disrespect. It all comes down to whether families and schools can help children develop this understanding.

(1)　下線部①が何を指すか，具体的に日本語で説明しなさい。

(2)　下線部②の(　　)内の語と語句を正しく並べ替えなさい。

(3)　空所(　③　)に入れるのに最も適切なものを1つ選び記号で答えなさい。

　　　ア　moistens　　イ　enriches　　ウ　extends　　エ　reflects

(4)　下線部④とはどのようなことか，具体的に日本語で説明しなさい。

(5)　英文の内容として最も適切なものを1つ選び記号で答えなさい。

　　　ア　ネットに熱中する子どもは，現実世界では人間関係を築くのが苦手である。

　　　イ　多くの子どもにとって，ネットが危険なのは，見知らぬ大人と出会うことである。

　　　ウ　子どもは，学校や部活と違う仲間を作り，仲間の輪をもっと広くするのがいい。

　　　エ　相手を否定しないよう，違うことでも「違う」と相手に言わない方がいい。

(☆☆☆○○○○)

【10】次の英文を読み，あとの問いに答えなさい。

　　Daniel Goleman is an internationally known psychologist. He was born in 1946. He published a book called *Emotional Intelligence* in 1995. The book puts forth the view that conventional measures of intelligence like IQ tests are totally inaccurate when used to predict an individual's success or failure in life. Mr. Goleman believes that a person's emotional make-up is a far more reliable (　1　) of how well that person will do in the world.

　　He believes that our early years are extremely important and, to some extent, determine our emotional health.

　　Mr. Goleman's ideas don't come as much of a surprise to most of us. We have all met people who seem to be intellectually (2) but have difficulty dealing with fellow human beings. Difficulty in dealing with human beings is equivalent to difficulty in dealing with society. And common sense tells us that an inability to deal with society is a large stumbling (3) to achieving personal or professional success.

The(4) ever conventional IQ tests has been raging since they were first invented. Do they have any validity at all? If so, what exactly do they meassure and what does it mean? Unfortunately, Mr. Goleman's book gives us no methods of measuring " emotional intelligence" at all.

However the fact that he addresses the question is enough to get us thinking. People who are likeable tend to like other people. People who are (5) and defensive find few friends and allies at home or at work. It stands to reason that people who deal well with other people are going to find more satisfaction and success than those who don't. Mr. Goleman also tells us that a stable emotional state, or the ability to control our emotional state, facilitates concentration. Again, this is not a surprising idea.

We all seem to be getting back to the fact that balance is essential for our wellbeing and, in a way, this is the essence of what Mr. Goleman is saying. IQ is great, but without a balanced human approach, it is not enough.

文中の(1)～(5)の空欄に当てはまる語を1つ選び記号で答えなさい。

(1)　ア　example　　　イ　heresy　　　　ウ　indicator
　　　エ　value
(2)　ア　aquatic　　　　イ　detachable　　ウ　federal
　　　エ　superior
(3)　ア　abode　　　　　イ　block　　　　　ウ　square
　　　エ　torch
(4)　ア　continuity　　　イ　contraction　　ウ　contradiction
　　　エ　controversy
(5)　ア　withdrawn　　　イ　popular　　　　ウ　sociable

　　エ　extrovert

【11】 Read the passage and answer the questions below.

　　We spend most of our lives either sleeping or working. With this in mind, it makes sense that everyone should (　a　) the most comfortable bed they can afford, and be in a job that makes them happy. It's important to have at least one of these things right. A good night's sleep means you can function better at your job. And a good job means it's not such (　b　) to get out of your bed in the morning.

　　Of course, there's no such thing as the perfect job. Every occupation comes with its stresses. I recently got my students to rank a list of occupations in order of how 　　A　　. Those that involved an element of danger, like police work and firefighting, came in at the top. But there was heated debate as to which occupations were the least stressful. A few students had put "student" at the [　1　] of their lists. "But you have to study all the time!" cried some other classmates, who had put "student" in their [　2　] five. "But," came the counter-argument from one person, "All you have to do is [　3　]."

　　Interestingly, the students that thought being a student was the least stressful thing a person could do had also experienced being a teacher themselves. These same students are also a joy to teach in class; they're here to learn. On most of my students' lists, at least being a teacher ranked a little higher on the stress scale than being a student.

　　Sure, as a teacher, you might not have any immediate threat to your life like a police officer. Nor could you accidentally kill someone like a doctor. But you do still (　c　) your students' lives. And this can be a stressful thing. Good teachers want to bring out the best in their students and encourage them to use whatever skill they're trying to teach. Good teachers are also good students—they themselves like to learn.

　　It's this aspect of being a teacher that makes me enjoy what I do. While discussing the idea of wealth with a student from Vietnam a while ago, I said that being a teacher means I'll never make millions. "But it would be nice to be rich so that I could visit my friends around the world whenever I wanted," I added. He asked me if ⌐B⌐ and I said yes, He considered what I'd said carefully before telling me: "Then, you are already rich."

His words resonated with me and ₋ᵧI was deeply moved by his observation. Who was the student now? Every day, people (d) different reasons to get out of their beds and go to work. For me, it's moments like the one I had with that Vietnamese student that make getting out of bed—even a comfortable one—that much easier.

(1) Choose the best phrase from among the four choices for each blank,
  (a)~(d). Write the number of the answer.

    a ① give up pursuing   ② refrain from
       ③ invest in   ④ do without

    b ① a chore   ② a pleasure
       ③ an honor   ④ a piece of cake

    c ① have an immediate threat to ② have an impact on
       ③ feel irresponsible for   ④ keep away from

    d ① do not desire any   ② fail to look for
       ③ are motivated by   ④ feel stressed with

(2) Choose the best combination of words for [1]~[3] from among the six choices. Write the number of the answer.

    ① 1 —top   2 —top   3 —study
    ② 1 —top   2 —bottom   3 —teach
    ③ 1 —top   2 —bottom   3 —study
    ④ 1 —bottom   2 —top   3 —teach
    ⑤ 1 —bottom   2 —top   3 —study
    ⑥ 1 —bottom   2 —bottom   3 —teach

(3) Put the appropriate phrases in ⌐A⌐ and ⌐B⌐ for the passage to

make sense. Each phrase should have more than 5 words.

(4)　Which of the following sentence is true in the passage? Write the numher of the answer.

①　Most students the writer is teaching think that being a student is more stressful than being a teacher.

②　The writer enjoys teaching students who used to be teachers and think that being students is the least stressful.

③　Those who used to behave well when they were students can become good teachers because they were treated better than other students by their own teachers.

④　For the writer, the talk with a Vietnamese student is the only experience which allows her to think that her work is meaningful.

(5)　As for the underlined part ア, why do you think the writer felt that way? Write the reason and your opinion about being 'rich' in your life. The length should be about 50 words.

(☆☆☆○○○)

【12】平成23年度から，小学校5，6年生では週1時間の「外国語(英語)活動」が必修となりました。平成32年度までには「活動」を3，4年生に早め，5，6「年生では「教科」にする方向で検討されています。このことについてあなたの考えを90～100語の英語で述べなさい。

(☆☆☆☆○○○)

【13】観点別評価の「コミュニケーションへの関心・意欲・態度」の観点は，何を評価することかを日本語で具体的に述べなさい。また，その際の評価規準を示しなさい。

(☆☆☆○○○)

【14】授業中に生徒が次の(1)と(2)の質問をしました。あなたは英語の先生としてどのように説明しますか。それぞれについて日本語で答えな

さい。(説明の一部に英語を交えても差し支えない)

(1) The party reached the summit.は受動態にできますが，The party reached the airport.は受動態にできないと聞きましたが，どうしてでしょうか。

(2) It's difficult for Ken to do the work in a day.とIt's difficult for Ken to finish the work in a day.の2つの文の違いについて説明しなさい。

(☆☆☆◎◎)

【高等学校】

【1】Read the following passage and answer the questions below.

Every time Parker Palmer's little granddaughter comes to visit, he observes her. He notices what she likes and doesn't like. He notices how she moves, what she does, and what she says. Then he writes his observations down. When his granddaughter is older, he will put his observations in a letter and give the letter to her. His letter will begin something like this: "Here is a sketch of who you were from your earliest days in the world. It is not a complete picture—only you can draw that. But it was sketched by a person who loves you very much. Perhaps these notes will help you do what $_\mathcal{P}$I finally did in my own life: Remember who you were when you first arrived and reclaim the gift of true self."

Dr. Palmer will give his granddaughter the letter when she is in her late teens or early 20s, when she will probably be deciding what kind of work she wants to do. Dr. Palmer hopes that if his granddaughter knows her "true self," she will choose work that is right for her.

Young people who are trying to decide on a career often ask themselves, "What should I do with my life?" Dr. Palmer thinks it is more useful to ask, "Who am I? What is my nature?" He points out that everything in the universe has a nature, which has its limits as well as its potentials. This is a truth that people who work daily with natural materials know. A potter, for example, cannot simply tell the clay what to do. The clay presses back on the potter's hands, telling her what it can and cannot do. If she fails to listen to the clay, her pottery will be frail and unattractive. An engineer cannot tell his materials what they must do. He must understand the nature of the steel or the wood or the stone he is working with. If he does not, the bridge or building he designs could collapse. Human beings, Dr. Palmer says, also have a nature, with limits as well as potentials. When choosing a career, we must understand the material we are working with, just as the potter understands the clay and the engineer the steel. To find work that is right for us, we must know our nature. Attempts to override that nature always fail.

It is not always easy for us to know exactly what our nature is. Sometimes we are discouraged from following our natural inclinations, and we lose track of what they are. When we are young, we are surrounded by expectations — the expectations of our families, our teachers, and, later, our employers. Often these people are not trying to understand our nature; instead, they are trying to ₁ <u>fit us into slots</u>. Sometimes racism, sexism, or tradition determines the slots people choose for us. For example, a little girl who wants to be a carpenter when she grows up is told that girls cannot be carpenters, but she could be a teacher. Or an oldest son who wants to be an artist is persuaded to take over the family business instead of studying art. We feel the pressure of others' expectations, and we betray our nature in order to be accepted.

Dr. Palmer maintains that if we lose track of our true self, it is possible to pick up the trail again. One way is to look for clues from our younger years, when we lived closer to our nature. That is how he found his way back to his true self. In his book *Let your Life Speak*, he writes:

In grade school, I became fascinated with the mysteries of flight. As many boys did in those days, I spent endless hours, after school and on weekends, designing, making, flying, and (usually) crashing model airplanes made of fragile wood. Unlike most boys, however, I also spent long hours creating eight- and twelve-page books about aviation. I would turn a sheet of paper sideways; draw a vertical line down and middle; make diagrams of, say, the cross-section of a wing; roll the sheet into a typewriter; and type a caption explaining how air moving across the wing creates a vacuum that lifts the plane. Then I would fold that sheet in half along with several others. I had made, staple the collection together down the spine, and painstakingly illustrate the cover.

I had always thought that the meaning of this paperwork was obvious: fascinated with flight, I wanted to be a pilot, or perhaps an aeronautical engineer. But recently, when I found a couple of these books in a cardboard box, I suddenly saw _アthe truth, and it was more obvious than I had imagined. I didn't want to be a pilot or anything related to aviation. I wanted to be an author, to make books — a task I have been attempting from the third grade to this very moment!

When he found _イthe books he had made as a boy, Parker Palmer realized that for most of his adult life he had not been following his natural inclinations. He says that he tried to ignore his nature, hide from it, and run from it, and he thinks he is not alone. He believes that there is a universal tendency to want to be someone else — but that it is more important to be oneself.

And so, Dr. Palmer observes his granddaughter. He hopes that someday his observations will help her remember what she was like when she was very young. He hopes that she will become the person she was born to be and find work that will bring her joy. He hopes, in short, that she will grow up to be the person [A].

(1) Choose the sentence from among four choices which could NOT have been written on the letter described in paragraph 1 and 2. Write the number of the answer.

① You are sure to be good at playing some musical instruments rather than playing sports.

②　You used to watch television very carefully when animals were on it.

③　You liked drawing pictures of flowers, trees and mountains.

④　You would often smile when you saw moving things such as cars and trains.

(2)　Choose the best sentence from among the four choices which explains the underlined part ア correctly. Write the number of the answer.

①　Dr. Palmer really wanted his granddaughter to become an author

②　Dr. Palmer gave up being an aeronautical engineer and started to write novels

③　Dr. Palmer didn't think about who he was and decided to write books

④　Dr. Palmer followed his natural inclinations and became an author

(3)　According to paragraph 3, which of the following sentences is true? Write the number of the answer.

①　Professional potter's works look very attractive because the potter believes he or she can do everything with the clay.

②　If you are to be an engineer, you have to learn the limits of each material used for constructing bridges or buildings as well as its potential.

③　When you choose your future career, you should first think about what kind of material you are the most familiar with.

④　When you think about what to do in the future, you need to learn every kind of occupations and you don't have to be worried about whether you can do it or not.

(4)　Choose the best phrase from among the four choices which is closest in meaning to the underlined part イ. Write the number of the answer.

①　give us opportunities to do what we want to do

②　decide what each of us should be

③　consider what kind of talent each of us has

④　find out whether each of us is useful to them or not

(5) What does the underlined part ウ indicate? Find the part from the same paragraph and write it. The part should have 10－15 words.

(6) Choose the best phrase from among the four choices which explains the underlined part エ. Write the number of the answer.

① the books on which Dr. Palmer wrote about his early days when he had spent many hours making and flying model airplanes with his friends

② the books on which Dr. Palmer described what his granddaughter was like on the very first days after her birth

③ the books on which Dr. Palmer mentions how he found his true self and chose work that was right to him

④ the books for which Dr. Palmer collected a lot of useful information when making an excellent model airplane

(7) Choose the best phrase from among the four choices for [　A　]. Write the number of the answer.

① she has always been

② she used to want to be

③ she is trying to be

④ who tries the best even in what she doesn't want to do

(☆☆☆○○○○)

【 2 】 Read the following passage and fill in the blanks [　A　]～[　F　] with appropriate sentence from among the eight choices. Write the number of the answer.

Second language learning and teaching are more important in the twenty-first century than ever before and are more important than even many language teachers appreciate. Most of us are familiar with traditional student populations: captive school children required to "pass" a foreign language (often for no obvious reason), college students satisfying a language requirement or working toward a BA in literature, young adults headed overseas for university courses, as missionaries or to serve as volunteers in the Peace Corps and similar organizations, and adults needing a L2 for vocational training or occupational purposes in the business world, aid organizations, the military, federal and state government, or the diplomatic and intelligence services. [A].

Less visible to many of us, but often with even more urgent linguistic needs, are the steadily increasing numbers of *in*voluntary language learners of all ages. Each year, millions of people are forced to cross linguistic borders to escape wars, despotic regimes, disease, drought, famine, religious persecution, ethnic cleansing, abject poverty, and climate change. [B]. In some instances, for example, migrant workers in Western Europe, the United States, and parts of the Arab world, the target language is an economically and politically powerful one, such as French, Spanish, German, English, or Arabic. Instruction is available for those with money and time to pursue it, but many such learners lack either. Worse, marginalized and living in a linguistic ghetto, they frequently have little or no access to target language speakers, interaction with whom could serve as the basis for naturalistic second language acquisition (SLA). [C]. When imperialist nation states use military force to annex territory, they typically oblige the inhabitants to learn the language of the occupier if they hope to have access to education, economic opportunity, or political power, often while relegating local languages to second-class status or even making their use illegal.

The overall picture is unlikely to change anytime soon. Advanced proficiency in a foreign or second language will remain a critical factor in determining the educational and economic life chances of all these groups, from college students and middle-class professionals, through humanitarian aid workers and government and military personnel, to migrant workers, their school-age children, and the victims of occupations and colonization. Moreover, if the obvious utilitarian reasons were not important enough, for millions of learners, especially the non-volunteers, acquiring a new language is inextricably bound up with creating a new identity and acculturating into the receiving community. [D]. For all these reasons, and given the obvious political implications of a few major world languages being taught to speakers of so many less powerful ones, a responsible course of action, it seems to me, as with education in general, is to make sure that language teaching (LT) and learning are as socially progressive as possible. LT alone will never compensate for the ills that create so many language learners, but at the very least, it should strive not to make matters worse.

[E]. Given the importance of language learning for so many people and so many different kinds of people, therefore, it would be reassuring to know that LT is being carried out efficiently by trained professionals and that language teachers and learners alike are satisfied with the end product. In fact, there is little evidence for either supposition. While individual programs are professionally staffed and producing good results, they are the exception. Around the world, people continue to learn languages in many ways, sometimes, it appears, with the help of instruction, sometimes without it, sometimes despite it, but there are many more beginners than finishers, (中略) the field remains divided on fundamental issues to a degree that would cause public consternation and generate costly lawsuits in true professions.

[F]. Since language learning is the process LT is designed to facilitate, an essential part of the rationale must surely be psycholinguistic plausibility, or consistency with theory and research findings about how people learn and use second foreign languages. But that is by no means the only motivation required. Given that the subject is language education, a solid basis in the philosophy of education should be expected too. Also of major importance are accountability, relevance, avoidance of known problems with existing approaches, learner-centeredness, and functionality.

(注) BA：文学士の称号 (Bachelor of Arts)　　L2：第二言語 (second language)　　SLA：第二言語習得 (second language acquisition) LT：言語指導 (language teaching)

① It is clear from the above examples — just a few of many possible — that the scope of second and foreign language learning and teaching in the twenty-first century is expanding and likely to continue to do so, and as varied as it is vast

② Many of these learners are poor, illiterate, uneducated, and faced with acquiring less powerful, often unwritten, rarely taught languages

③ In some cases, involuntary learners are not created by people moving into new linguistic zones but by powerful languages coming to them

④ Even if they have a high level of competence in a L2, they aren't necessarily able to live an easy life

⑤ Occasionally, SLA is a path to resistance for them ("Know thine enemy's language"), but in all too many cases, it is simply necessary for survival

⑥ Against this backdrop, it seems reasonable to suggest that new proposals for LT should strive to meet some minimum criteria, with the justification for any serious approach needing to be multi-faceted

⑦ Typically, these students are literate, well educated, relatively affluent, learning a major world language, and, the school children aside, doing so voluntarily

⑧ On the other hand there are some cases where professional SLA instructions are not desired or do not work well

(☆☆☆☆◎◎◎◎)

【3】 Read the following passage and answer the questions below.

　The relationship between writing and speaking is important for language testing, among other reasons, because of the question to what extent writing can be seen as a special case of L2 language use and to what extent writing represents a distinctly different ability from speaking, drawing on many of the same linguistic resources but also relying on distinctly different mental processes. A good deal of literature in both first- and second-language studies has addressed the differences between speaking and writing from a number of different perspectives. As Grabe and Kaplan (1996) point out, linguists and educational researchers have historically held contradictory positions about the relationship between writing and speaking: traditional linguistic inquiry has held that speech is primary and written language is merely a reflection of spoken language, while educational research has taken the stance that the written form of the language is [　A　] than oral language. However, in recent years a consensus has been emerging to reconcile these two positions: [　B　] is inherently superior to the other, but oral and written texts do vary across a number of dimensions, including (but not limited to) textual features, sociocultural norms and patterns of use, and the cognitive processes involved in text production and comprehension.

A useful summary of some of the differences between speaking and writing can be found in Brown (1994). Brown provides the following list of the characteristics that ordinarily differentiate written language from spoken language:

- Permanence: oral language [　C　], while written language is permanent and can be read and reread as often as one likes;
- Production time: writers generally have more time to plan, review, and revise their words before they ate finalized, while speakers must plan, formulate, and deliver their utterances within a few moments if they are to maintain a conversation;
- Distance between the writer and the reader in both time and space, which [　D　] that is present between speaker and listener in ordinary face-to-face contact and thus necessitates greater explicitness on the part of the writer;
- Orthography, which [　E　] compared to the richness of devices

available to speakers to enhance a message (e.g. stress, intonation, pitch, volume, pausing, etc.);

● Complexity: written language tends to be characterized by longer clauses and more subordinators, while spoken language tends to have shorter clauses connected by coordinators, as well as more redundancy (e.g. repetition of nouns and verbs);

● Formality: because of the social and cultural uses to which writing is ordinarily put, writing tends to be more formal than speaking;

● Vocabulary: written texts tend to contain a wider variety of words, and more lower-frequency, words, than oral texts.

While Brown's list is a valuable, if somewhat oversimplified, starting point for discussing speaking/writing differences, the fact that the differences between speaking and writing go far beyond these surface textual feature is becoming widely recognized. In particular, speaking and writing are frequently used in different settings, for different reasons, and to meet different communicative goals. Furthermore, the cognitive processes involved in writing differ in important ways from those used in speaking. (中略)

As Grabowski (1996) notes, very few of the surface differences between speaking and writing result from the inherent properties of speaking and writing under ordinary circumstances. In fact, only the first two items on Brown's list (permanence and production time) can be seen as fundamental in this sense: writing ordinarily leaves a physical trace, which can later be referred to either by the writer or by the reader, while speaking, unless it is recorded, ア<u>does not</u>, and the physical act of writing takes longer than the physical act of speaking. All other differences between spoken and written texts either arise from these two fundamental differences, or can be ascribed to the fact that writing and speaking are for the most part used in different contexts and for different purposes. Grabowski lists イ<u>a number of conditions under which writing tends to be chosen over speaking</u>, noting that while the choice is frequently based on social or conventional norms, other factors such as the costs and benefits of one mode of communication vis-á-vis the other also play a role. For example, it may be less costly to send an e-mail message than to make a long-distance phone call; on the other hand, if the message is [　F　] the advantage of speed may be more important than a saving of money.

(1)　Choose the best phrase from among the four choices for [　A　]. Write the number of the answer.
  ①　less 'correct' and therefore can be less valued
  ②　less 'correct' but actually more highly valued
  ③　more 'correct' and therefore should be more highly valued
  ④　more 'correct' but actually less valued

(2)　Choose the best phrase from among the four choices for [　B　]. Write the number of the answer.
  ①　both oral and written language
  ②　either oral or written language
  ③　not only oral but also written langage
  ④　neither oral nor written language

(3)　Choose the best phrase from among the six choices for [　C　], [　D　], and [　E　]. Write the number of the answer.
  ①　enables them to be in the same situation
  ②　eliminates much of the shared context
  ③　is transitory and must be processed in real time
  ④　provides a lot of nonverbal messages
  ⑤　carries a limited amount of information
  ⑥　remains for a while and will be remembered

(4)　Add some English words which are omitted after the underlined part ア. The number of words should be within 5 words.

(5)　Think about a concrete example of the underlined part イ (which is not included in this passage) and describe the situation and why you think so in

English.

(6)　Write the word for [　F　] in order for the passage to make sense. The word should start with the letter "u".

(7)　L2 learners usually have to practice both having daily conversation and making a public speech if they want to improve their speaking skills. When they do the latter, teachers usually have them write the script first and then practice speaking. Write your opinion about the activity of writing what they will talk about before they actually talk.

　　　It should　　1) include advantages and disadvantages with specific reasons or details to support your opinion.

　　　　　　　　　2) include some information from the passage.

　　　　　　　　　3) have 100-150 words.

（☆☆☆○○○○○）

解答・解説

【中高共通】

【１】Conversation 1　B　　　Conversation 2　D　　　Conversation 3　C　　　Conversation 4　B

〈解説〉それぞれの会話についての質問に適切に答えること。Conversation 1　Dr. Lovecraftの未来を予見する方法を聞かれている。Manの1回目の発言のthe relative以降で天体の位置関係について述べている。　Conversation 2　Georgeがタバコをたしなむ理由を聞かれている。Manの1回目の発言のIt helps以下で，タバコを吸うとリラックスできると言っている。　Conversation 3　Ms. Jonesが言っている広告の目的を聞かれている。Womanの2回目の発言でto discover their latent needsと言っている。latent「隠れた。潜在の」。　Conversation 4　指示文に注意すること。Saviniが主張していないことを選択する。Aは，Manの

2回目の発言でdeforestationと言っている。Cは，Manの1回目の発言の
humans以下で言っている。Dは，Manの2回目の発言のcomplete以下で
言っている。したがって，正解はBである。beyond our grasp「手の届
く範囲外」。

【2】〔Passage 1〕　　Question 1　C　　　Question 2　A
　　〔Passage 2〕　　Question 1　D　　　Question 2　B
〈解説〉まとまりのある英文を聞き取って理解し，その内容についての質
　　問に適切に答えること。　〔Passage 1〕　　Question 1　風力発電の問題
　　点を答える。Womanがスクリプト6文目でnoise pollution is a concernと
　　言っている。　Question 2　風力発電がもっと人気が出るために必要な
　　ことを答える。Womanがスクリプト最後の文でAs technology develops
　　to address this issueと言っている。　〔Passage 2〕　　Question 1　4つの
　　選択肢からスクリプトの内容と合っているものを選ぶ。Manがスクリ
　　プト5文目graffitiからmessagesまでで「落書きには社会的政治的に深い
　　メッセージがある」と言っている。　Question 2　ある市が落書きを価
　　値あるものと見なしている証拠を答える。Manが最後から2文目で「自
　　治体の中には，落書き芸術専用の場所を指定したところもある」と言
　　っている。

【3】〔Conversation 1〕　　Question No.1　Because real estate in his neighborhood
　　is valuable.　　Question No.2　Because his legal fees are very expensive.
　　〔Conversation 2〕　　Question No.1　Because the bank's security system was
　　still working.　　Question No.2　She has been working on the new contracts
　　since five AM.
〈解説〉会話を聞いて，質問に対して適切な英語で答えること。
　　〔Conversation 1〕　　不動産の売買に関する話題である。登場人物の整
　　理を確実にすること。ここでは男性(Mr. Miller)が売主で，女性(Ms.
　　Banks)が不動産屋である。Millerが，買い手の様子はどうかと聞いてい
　　る場面である。Banksが，なぜMillerは買い手の申し出を断るべきと考

えているのか聞かれている。　Question No.1　Womanの4回目の発言2文目で「隣の不動産の値段を考えると，あなたの家はもっと高い値が付く」と言っている。　Question No.2　Millerはなぜお金が必要なのか聞かれている。Manの3回目の発言2文目で「訴訟費用がとにかく高すぎるからだ」と言っている。legal fee「訴訟費用」。

〔Conversation 2〕　昨夜の停電の間の銀行強盗未遂事件について2人が話している場面である。　Question No.1　強盗が銀行からなぜお金を奪えなかったか答える。Manの4回目の発言2文目にits security system has a backup generator「警報システムに停電用の発電機があった」とあるので，停電時でも警報システムは作動していたことがわかる。Question No.2　Helenがニュースを見ていなかった理由を答える。Womanの1回目の発言で，「朝5時から新規契約の件でずっとここにいたので，ニュースは全く見ていない」と言っている。

【4】睡眠不足は，重大な事故につながることもあり，睡眠は，ますます大切なものと認識されている。ジョン・グッドソン教授は，狩猟民族の睡眠習慣の研究をした。彼らは，電気，電話，コンピュータ等を持っていないが，私たちとほぼ同じ睡眠時間で，日没後数時間たってから寝ていた。彼らは誰も不眠症に悩んでおらず，適度な睡眠時間と日中多くの運動をすることが，安らかな睡眠にとって重要な要因であることが分かった。(193文字)

〈解説〉長文を聞いて，その概要を150字以上200字以内の日本語でまとめる問題。英文は2度聞くことができるので，1回目は名詞や数字などに注意して聞き，2回目で確認するようにするのが原則である。ただ，この問題は「概要」を求めているので，全体の流れをつかむことが重要である。そのためにはまず，キーワードに注意することである。ちなみに，このスクリプトは255語あるが，sleepという単語が10回出てくる。特に第1段落冒頭の2文までに4回も出てくるので，1回目でsleep関連の話題だということがつかめるはずである。次に，surprisingやnoticeable，very few，important等の強調する表現に注意することであ

る。概要を求められる場合には以上の方法で聞き取るようにすればよい。

【5】(1) ウ　(2) ア　(3) イ　(4) エ　(5) ウ

〈解説〉(1)　「インフルエンザの流行のせいで」の意味である。epidemicは伝染病などの突発的におこるよくないものの「発生。流行」という意味がある。　(2)　直後に前置詞fromがあることに注意。abstain from smokingを直訳すると「喫煙を控える」，つまり「禁煙する」の意味である。　(3)　空欄を含む文は「食べられるが，色が鮮やかなほうではない」の意味である。oneは可算名詞の繰り返しを避けるために用いられる。　(4)　空欄を含む文は「適切な治療を受けないと慢性病になる」の意味である。　(5)　give in toで「〜に譲歩をする」の意味である。ここでは，娘の要求に簡単に譲歩する様子が述べられている。

【6】(1) エ　(2) エ　(3) ア　(4) イ　(5) ウ

〈解説〉(1)「〜は言うまでもなく」の意味である。　(2)「(苦難などを)経験する，耐え抜く」の意味である。　(3)「(考えなどを)思いつく」の意味である。　(4)「あからさまに示す，自慢げに見せる」の意味である。　(5)「〜に関しては」の意味である。withはinでも可能である。

【7】(1)　記号…ウ　　適切な形…its　　(2)　記号…ア　　適切な形…Almost all (of the)　　(3)　記号…ア　　適切な形…Information
(4)　記号…イ　　適切な形…should　　(5)　記号…エ　　適切な形…is

〈解説〉(1)　会社はitで受ける。その所有格である。　(2)　数量を示す「ほとんどの」という意味で用いるので，Almost allまたはAlmost all of theとしなければならない。　(3)　情報は不可算名詞なので単数形である。　(4)　chemicalsまでが主語なので，theyは不要である。
(5)　原級による比較である。最初の主語の動詞に一致させる。

【8】(1)　4番目…ア　　7番目…キ　(2)　4番目…オ　　7番目…カ
(3)　4番目…エ　　7番目…イ　(4)　4番目…コ　　7番目…ケ
(5)　4番目…ク　　7番目…ウ

〈解説〉(1)　該当部分は，Tom finally realized his dream of becoming an English teacher(イ→コ→ケ→ア→カ→ウ→キ→エ→ク→オ)となる。英文の意味は「Tomは英語教師になるという夢を最後にかなえたが，(夢のために)他の多くの物を犠牲にした」である。　(2)　該当部分は，print out one for you if there are none left(ウ→ア→コ→オ→イ→キ→カ→ク→エ→ケ)となる。英文の意味は，「会議室には資料が積んであるはずだが，もしなければあなたのためにそれを印刷しよう」である。(3)　該当部分は，was wrong of them not to inform their teacher of the delay(ア→ウ→オ→エ→コ→ケ→イ→カ→キ→ク)となる。英文の意味は，「彼らが先生に遅刻を知らせなかったのはよくないことだった」である。善悪の判断や性質などについていう場合は，forではなくてofを使う。なお，informの用法にも注意すること。　(4)　該当部分は，be happy to go along with your proposals as long(オ→キ→ア→コ→イ→ク→ケ→ウ→エ→カ)となる。英文の意味は，「両親も満足さえすればあなたの提案で私は満足だ」である。　(5)　該当部分は，Most of victims were carried on stretchers but several were able to(エ→ケ→オ→ク→カ→コ→ウ→ア→キ→イ)となる。英文の意味は，「ほとんどの犠牲者は担架に乗せられて運ばれたが，数名は歩くことができた」である。

【9】(1)　インターネットに夢中になる子どもは，他人との普通の人間関係の構築に問題を抱えているということ。　(2)　offers children the opportunity to stay in touch with　(3)　イ　(4)　仲間として受け入れられるような振舞いをしなければ，排除や無視をされてしまうという心理的な圧力。　(5)　ウ

〈解説〉(1)　第1段落1文目childrenからothersまでの内容を受けている。hook on ～「～に夢中になる」。　(2)　下線部②は，(インターネットは，)「子どもたちが友人たちといつも一緒にいられる機会を提供する」

という意味になる。　(3)　第5段落3文目Whileからcrimesまでで「自動車は事故の危険を伴っており，犯罪の道具として使われる一方で」とあるので，この反対の趣旨を表す単語を選べばよい。　(4)　第8段落の下線部④の直後のto gainからpeersまでの部分(不定詞の形容詞用法)の意味を考えればよい。　(5)　正答のウの内容は，第9段落1文目Childrenからclubsまでで記述されている。　ア　第1段落2文目that以下で「必ずしもそうではない」と述べている。　イ　第4段落後半のbut以下で「そうではなくて普段の友人から認めてもらうという圧力である」とある。　エ　第10段落1文目で「他人の意見に賛成しないことも友人関係には必要なことで，失礼なことではない」と述べている。

【10】　(1)　ウ　　　(2)　エ　　　(3)　イ　　　(4)　エ　　　(5)　ア

〈解説〉(1)　空欄直後のof以下は「本人が社会でどの程度役に立つか」という意味なので，ウ「指標」が適切である。　(2)　第3段落2文目peopleからbeingsまでの大意は「IQは高いが扱いにくい人」となる。したがって，エ「優れて」が適切である。　(3)　空欄直後のto以下は「個人的または職業的な成功」の意味である。この部分と第3段落4文目an inabilityからsocietyまでで「社会との関係をうまく結べない」という意味になる。両者を考えれば，イ「障害」が適切である。

(4)　第4段落1文目overから3文目meanまででは，IQに関する疑問点が述べられている。したがって，エ「論争」が適切である。　(5)　第5段落2文目は「好かれやすい人は他人に好意を持つ傾向がある」の意味であり，これと対照的に次の部分が述べられている。したがって，defensiveと関係するア「積極的でない」が適切である。

【11】　(1)　a　③　　b　①　　c　②　　d　③　　(2)　⑤
(3)　A　stressful they thought the jobs were　　B　I had many friends around the world　　(4)　②　　(5)　I think it's because the writer realized that the student didn't think being rich always means having a lot of money. I also think being rich in material is not so important. Family, good job, and

friends can make your life a better one and make you satisfied more than a lot of money. (54 words)

〈解説〉(1)　a　第1段落冒頭の文で「人生は寝ているか働いているかだ」と述べて，続く2文目ではこの両面について述べている。第2文の後半の記述を参考にすれば，前半の「寝ることにお金をかける」という趣旨がわかる。したがって，③「金を使う」が正解。　b　空欄部分の説明がto get以下なので，「朝ベッドから起きる」という内容は①「雑用」が適切。　c　第4段落4文目で「このことはストレスを生じる可能性がある」と述べている。したがって解答は①か②だが，①は「脅威」なので不適切。②「強い影響を与える」が適切となる。　d　第6段落3文目to getからto workまでは「毎日起きて働きに出かける」の意味で直前の部分の説明である。したがって，③「(異なる理由によって)動機づけられている」が適切である。　(2)　1または2にstudyは入らないので，3である。第2段落7文目は，前の文の発言を受けて「学生はいつも勉強しなければならない」と述べているので，ストレスが多いという趣旨である。したがって，⑤が適切である。　(3)　A　第2段落2文目Everyから3文目occupationsまでで「どんな職業にもストレスが伴う。そこで，学生たちにそのリストを作らせた」の意味である。B　第5段落3文目so thatからwantedまでの発言を聞いて，その学生が筆者に尋ねた内容である。　(4)　正答の②は，第3段落1文目the studentsから2文目in classまでで「学生は最もストレスが少ないと思った受講生たちが，かつては教員を経験した者たちで，彼らを教えるのは喜びだ」と述べていることから判断できる。　①　第3段落3文目On以下で「教員の方が学生よりもストレスが若干上だ」と述べている。③　論旨にはない。　④　問題文のthe only以下の内容は本文にはない。(5)　解答例は，「豊かであるということは必ずしもお金をたくさん持っているということではない」とうい観点から書いている。以下に解答例とは異なる表現の英文を示すので，参考にしてほしい。I suppose the writer knew the Vietnamese student understood what is rich and happy. He believes that richness and happiness are not always given by money. He means that he won't become happy without friends even if he has a lot of money to buy anything he likes. (48 words)

【12】 I totally agree with English language education in elementary school. It is partly because research suggests that language learning should be as early as possible. And English is the fundamental tool for being embraced by the international community. As you know, for a long time, the teaching of English in Japanese junior and senior high school has been focusing on grammar and English-Japanese translation, and making little of communication activities. If English is successfully placed into the curriculum at elementary school, it is possible that there will be a big change in English education in Japan. (96 words)

〈解説〉解答例は,「小学校から英語を教えることに賛成であり, 従来の文法, 英作文中心の授業からコミュニケーション活動重視へと変えていくべき」という主旨で書かれている。以下に一部反対の立場(3, 4年生での導入には反対だが, 5, 6年生での実施には賛成)からの英文を示すので, 参考にしてほしい。I don't entirely agree to English language education in elementary school. It is necessary that Japanese language education should be more stressed than now at elementary school. I agree to start English language education in the fifth and sixth grades at elementary school. These are important stage for the connection to junior high school. In these grades, the international understanding curriculum is especially needed. If pupils in these grades realize what and why such education of English is required in the curriculum, their interest in English at junior high school will be more enhanced. (94 words)

【13】 コミュニケーションに取り組む様子やコミュニケーションを継続させようとする努力の様子がみられるかどうかを評価する。したがって, そこで用いられる英語の正確さや適切さなどの運用の能力などは評価しない。

〈解説〉指導においては，各教科・科目の目標だけでなく，領域や内容項目レベルの学習指導のねらいが生徒の学習状況としてどの程度実現されているかを具体的に想定する必要があり，評価規準はこれを具体的に示したものである。「コミュニケーションへの関心・意欲・態度」の観点は，コミュニケーションに関心をもち，積極的に言語活動を行い，コミュニケーションを図ろうとするかをみるものである。解答例では，この観点からの態度の例を表している。

【14】(1)　前の文は，言わばニュースバリューとしての価値を持つが，後ろの文のthe airportは，誰もが容易に到着でき，到着したところで影響を受けるものではなく，情報としての価値を持たないからで，後の文は通常の文脈ではあり得ない文であるということになるからです。
(2)　前の文は，「ケンが一日で仕事をするのは難しい。(ケンは仕事を始めていない。)」という意味で，後ろの文は，「ケンが一日で仕事を終えるのは難しい。(ケンは仕事をすでに始めている。)」という意味。前の文のto doは，これから始めることを意味します。
〈解説〉(1)　解答例の「情報の価値」以外にも，受動態を使う場合については様々なポイントがある。動作主が不明か不要な場合や，by以下で明示して強調する場合である。また，他動詞であれば何でも受動態にできるわけではなく，動詞の性格によっては不可能な場合もあるので，注意が必要である。　(2)　後の文のfinishは「終える，完了する」という意味なので，finish the work in a dayでは「1日で(すでに始めた)仕事を完了させる」という意味になる。

【高等学校】

【1】(1)　①　　(2)　④　　(3)　②　　(4)　②　　(5)　I didn't want to be a pilot or anything related to aviation. (12 words)　　(6)　④　　(7)　①
〈解説〉(1)　①　第1段落6文目a sketchから7文目pictureまでは，「幼児のころからの描写だが完全なものではない」と述べているので，将来的な事には触れていないと思われる。　(2)　正答の④については，第5

段落のDr. Palmerの本からの引用箇所(以下，「引用箇所」と略記)の最後の3文で「小さいころに自分が作った本を見て，作家になろうと思った」という内容が述べられている。　①　論旨にはない。　②　第5段落の引用箇所の最後から2行目に，I didn't 〜 aviation「パイロットや航空関係の職には就こうとは思わなかった」とある。aeronautical engineerは「航空技術者」の意。　③　第5段落の引用箇所の最後の1文にI wanted to be an authorとある。　(3)　正答の②について，第3段落3文目と，8〜9文目でそれぞれ「宇宙のすべての物には本来の性質があり，それは可能性と同時に限界もある」と「技術者は材料がどうあるべきかについては語れないし，彼が使う鉄や木や石の性質を理解せねばならない」とある。　①　第3段落6文目に「粘土が陶工の両手に反発して，その感じでできることとできないことが分かる」とある。③　第3段落12文目Whenからworking withまでで「職業を選ぶときには，使用する材質について理解しなければならない」とあり，「最もなじみのある材質」とは言っていない。　④　第3段落最後から2文目で「自分に合う職業を探すには，自分の性質を知らねばならない」とあるので，「すべての職業について学ぶ」というこの英文は誤りである。(4)　第4段落4文目のOffenからnatureまでは「これらの人々は私たちの性質を理解しようとはしない」の意味である。また，slotは「定位置。溝」の意味なので，下線部は，いわゆる「型にはめる」と考えればよい。したがって，②が正解である。　(5)　下線部ウを含む文は「真実は自分が想像したよりも明白だった」の意味である。具体的な内容は直後の1文である。　(6)　第5段落の引用箇所の3文目I以下で「長い時間かけて航空機関係の本を手作りした」と述べられている。　(7)　第7段落3文目で「孫娘が生まれたときの性格で成長して，喜びの持てる職業に就くことを彼は望んでいる」と述べられている。つまり，「今まで成長してきたように」という意味が適切である。

【2】A　⑦　　B　②　　C　③　　D　⑤　　E　①　　F　⑤
〈解説〉A　空欄Aの前の文は「実業界，援助機関，軍，連邦や州の政府，

外交や情報機関」という意味である。選択肢⑦では「典型的に，これらの学生は教養があり，教育も十分で世界の主要な言語を学んでいる」と記述されており，適切。　B　空欄Bの前では，戦争や宗教的迫害などから逃れる人々について記述され，空欄Bに続く文のmigrantからEuropeまでは「西ヨーロッパの移民」の意味である。これらの人々は経済的にも困窮し，教養もあまり高くないと考えられる。したがって，選択肢②が適切である。　C　空欄Cに続く文のimperialistからpowerまでは，帝国主義の国々がとった植民地政策について述べている。選択肢③は必要にかられて第2言語が必要になった状況を述べていて，by powerful以下はこれに合致するので適切。　D　第3段落2文目Advancedからgroupsまでで，「これらのグループでは，依然として母語以外の言語が教育や経済的に有利な決定的要素であり続ける」と述べている。この趣旨が選択肢⑤のbut以下の「あまりにも多くの場合で，生存には必要不可欠である」と合致する。　E　第3段落最後から2文目後半のlanguageからpossibleまでは「言語の指導と習得はできる限り社会的に進展するものである」の意味である。選択肢①のthe scopeからdo soまでは「第2言語と外国語の習得と指導の21世紀の見通しは，広がり続きそうである」の意味であり，適切。　F　第4段落4文目peopleからfinishersまでは，世界中で人々が様々な方法で言語を学んでいる様子が記述されている。選択肢⑥のbackdropは「背景」の意味であり，上述の状況を指していることから，適切である。

【３】(1)　③　　(2)　④　　(3)　C　③　　D　②　　E　⑤
(4)　leave a physical trace (4 words)　　(5)　When you want to celebrate your friend's wedding, you tend to write a greeting card or a letter because it is more formal and the receiver can keep it and occasionally it reminds him or her of your kindness. It is better than temporary conversation.　　(6)　urgent
(7)　I think there are some advantages and disadvantages in having learners write a script before they make a speech when you want to improve their speaking skills.

One of the strong points of the activity is that written script can be read or reread. Of course the teacher can correct their mistakes and give them advice. Then learners can revise it again and again and make the best statement. In this way, they can improve both writing skills and speaking skills at the same time.

On the other hand, that kind of process is not enough to improve speaking skills. In this case, learners tend to memorize all the words of the script, which cannot necessarily be applied to natural conversation. If learners need to have ability to maintain a conversation, they need to practice delivering their utterances within a few moments. (142 words)

〈解説〉(1)　空欄Aを含む文の前半のtraditionalからspoken languageまでは，伝統的な言語学の調査では，発話が主要なもので書き言葉は話し言葉の投影に過ぎないという内容である。一方，続くeducationalからof the languageまではこの逆の論理なので，「書き言葉は話し言葉よりも上位だ」と考えればよい。したがって，③が適切である。　(2)　空欄Bを含む文のa consensusからtwo positionsまでは，「これら2つの相互関係を調和させる考えがでてきた」の意味である。したがって，どちらが優位だという考えではないので，④が適切である。　(3)　C　空欄直後にwhileがあるので，written language is permanent「書き言葉は永続的である」と逆の意味で考えればよい。したがってtransitoryを含む③が適切である。　D　書き手と読み手の時間と空間的な広がりの距離感について述べている。whichの先行詞はDistanceなので，書き手と読み手では共通の文脈はまずないと考えるのが適切である。したがって，②が適切である。　E　orthographyとは「正しい綴り。文字体系」の意味である。したがって，compared以下では，話し手の優位性が記述されているので，⑤が適切である。　(4)　下線部アの直前のwritingからrecordedまでは，普通の状況での書くことの特性について述べられており，leaves a physical traceとして「物理的な痕跡を残す」と記述されている。問題の箇所はこの部分の省略についての出題である。解答の場合は三単現に注意すること。　(5)　ここでは，結婚祝いのカードを

郵送する場面を設定している。英文には記述されていないが，「(メールなどよりも)形式的だが，カード自体が保存されて友人の真心が後々まで伝わる」ことが述べられている。remind A of Bで「AにBのことを思い出させる」の意味である。　(6)　空欄の後のthe advantage以下の意味は「金額よりも速さを優先する」の意味である。したがって，このような状況は「火急の。一時も無駄にできない」場合なので，urgentが適切である。　(7)　条件が3点あることに注意すること。全くの自由英作文ではない。特に，2番目の「文章からの情報も盛り込むこと」を忘れないようにする。解答例では，2，3，4文目が長所として述べられている。一方，最後の1文は短所として記述されている。

●書籍内容の訂正等について

　弊社では教員採用試験対策シリーズ（参考書，過去問，全国まるごと過去問題集），公務員試験対策シリーズ，公立幼稚園・保育士試験対策シリーズ，会社別就職試験対策シリーズについて，正誤表をホームページ（https://www.kyodo-s.jp）に掲載いたします。内容に訂正等，疑問点がございましたら，まずホームページをご確認ください。もし，正誤表に掲載されていない訂正等，疑問点がございましたら，下記項目をご記入の上，以下の送付先までお送りいただくようお願いいたします。

> ① **書籍名，都道府県（学校）名，年度**
> 　（例：教員採用試験過去問シリーズ　小学校教諭 過去問　2025年度版）
> ② **ページ数**（書籍に記載されているページ数をご記入ください。）
> ③ **訂正等，疑問点**（内容は具体的にご記入ください。）
> 　（例：問題文では"ア～オの中から選べ"とあるが，選択肢はエまでしかない）

〔ご注意〕

○ 電話での質問や相談等につきましては，受付けておりません。ご注意ください。

○ 正誤表の更新は適宜行います。

○ いただいた疑問点につきましては，当社編集制作部で検討の上，正誤表への反映を決定させていただきます（個別回答は，原則行いませんのであしからずご了承ください）。

●情報提供のお願い

　協同教育研究会では，これから教員採用試験を受験される方々に，より正確な問題を，より多くご提供できるよう情報の収集を行っております。つきましては，教員採用試験に関する次の項目の情報を，以下の送付先までお送りいただけますと幸いでございます。お送りいただきました方には謝礼を差し上げます。

（情報量があまりに少ない場合は，謝礼をご用意できかねる場合があります）。

◆あなたの受験された面接試験，論作文試験の実施方法や質問内容

◆教員採用試験の受験体験記

送付先	○電子メール：edit@kyodo-s.jp
	○FAX：03-3233-1233（協同出版株式会社　編集制作部 行）
	○郵送：〒101-0054　東京都千代田区神田錦町2-5
	協同出版株式会社　編集制作部 行
	○HP：https://kyodo-s.jp/provision（右記のQRコードからもアクセスできます）

　※謝礼をお送りする関係から，いずれの方法でお送りいただく際にも，「お名前」「ご住所」は，必ず明記いただきますよう，よろしくお願い申し上げます。

教員採用試験「過去問」シリーズ

京都市の
英語科 過去問

編　集	Ⓒ 協同教育研究会
発　行	令和6年1月25日
発行者	小貫　輝雄
発行所	協同出版株式会社
	〒101-0054　東京都千代田区神田錦町2‐5
	電話　03－3295－1341
	振替　東京00190－4－94061
印刷所	協同出版・POD工場

落丁・乱丁はお取り替えいたします。

2024年夏に向けて
―教員を目指すあなたを全力サポート！―

●通信講座
志望自治体別の教材とプロによる
丁寧な添削指導で合格をサポート

●公開講座 (＊1)
48のオンデマンド講座のなかから、
不得意分野のみピンポイントで学習できる！
受講料は6000円〜　＊一部対面講義もあり

●全国模試 (＊1)
業界最多の **年5回** 実施！
定期的に学習到達度を測って
レベルアップを目指そう！

●自治体別対策模試 (＊1)
的中問題がよく出る！
本試験の出題傾向・形式に合わせた
試験で実力を試そう！

　上記の講座及び試験は，すべて右記のQRコードからお申し込みできます。また，講座及び試験の情報は，随時，更新していきます。

＊1・・・ 2024年対策の公開講座、全国模試、自治体別対策模試の
　　　　情報は、2023年9月頃に公開予定です。

協同出版・協同教育研究会
https://kyodo-s.jp

お問い合わせは
通話料無料の
フリーダイヤル

0120 (13) 7300
いいみ　なさんおうえん

受付時間：平日（月〜金）9時〜18時　まで